AMERICAS

AMERICAS

Study Guide

Bernadette M. Orr
with Bárbara Cruz

Americas is a coproduction of WGBH Boston and Central Television Enterprises
for Channel 4, U.K., in association with the School for International
and Public Affairs at Columbia University, the Latin American and Caribbean Center
at Florida International University, and Tufts University.

The *Americas Study Guide* is part of a college credit course from

The Annenberg/CPB Collection

OXFORD UNIVERSITY PRESS
New York   Oxford
1993

Oxford University Press

Oxford   New York   Toronto
Delhi   Bombay   Calcutta   Madras   Karachi
Kuala Lumpur   Singapore   Hong Kong   Tokyo
Nairobi   Dar es Salaam   Cape Town
Melbourne   Auckland   Madrid

and associated companies in

Berlin   Ibadan

Published by Oxford University Press, Inc.,
200 Madison Avenue, New York, New York 10016

Oxford is a registered trademark of Oxford University Press

Library of Congress Cataloging-in-Publication Data
Orr, Bernadette M.
Americas : study guide / by Bernadette M. Orr, with
Bárbara Cruz.
p. cm. Includes bibliographical references.
ISBN 0-19-507793-8
1. Latin America. 2. Caribbean Area. I. Cruz, Bárbara
II. Americas (Television program) III. Title.
F1408.07 1992 980'.0071'1759--dc20   92-25767

This book was developed for use by students enrolled in the
Americas telecourse. The telecourse consists of ten one-hour
public television programs; a reader, *Americas: An Anthology*,
edited by Mark B. Rosenberg, A. Douglas Kincaid, and Kathleen Logan; a textbook, *Modern Latin America*, by Thomas E.
Skidmore and Peter H. Smith; this study guide; and an optional book entitled *Americas: New Interpretive Essays*. All of the
publications are available from Oxford University Press.

Americas was produced for PBS by WGBH Boston and
by Central Television Enterprises for Channel 4, U.K., in association with the School of International and Public Affairs
at Columbia University, the Latin American and Caribbean
Center at Florida International University, and Tufts University.

Major funding for *Americas* was provided by the Annen-
berg/CPB Project, with additional funding from the Carnegie
Corporation of New York*, the John D. and Catherine T.
MacArthur Foundation, the Rockefeller Foundation, the Corporation for Public Broadcasting, and public television view-
ers.

Americas is closed-captioned for the hearing-impaired.

For further information about the print components of the
Americas television course, contact:

> *Americas*
> Oxford University Press
> Attention: College Sales Coordinator
> 200 Madison Avenue
> New York, NY 10016

For more information about television course licenses and
off-air taping, contact:

> *Americas*
> PBS Adult Learning Service
> 1320 Braddock Place
> Alexandria, VA 22314–1698
> 1–800–ALS-ALS8

For more information about *Americas* videocassettes and print
materials, off-air taping and duplication licenses, and other
video and audio series from the Annenberg/CPB Collection,
contact:

> *Americas*
> The Annenberg/CPB Collection
> P.O. Box 2345
> South Burlington, VT 05407–2345
> 1–800–LEARNER

*The Carnegie Corporation of New York is not responsible for any state-
ments or views expressed in the *Americas* programs or materials.

Cover Image: Peter Martinez
Cover Design: Gaye Korbet, WGBH Design

9 8 7 6 5 4 3 2 1

Printed in the United States of America
on acid-free paper

Acknowledgments

We would like to thank the Annenberg/CPB Project, whose support made this telecourse possible. We would also like to thank the Carnegie Corporation of New York, the John D. and Catherine T. MacArthur Foundation, the Rockefeller Foundation, and the Corporation for Public Broadcasting, as well as Channel 4, U.K.

We also wish to acknowledge the direction and guidance of Mark B. Rosenberg of the Latin American and Caribbean Center at Florida International University, the Project Education Director, who began thinking about creating a telecourse about Latin America and the Caribbean in late 1982; Alfred C. Stepan, former Dean of the School of International and Public Affairs at Columbia University, who joined the endeavor as Chair of the Academic Advisory Board in 1984; and Peter Winn of Tufts University, who became Project Academic Director in 1985.

In addition, our distinguished board of academic advisors, listed below, provided invaluable assistance in developing both the television programs and the print materials for the telecourse. Margaret E. Crahan provided valuable guidance on three of the units: Unit 2, Legacies of Empire: From Conquest to Independence; Unit 8, Miracles Are Not Enough: Continuity and Change in Religion; and Unit 11, Fire in the Mind: Revolutions and Revolutionaries. Peter H. Smith provided direction on two of the units: Unit 3, The Garden of Forking Paths: Dilemmas of National Development; and Unit 10, Get Up, Stand Up: The Problems of Sovereignty. Albert Fishlow assisted with Unit 4, Capital Sins: Authoritarianism and Democratization. M. Patricia Fernández Kelly and Alejandro Portes reviewed Unit 5, Continent on the Move: Migration and Urbanization. Kay Barbara Warren and Anthony Maingot provided guidance on Unit 6, Mirrors of the Heart: Color, Class, and Identity. Cornelia Butler Flora, Helen Safa, and Marysa Navarro-Aranguren helped create Unit 7, In Women's Hands: The Changing Roles of Women. Jean Franco advised on Unit 9, Builders of Images: Writers, Artists, and Popular Culture. Franklin Knight greatly assisted with Unit 10, Get Up, Stand Up: The Problems of Sovereignty, and also reviewed the print materials for Unit 6. Cynthia Arnson assisted with Unit 11, Fire in the Mind: Revolutions and Revolutionaries, and Rubén Rumbaut helped create Unit 12, The Americans: Latin American and Caribbean Peoples in the United States.

The development of the educational print materials was a long process which involved the input of many people in addition to the academic advisory board. Our utilization advisory board, listed below, helped create the structure for the telecourse materials and reviewed the materials for level and curriculum fit. Special thanks go to Pam Quinn, Chief Utilization Advisor. Bárbara Cruz, formerly of the Latin American and Caribbean Center at Florida International University, wrote the pilot lesson plan, which was reviewed and tested before the rest of the materials were developed. She also participated in the development of the structure and focus for both the study guide and the faculty guide, and contributed to some chapters. Nancy Lane, Edward Harcourt, David

Roll, Christopher Johnson, and Donna Ng of Oxford University Press oversaw the publication and promotion of the books.

A special note of thanks goes to the producers, especially to Senior Editor Adriana Bosch Lemus, WGBH staff, and others whose cooperation helped us create these materials: David Ash, Marc de Beaufort, Pam Benson, Javier Betancourt, Peter Bull, Elizabeth Buxton, Yezid Campos, Margaret Carsley, Tania Cypriano, Ann Downer, Orna Feldman, Rachel Field, Andrew Gersh, Karen Jersild, Kevin Keogan, Gaye Korbet, Julie Mallozzi, Juan Mandelbaum, Rebecca Marvil, Elizabeth Nash, Marisol Navas, Debbie Paddock, Lourdes Portillo, Christina Ragazzi, Jane Regan, João Resende-Santos, Margo Shearman, Virginia Sietz, Roderick Steel, Ann Strunk, Fay Sutherland, Andrés di Tella, Raymond Telles, Joseph Tovares, Mauricio Vélez, Ann Weinstock, Sonia Walrond, Veronica Young, and Jeanne Zimmerman.

Bernadette M. Orr
Author

Patricia Crotty
Project Director, Educational Print and Outreach

Beth Kirsch
Director, Educational Print and Outreach

Judith Vecchione
Executive Producer

WGBH Educational Foundation
Boston, MA

The Americas *Project*

Utilization Advisory Board

Pam Quinn
Chief Utilization Advisor
Center for Telecommunications,
Dallas Community College

Dennis Cudd
Central Piedmont Community College

Ethel McClatchey
Los Angeles Community College

Dr. Joyce Nielson
Western Illinois University

Wayne Prophet
University of Iowa

Dr. Kenneth Sharpe
Swarthmore College

WGBH Boston

Peter McGhee
Vice President for
National Program Productions

Brigid Sullivan
Vice President for
Special Telecommunications Services

Judith Vecchione
Executive Producer, Americas

Beth Kirsch
Director
Educational Print and Outreach

Patricia Crotty
Project Director
Educational Print and Outreach

What forces contributed to the heavy international debt burdens confronting many countries in the region?

Why do rural people continue to migrate to urban areas even as the cities become increasingly unlivable? How does domestic and international migration affect families and countries?

How have women reconciled their traditional places in family, church, and community with the expression and exercise of political and economic power?

What are some of the possible future trends for U.S. relations with Latin America and the Caribbean and for the region's political, economic, and social development?

COURSE OBJECTIVES

The *Americas* telecourse is designed to help you:

increase your knowledge and understanding of the nations of Latin America and the Caribbean

see the people of the Americas as creative and productive, actively confronting their problems, and becoming a force on the global scene

become aware of the long-standing economic, political, social, and cultural ties that link the United States with the other nations of the Americas

gain insight into the future of the nations of the Americas and the impact they will have on this country in coming years

COURSE COMPONENTS

The 13–unit *Americas* telecourse consists of the following components:

- 10 one-hour video programs

- this study guide

- the reader, *Americas: An Anthology,* by Mark B. Rosenberg, A. Douglas Kincaid, and Kathleen Logan, published by Oxford University Press

- the textbook, *Modern Latin America* (3d edition, 1992), by Thomas E. Skidmore and Peter H. Smith, published by Oxford University Press

A book of essays written by members of the *Americas* academic advisory board entitled *Americas: New Interpretive Essays,* edited by Alfred Stepan and published by Oxford University Press, is available as an optional component of the television course.

THE STUDY UNITS

Unit 1

The Introduction (a print-only unit) lays out the structure of the course, including the key themes and issues to be studied. It also surveys the geography and peoples of the region.

Unit 2

Legacies of Empire: From Conquest to Independence (a print-only unit) provides a brief history of the region. The readings outline the precolonial period and trace the history of the Spanish and Portuguese conquest, the years of empire, and the early independence period of the 1800s.

Unit 3

The Garden of Forking Paths: Dilemmas of National Development (program 1) examines the twentieth-century development of the nations and national economies of the Americas. The program focuses on Argentina and includes the Perón years,

Contents

Preface: The *Americas* Telecourse   *xi*

Unit 1   The Introduction   *1*

Unit 2   Legacies of Empire: From Conquest to Independence   *10*

Unit 3   The Garden of Forking Paths: Dilemmas of National Development   *22*

Unit 4   Capital Sins: Authoritarianism and Democratization   *35*

Unit 5   Continent on the Move: Migration and Urbanization   *47*

Unit 6   Mirrors of the Heart: Color, Class, and Identity   *60*

Unit 7   In Women's Hands: The Changing Roles of Women   *74*

Unit 8   Miracles Are Not Enough: Continuity and Change in Religion   *87*

Unit 9   Builders of Images: Writers, Artists, and Popular Culture   *100*

Unit 10   Get Up, Stand Up: The Problems of Sovereignty   *112*

Unit 11   Fire in the Mind: Revolutions and Revolutionaries   *126*

Unit 12   The Americans: Latin American and Caribbean Peoples in the United States   *143*

Unit 13   Course Review   *156*

Appendix: Answers to Self-Test Questions   *168*

Preface: The Americas *Telecourse*

COURSE OVERVIEW

Before the end of this century, people of Latin American and Caribbean origin will constitute the largest minority in the United States.

The 33 sovereign states that make up Latin America and the Caribbean represent the United States' most important trade partners in the developing world and most reliable source of many strategic resources, including oil. In the next century, our relationship with this vital region will take on even greater significance. Yet much about the history, politics, economics, social structures, and complex relationships of this important region with other world powers eludes us. Too often, our perspective is colored by stereotypes, broad generalizations, and incomplete or inaccurate information.

Americas, an innovative 10–part television series and 13–unit complete television course, brings to life a startlingly diverse region that encompasses great wealth and desperate poverty, countries as tiny as Jamaica and as enormous as Brazil, with democratic and authoritarian governments and a complex, multicultural heritage. The series provokes a re-examination of U.S. relations with its hemispheric neighbors and with people of Latin American and Caribbean origin living in the United States by highlighting key issues and events of the twentieth century, providing a new perspective that extends far beyond the limited images and crisis-driven headlines of the nightly news.

Americas presents the human face of important

issues from representative countries. [...] range from personal or family issues, [...] moments in history, to aspects of local [...] national culture. In each case, individu[...] nity and country examples illuminate [...] processes affecting the region as a whol[...]

The challenges facing the countrie[...] America and the Caribbean are dauntin[...] responses of the peoples of the region [...] been positive and innovative. Many of [...] egies, crafted in response to local conditi[...] instructive lessons applicable far be[...] boundaries of their particular situation. [...] had international impact in widely dive[...] witness the new social and political ro[...] Catholic Church in Latin America, the [...] ment of unique popular music that enh[...] tural identity in the Caribbean states, an[...] ticlass coalitions forged by women in the [...] of the Americas.

In its explorations of the forces unde[...] contemporary problems and achievement[...] America and the Caribbean, *Americas* [...] these and other questions:

- What is the meaning of sovereignt[...] Americas? Why are sovereignty and na[...] so important throughout the region?

- Has foreign intervention in the region'[...] and economic affairs helped or hind[...] goals of democracy and stability?

the military dictatorship of the 1970s, the Malvinas/Falklands War, and the return to civilian government.

Unit 4

Capital Sins: Authoritarianism and Democratization (program 2) begins in the 1960s, when many nations' economic and political systems were in disarray and a move toward authoritarian government swept the region. The film focuses on Brazil, a major and influential nation in the region, whose experience of military rule, economic growth, and redemocratization was echoed elsewhere in the Americas. The program also considers the legacy of the military period and the prospects for future economic and political development in Brazil.

Unit 5

Continent on the Move: Migration and Urbanization (program 3) explores the causes and effects of one of the most important forces transforming the Americas: the migration of vast numbers of people within the region. Set in Mexico, the unit focuses on the steady flow of rural migrants to congested cities, in search of jobs, education, and a better future for their children. Following the fortunes of a migrant family, the film looks at the reality of migrants' lives and the difficult choices that must be made.

Unit 6

Mirrors of the Heart: Color, Class, and Identity (program 4) is set on the island of Hispaniola, shared by the countries of Haiti and the Dominican Republic—nations with very different languages, histories, and cultural identities—and in Bolivia, a country with a large indigenous population. It examines the issues of race, class, and ethnic identities in the region and considers how they continue to be redefined by individuals, communities, and nations.

Unit 7

In Women's Hands: The Changing Roles of Women (program 5) looks at how women in the region are adopting, by choice or necessity, new economic and political roles that break traditional stereotypes about gender and family. The spotlight is on Chile, where the social and political turmoil of the 1970s and 1980s challenged women of every social class and provoked many women into political activism and a new understanding of feminism.

Unit 8

Miracles Are Not Enough: Continuity and Change in Religion (program 6) travels to Brazil to observe the explosion of theological debate, social activism, and spiritual revival which is changing a region where religion has long been important in society and politics. The program explores the diversity of religious beliefs and practices in the Americas, where institutional churches coexist with indigenous and African religions and with newer Pentecostal movements.

Unit 9

Builders of Images: Writers, Artists, and Popular Culture (program 7) reflects on the extraordinary creative ferment that has given the region a prominent place on the global artistic map, tracing the evolution of the visual arts, music, and literature in Latin America and the Caribbean. The challenges of artists in the region to define an authentically American voice and their effectiveness in raising important social and political issues are highlighted in this program, which is set in Puerto Rico, Brazil, Mexico, and Argentina.

Unit 10

Get Up, Stand Up: The Problems of Sovereignty (program 8) examines the ways in which nations in the Americas struggle to maintain economic and vereignty in the face of strong pressures, reign and domestic. Set in Colombia, Ja- a, and Panama, the program explores a wide age of threats to sovereignty, from domestic guerrilla movements to the power of drug lords, to economic dependency and foreign intervention.

Unit 11

Fire in the Mind: Revolutions and Revolutionaries (program 9) looks at the reasons for and composition of revolutionary movements in the region. Set in El Salvador and Peru, the program compares and contrasts the two countries' revolutionary struggles and links these movements to earlier twentieth-century revolutions in Mexico, Cuba, and Nicaragua.

Unit 12

The Americans: Latin American and Caribbean Peoples in the United States (program 10) returns to the United States to explore how communities of Latin American and Caribbean origin are challenging and redefining the U.S. sense of national identity. Using the examples of the long-established Mexican-American community in southern California, Cuban-Americans in Miami, and the Puerto Rican and non-Hispanic Caribbean communities of New York City, the program considers the issues of assimilation and cultural identity, and looks at the growing impact of these communities on the local and national political and cultural scenes.

Unit 13

Course Review (a print-only unit) summarizes the themes and materials of the course and suggests applications of what students have learned in the course to issues of vital importance in the Americas today.

The Analytic Framework

The *Americas* television course was designed around an analytic framework that defines the special character of the region and will guide you through a large body of information. This four-part framework underlies every unit of the course.

International Relations

The region's distinct relationship to the world order results from its experience of conquest, colonization, and settlement, and from the manner in which it was integrated into global economic, political, and cultural systems. The dynamic tension among these elements defines the region as much as its language, culture, and religion, and shapes its key ideals and values.

The region's relatively late incorporation into the world economy has produced complex and often problematic relationships with the major industrial powers. Particularly important is the region's paradoxical stance toward the United States, which is perceived as both benefactor and aggressor, a success story and a cautionary tale, the home of liberal democratic ideals and the source of Yankee imperialism.

Tension

The history of the region's relationships with the rest of the world helps to explain the Americas' high levels of internal tension and social and political instability. The strain shows in a history of authoritarian governments, glaring inequalities of income, and economic policies that have led to some of the highest national debts in the world. These problems are not solely the products of colonial legacies and external constraints, though; they also stem from such internal factors as the concentration of land ownership, the weakness of key democratic political institutions, and the conscious decisions of particular political leaders and social groups to maintain a monopoly on power.

Innovation

The social and political realities of the Americas have spawned innovative cultural, economic, political, and religious responses. New movements that empower women, peasants, and other marginalized groups have arisen, and new literary, musical, and theatrical forms are dissolving national and international cultural barriers. Common to these innovations is the push toward social participation, which is on the rise throughout the region.

Transformation

Ever since the idea of the New World captured the imagination of the European conquerors, a complex process of reciprocal transformation has characterized Latin America's relationship to the world. Transformation born of tension and innovation is still evident today, as the new forms pioneered in the Americas are altering the world's intellectual and imaginative landscape.

Latin American and Caribbean literature and the theology of liberation claim worldwide attention. Multiclass coalitions in which women have set forth new political agendas serve as models for organizing women in other parts of the world. In response to the region's crisis, Latin American social scientists have produced some of the field's most original thinking on the economic and political problems of developing countries. And, paradoxically, the size of the region's foreign debt has given it enormous leverage in the world economy while its importance in international trade continues to expand.

In geopolitical terms, the countries of the Americas have emerged as key actors. For example, Brazil's resources and economic strength promise to make it a growing global force in the coming decades; Cuba has exercised an influential role in the region and throughout the developing world; and Mexico has become increasingly important as a potential member of a North American Free Trade Zone.

THE TELEVISION PROGRAMS

The 10 one-hour television programs, corresponding with Units 3 through 12 of the telecourse, examine the contemporary history, politics, culture, economics, religion, and social structures of this important region, as well as past, present, and future influences of change. Moving personal stories help to illustrate larger themes.

THE STUDY GUIDE

Ten of the 13 study guide units correspond directly to the 10 television programs, two print-only units precede the television programs, and a final print-only unit concludes the course. The study guide is designed to prepare you to view each

television program critically, and to help you evaluate your understanding of what you have seen. It also integrates the program material with assigned readings in the textbook and anthology, and reinforces the themes of the telecourse.

The study guide is not a substitute for the assigned and supplementary readings, and it may not cover all the material your instructor will expect you to master in each unit. Be sure you understand clearly which additional material you are responsible for in each unit. Use the study guide as a tool to organize your learning and to aid your comprehension of each unit's key concepts, not as a replacement for any of the print or television components of the course.

Each unit of the study guide includes the following sections:

· **Unit Summary:** provides an outline of the material presented in the textbook and anthology readings for the unit, as well as a description of the television program, if there is one.

· **Key Issues:** lists critical questions that address the learning objectives for each unit.

· **Glossary:** defines key terms, individuals, and concepts presented in the unit, with pronunciation guides for any non-English words.

· **Overview:** summarizes the information covered in the unit, integrating the program with the material included in the reading assignment.

· **Reading Assignment:** indicates required readings from the textbook and anthology.

· **Unit Review:** states the learning objectives of the unit.

· **Self-Test Questions:** includes multiple choice, true or false, and identification/short answer questions to prepare you for examinations. Correct answers with sources are provided at the back of the book.

· **Questions to Consider:** poses open-ended questions that encourage critical thinking about the issues presented in the unit.

- **Resources:** lists nonfiction, fiction, films, recordings, and other materials to encourage you to pursue questions or interests that may develop as you complete the unit.

THE ANTHOLOGY

Americas: An Anthology
Edited by Mark B. Rosenberg, A. Douglas Kincaid, and Kathleen Logan
380 pages
Oxford University Press, 1992
ISBN 0–19–507792–X

Key source materials, tailored to fit the structure of the television course, make this anthology a valuable resource. *Americas: An Anthology* brings together vivid accounts of places and events, speeches, profiles, interviews from national newspapers and magazines, oral histories, excerpts from a wide range of literature, policy papers, and other readings. Many of the readings are translations from Spanish, Portuguese, and French sources.

Each chapter contains an introduction that sets the stage for the readings and linking them to the film and the other print components of the course.

THE TEXTBOOK

Modern Latin America
Third Edition
Thomas E. Skidmore and Peter H. Smith
approximately 450 pages
Oxford University Press, 1992
ISBN 0–19–507648–6 (hardcover)
ISBN 0–19–507649–4 (paperback)

Modern Latin America, the textbook for this course, is a critically acclaimed text already widely used in colleges and universities. The authors, one of whom is a member of the *Americas* academic advisory board, have updated the book to coincide with the television course premiere. The textbook is an important companion to the television programs, setting each film into historical context. Its in-depth, case study approach guides you through the major countries and the region as a whole in a straightforward, clear, and readable style.

THE BOOK OF ESSAYS

Americas: New Interpretive Essays
Edited by Alfred Stepan
approximately 320 pages
Oxford University Press, 1992
ISBN 0–19–507794–6 (hardcover)
ISBN 0–19–507795–4 (paperback)

Americas: New Interpretive Essays is an optional addition to the television course for upper-level courses and is a supplement to traditional courses on Latin American and Caribbean studies. The book is composed of original essays written as a companion to the series by leading scholars who are members of the *Americas* academic advisory board. Each essay expands on the themes and materials presented in the program and other print materials of the course, with the goal of presenting the most current and innovative interpretations in each issue area. The authors are prominent social scientists and humanists in Latin American and Caribbean studies. The editor, Alfred Stepan, is Burgess Professor of Political Science at Columbia University and an internationally recognized Latin American scholar.

Taking the *Americas* Telecourse

Find out the following information as soon after registration as possible:

- What books are required for the course

- If and when an orientation session has been scheduled

- When *Americas* will be broadcast in your area

- When course examinations are scheduled (mark these in your calendar)

· If any additional on-campus meetings have been scheduled (plan to attend as many review sessions, seminars, and other meetings as possible)

To learn the most from each unit:

1. Before viewing the television program, read the Unit Summary, Key Issues, Glossary, and Overview in the study guide. Pay particular attention to the questions listed in the Key Issues section.

2. Read the textbook and anthology assignment listed in the study guide and any supplementary material assigned by your instructor. Take notes as you read on any information that relates to the Overview from the study guide.

3. View the program, keeping the Key Issues questions in mind. Be an active viewer. Some students find that taking notes while viewing the programs is helpful. If your area has more than one public television station, there may be several opportunities for you to watch the program. Many public television stations repeat a program at least once during the week it is first shown. The programs may also be available on videocassette at your school, or you can tape them at home if you own a VCR.

If you don't have a VCR, you can make an audiocassette of the program for review.

4. Read the Unit Review section of the study guide, to reinforce the key points of what you have seen.

5. Take the Self-Test, read through the Questions to Consider, and complete any other questions, activities, or essays assigned by your instructor.

6. Keep up with the course on a weekly basis. Each unit of the course builds upon knowledge gained in previous units. Stay current with the programs and readings. Make a daily checklist and keep weekly and term calendars, noting your scheduled activities such as meetings or examinations as well as blocks of time for viewing programs, reading, and completing assignments.

7. Keep in touch with your instructor. If possible, get to know him or her. You should have your instructor's mailing address, phone number, and call-in hours. Your instructor would like to hear from you and to know how you are doing. He or she will be eager to answer any questions you have about the course.

AMERICAS

Unit 1

The Introduction

The peoples and nations of Latin America and the Caribbean vary greatly, and have richly diverse histories, economic and political systems, cultures, and social structures. © Robert Frerck/Odyssey Productions

UNIT SUMMARY

Unit 1 serves as an introduction to Latin America and the Caribbean and to the major themes of this television course. The text and anthology readings briefly outline the diverse physical geography and demographic characteristics of the region and explain two important perspectives on its social, political, and economic development: modernization theory and dependency theory. Unit 1 does not include a television program.

KEY ISSUES

· Who are the major groups of people whose presence in Latin America and the Caribbean has contributed to the complexity and diversity of today's societies?

· What were the differences among the nonindigenous groups in terms of their motivations and methods of arriving in the region?

· What are the most important features of Latin America's physical geography, and how have they influenced its economic development?

· What two major theories have scholars used to explain Latin America's unique patterns of social, economic, and political development? What are some important criticisms of the two theories?

· What are the four primary themes of this course?

GLOSSARY

altiplano (all-tee-PLAH-no):   plateau in the Andes located about 12,000 feet above sea level. Bolivia's capital city, La Paz, is built upon the *altiplano*.

Creole (CREE-ohl):   languages of combined African and European origin spoken widely in the Caribbean, especially by those without much formal education. Creole, with French, is the official language of Haiti. Also used to describe persons of European descent born in Spanish America.

dependency theory: perspective on Latin American political and economic history developed by Latin American scholars in the 1970s and 1980s; argues that Latin American countries have not been able to pursue independent development goals because their economies are tied to and dependent on the growth of other nations, particularly the industrialized economies of North America and Western Europe. Some proponents of this view also maintain that economic dependency leads almost inevitably to political authoritarianism.

gross national product (GNP):   the total value of production in any country during the course of one year. GNP per capita is the total production divided by the number of citizens, giving a figure of average income per person that is a very rough estimate of the average standard of living in the country.

modernization theory: theory developed by North American scholars in the late 1950s and early 1960s which proposed that economic growth and industrialization had been delayed in Latin America and the Caribbean, but would eventually occur there as it had in the United States. Proponents of this view also argued that the processes of growth and industrialization would bring about political democracy and greater social equity in the region.

Quechua (KETCH-oo-ah):   language spoken by most indigenous peoples in the Andes. *Quechua* and Spanish are the official languages of Peru.

OVERVIEW

Although most North Americans know very little about their neighbors to the south, the history, development, and future of Latin America and the Caribbean are of vital concern to the United States. Too often, our perspective is narrowed by stereotypes that, while perhaps explaining a part of reality, are insufficient and even harmful to understanding the region as a whole. Yet the two continents in the Western Hemisphere are bound by historical, political, and economic links that remain strong today. The aim of this telecourse is to increase awareness of the complexity, variety, and unique historical experience that characterize the 33 nations of Latin America and the Caribbean.

Latin America is a region of enormous natural contrast. It contains numerous mountain ranges, including the Andes, the world's second highest mountains, which run the length of western South America. At lower elevations the climate tends to be tropical, with high average temperatures and lush, year-round vegetation. The lowlands along Latin America's ocean shores and the cooler inland plateaus and valleys are the location for most of the region's major human settlements, although many indigenous people continue to live in highland mountainous areas from Central America through the Andes, as well as in the dense jungles and rain forests of the interior. The many important river systems have made hydroelectricity an important and common source of power. The 3,300 mile–long Amazon, the world's longest river, is surrounded by tropical rain forest. This immense forest is home to millions of animal, insect, and plant species, many of which have valuable medical uses throughout the world, while many more have yet to be studied by modern scientists.

The people of Latin America and the Caribbean are also strikingly diverse. Their societies exhibit complex class and ethnic groupings, with much intermingling among the descendents of the many indigenous groups and others who arrived over the course of five centuries. The Spanish and Portuguese were the first Europeans to arrive in the fifteenth and sixteenth centuries, followed by the French, English, and Dutch in the seventeenth and eighteenth centuries. While the indigenous populations of the Indians were decimated by Old World diseases and the experience of conquest and colonization, and some were completely eradicated, many others did manage to survive. Their descendents form the ethnic majority in a few countries and, in 1990, totaled about 20 million of the region's approximately 440 million inhabitants.

Africans were brought in large numbers to work as slaves in the plantations of Brazil and the Caribbean, in an inhuman commerce that began in the early sixteenth century and persisted until the midnineteenth century. Finally, immigrants from Asia and from Eastern and Southern Europe came as laborers and settlers to Latin America and the Caribbean during the late nineteenth and early twentieth centuries.

Themes of the Television Course

This course uses case studies in specific countries to illustrate issues that affect countries throughout the region. There are four organizing themes in the *Americas* telecourse. First, Latin America and the Caribbean have a distinct historical relationship to the rest of the world based on their experience of conquest, colonization, and settlement. The region also has a unique economic history. For years, economic investment and growth in Latin America and the Caribbean were tied almost exclusively to the exploitation of natural resources by the European colonizers. Industrialization was late in arriving, and its benefits typically were restricted to small circles of manufacturers, landowners, and exporters. In modern times, much of the region's economic growth has been fueled by production of goods for export to Europe and North America. Consequently, economic stability has always been highly dependent on fluctuations in global prices and demand cycles.

A second theme is that these characteristics, along with key domestic political and economic choices, have created numerous internal tensions. Frequent political and social upheavals in many Latin American and Caribbean countries have resulted from the struggles among various interests groups. Elites strive to maintain their privileged position; peasants and working classes push for a greater share of economic benefits in the form of increased wages and lower prices; and middle-class professionals, students, and others try to increase their share of economic and political power. Military regimes throughout the region have often reacted to social tensions by imposing strict controls over political and civil liberties. The United States has a history of intervening in the internal politics of the region, perceiving in the social and political unrest a threat to its own economic, political, and strategic interests.

Third, the peoples of Latin America and the Caribbean have shown great creativity and developed many innovative responses to their social and political situations. The typical North American images of the passive peasant or downtrodden slum resident contrast sharply with the social and political reality of the region, where impoverished and disenfranchised groups are creating new modes of social organization, economic activity, and political advocacy. The efforts of Latin America's

Latin America and the Caribbean

UNITED STATES

Gulf of Mexico

MEXICO

Mexico City

BAHAMAS

Havana

CUBA

HAITI

DOMINICAN REPUBLIC

PUERTO RICO

JAMAICA

BELIZE

CARIBBEAN SEA

ATLANTIC OCEAN

GUATEMALA

EL SALVADOR

HONDURAS

NICARAGUA

COSTA RICA

PANAMA

VENEZUELA

Caracas

BARBADOS

TRINIDAD & TOBAGO

GUYANA

SURINAME

FRENCH GUIANA

Magdalena

Bogotá

Orinoco

COLUMBIA

ECUADOR

Quito

Amazon

PERU

Lima

BRAZIL

La Paz

BOLIVIA

ANDES

ALTIPLANO

PARAGUAY

Rio de Janeiro

PACIFIC OCEAN

Rio de la Plata

Santiago

Montevideo

Buenos Aires

URUGUAY

CHILE

ARGENTINA

N

S

0   500   1000   1500 Miles

Strait of Magellan

FALKLAND ISLANDS (ISLAS MALVINAS)

Cape Horn

religious and social movements on behalf of human rights stand as moving testimony to the courage, creativity, and political sophistication of even the most disadvantaged groups. Popular cultures in Latin America and the Caribbean have proved both durable and resilient, generating new styles of dance, music, literature, and theater. Many of these new arts incorporate traditional elements within modern forms.

Fourth, these innovations continue to affect Latin America's relationship to the world order. The nations of Latin America and the Caribbean are highly interdependent, not only on one another, but on political, social, and economic trends around the world. This interdependence takes many forms: emigration of the region's inhabitants to the United States and other countries, and the weight of the region's debt to world banks are two examples. Others include the impact of Latin American and Caribbean literature, now routinely translated into many languages, and the international appeal of music and dance originating in the region, from the samba and bossa nova to "salsa" and reggae. In addition, church activism in Latin America and the Caribbean has served as a model for popular movements seeking social change in other parts of the world.

Perspectives on Latin America's Economic Development

Scholars have attempted to develop theories to explain why Latin America and the Caribbean, a region of rich natural and human resources, should still experience widespread underdevelopment and poverty. Two of the most important of these explanations are modernization theory and dependency theory.

Modernization theory, which was developed primarily by North American political economists in the late 1950s and early 1960s, argued that economic growth and development were the key to social and political democracy. Industrialization had been delayed in Latin America and the Caribbean, these scholars argued, but sustained economic growth would bring an end to feudal traditions and military dictatorships. This generally optimistic view was not borne out by historical events. During the 1960s and 1970s, economic growth faltered and authoritarian military governments took power in countries throughout the region. In Brazil and Chile the military regimes presided over periods of rapid economic growth combined with severe political restrictions, and widespread violations of human rights. Apparently, the historical linkage between industrialization and democracy experienced in Western Europe and North America was not to be repeated in Latin America.

Dependency theory, on the other hand, was much more pessimistic about the prospects for achieving both sustained economic growth and political democracy. Dependency theorists, mostly Latin American scholars writing in the late 1960s and 1970s, argued that their countries' economies were tied to and dependent on the growth of other economies, particularly those of the industrialized nations of North America and Western Europe. Some of them believed this economic dependency would lead almost inevitably to political authoritarianism, since the benefits of growth were few and were restricted to a small elite whose primary goal was to protect its privileged position.

More recent history offers some evidence that dependency theory is not a completely accurate interpretation of why and how Latin America's development has differed from that of North America and Europe. For example, dependency theory is insufficient to explain the transitions from military rule in the late 1980s, or the many variations in the national experiences of countries as different as Haiti and Costa Rica, Mexico and Brazil, Argentina and Peru. Both modernization and dependency theories, however, offer important perspectives that will be helpful throughout this course as we attempt to foster a more sophisticated understanding of the reality of Latin America and the Caribbean today.

ASSIGNMENT

1. Read *Modern Latin America*, 3d ed., pp. 3–13.

    The prologue, "Why Latin America?" discusses the most striking paradoxes of the region in terms of its history, political systems, and economic development. The chapter also critiques some of the most common stereotypes of Latin America and the Caribbean and explains the two interpretive theories of modernization and dependency.

2. Read *Americas: An Anthology,* chapter 1, pp. 3–16.

This brief introduction provides the reader with a geographic, economic, political, and cultural overview of the region. Particular attention is given to describing the four themes of the course.

UNIT REVIEW

After reading the assignments, you should be able to:

· Identify the major groups of people whose presence in Latin America and the Caribbean has contributed to the complexity and diversity of today's societies in the region.

· Explain the different motivations and methods that characterized the arrival of non-indigenous groups to the region.

· Recognize the most important features of Latin America's physical geography, and the impact those features have had on the region's economic development.

· Understand two major theories that scholars have used to explain the unique patterns of social, economic, and political development in Latin America and the Caribbean, and identify some important criticisms of those theories.

· Describe the four basic themes of the course.

SELF-TEST QUESTIONS

Multiple Choice

*Mark the letter of the response that **best** answers the question or completes the statement.*

_____ 1. The second highest mountain range in the world can be found in South America. It is:
   a. the Sierra Nevada.
   b. the Andes.
   c. the Himalayas.
   d. the Serra do Mar.

_____ 2. Modernization theory, as applied to Latin American history:
   a. was developed by European social scientists.
   b. maintains that economic growth is necessary for stable political democracy.
   c. proposes that rural society is the key to economic growth.
   d. places great hope on the emergence of a well-educated upper class.

_____ 3. The world's longest river, found in South America, is the:
   a. Rio Grande.
   b. Orinoco.
   c. Nile.
   d. Amazon.

_____ 4. Creole is: *(Mark all that apply.)*
   a. a term used to describe persons of European descent born in Spanish America.
   b. one of the official languages of Brazil.
   c. a term used to describe persons of indigenous ancestry.
   d. a language with African roots spoken widely in Haiti and elsewhere in the Caribbean.

_____ 5. Which of the following statements are true about dependency theory? *(Mark all that apply.)*
   a. It was developed by Latin American scholars in the 1960s and 1970s.
   b. It associated economic dependence with political authoritarianism.
   c. It considered Latin America as a region to be highly dependent on economic forces outside its control.

Contents

Preface: The *Americas* Telecourse   *xi*

Unit 1   The Introduction   *1*

Unit 2   Legacies of Empire: From Conquest to Independence   *10*

Unit 3   The Garden of Forking Paths: Dilemmas of National Development   *22*

Unit 4   Capital Sins: Authoritarianism and Democratization   *35*

Unit 5   Continent on the Move: Migration and Urbanization   *47*

Unit 6   Mirrors of the Heart: Color, Class, and Identity   *60*

Unit 7   In Women's Hands: The Changing Roles of Women   *74*

Unit 8   Miracles Are Not Enough: Continuity and Change in Religion   *87*

Unit 9   Builders of Images: Writers, Artists, and Popular Culture   *100*

Unit 10   Get Up, Stand Up: The Problems of Sovereignty   *112*

Unit 11   Fire in the Mind: Revolutions and Revolutionaries   *126*

Unit 12   The Americans: Latin American and Caribbean Peoples in the United States   *143*

Unit 13   Course Review   *156*

Appendix: Answers to Self-Test Questions   *168*

Preface: The Americas *Telecourse*

COURSE OVERVIEW

Before the end of this century, people of Latin American and Caribbean origin will constitute the largest minority in the United States.

The 33 sovereign states that make up Latin America and the Caribbean represent the United States' most important trade partners in the developing world and most reliable source of many strategic resources, including oil. In the next century, our relationship with this vital region will take on even greater significance. Yet much about the history, politics, economics, social structures, and complex relationships of this important region with other world powers eludes us. Too often, our perspective is colored by stereotypes, broad generalizations, and incomplete or inaccurate information.

Americas, an innovative 10–part television series and 13–unit complete television course, brings to life a startlingly diverse region that encompasses great wealth and desperate poverty, countries as tiny as Jamaica and as enormous as Brazil, with democratic and authoritarian governments and a complex, multicultural heritage. The series provokes a re-examination of U.S. relations with its hemispheric neighbors and with people of Latin American and Caribbean origin living in the United States by highlighting key issues and events of the twentieth century, providing a new perspective that extends far beyond the limited images and crisis-driven headlines of the nightly news.

Americas presents the human face of important issues from representative countries. Its stories range from personal or family issues, to pivotal moments in history, to aspects of local and international culture. In each case, individual community and country examples illuminate the larger processes affecting the region as a whole.

The challenges facing the countries of Latin America and the Caribbean are daunting, but the responses of the peoples of the region have often been positive and innovative. Many of their strategies, crafted in response to local conditions, offer instructive lessons applicable far beyond the boundaries of their particular situation. Some have had international impact in widely diverse areas: witness the new social and political roles of the Catholic Church in Latin America, the development of unique popular music that enhances cultural identity in the Caribbean states, and the multiclass coalitions forged by women in the countries of the Americas.

In its explorations of the forces underlying the contemporary problems and achievements of Latin America and the Caribbean, *Americas* examines these and other questions:

· What is the meaning of sovereignty in the Americas? Why are sovereignty and nationalism so important throughout the region?

· Has foreign intervention in the region's political and economic affairs helped or hindered the goals of democracy and stability?

- What forces contributed to the heavy international debt burdens confronting many countries in the region?

- Why do rural people continue to migrate to urban areas even as the cities become increasingly unlivable? How does domestic and international migration affect families and countries?

- How have women reconciled their traditional places in family, church, and community with the expression and exercise of political and economic power?

- What are some of the possible future trends for U.S. relations with Latin America and the Caribbean and for the region's political, economic, and social development?

COURSE OBJECTIVES

The *Americas* telecourse is designed to help you:

- increase your knowledge and understanding of the nations of Latin America and the Caribbean

- see the people of the Americas as creative and productive, actively confronting their problems, and becoming a force on the global scene

- become aware of the long-standing economic, political, social, and cultural ties that link the United States with the other nations of the Americas

- gain insight into the future of the nations of the Americas and the impact they will have on this country in coming years

COURSE COMPONENTS

The 13–unit *Americas* telecourse consists of the following components:

- 10 one-hour video programs

- this study guide

- the reader, *Americas: An Anthology*, by Mark B. Rosenberg, A. Douglas Kincaid, and Kathleen Logan, published by Oxford University Press

- the textbook, *Modern Latin America* (3d edition, 1992), by Thomas E. Skidmore and Peter H. Smith, published by Oxford University Press

A book of essays written by members of the *Americas* academic advisory board entitled *Americas: New Interpretive Essays*, edited by Alfred Stepan and published by Oxford University Press, is available as an optional component of the television course.

THE STUDY UNITS

Unit 1

The Introduction (a print-only unit) lays out the structure of the course, including the key themes and issues to be studied. It also surveys the geography and peoples of the region.

Unit 2

Legacies of Empire: From Conquest to Independence (a print-only unit) provides a brief history of the region. The readings outline the precolonial period and trace the history of the Spanish and Portuguese conquest, the years of empire, and the early independence period of the 1800s.

Unit 3

The Garden of Forking Paths: Dilemmas of National Development (program 1) examines the twentieth-century development of the nations and national economies of the Americas. The program focuses on Argentina and includes the Perón years,

26. In addition to the *altiplano,* where else do indigenous peoples live in Central and South America?

27. Dependency theory:

28. Per capita GNP:

QUESTIONS TO CONSIDER

1. What historical forces have given the countries of Latin America and the Caribbean a certain unity, despite their many differences?

2. How are the physical geography and demographic makeup of Latin America and the Caribbean different from that of the United States? How are they similar?

3. What are your reasons for taking this course? What do you hope to learn, and why do you think it is important to study Latin America and the Caribbean?

RESOURCES

Nonfiction

Beezley, William H., and Judith Ewell, eds. *The Human Tradition in Latin America: The Nineteenth Century, and The Twentieth Century.* 2 vols. Wilmington, Del.: Scholarly Resources, 1987. This two-volume set is a collection of 23 biographies of "ordinary" people in independent Latin America.

Collier, Simon, Harold Blakemore, and Thomas E. Skidmore, eds. *The Cambridge Encyclopedia of Latin America and the Caribbean.* New York: Cambridge University Press, 1985. This essential reference offers a very thorough overview of the physical and human geography of the region.

Keen, B., ed. *Latin American Civilization: History and Society, 1492 to the Present.* Boulder, Colo.: Westview Press, 1986. Anthology of primary sources that provides various perspectives on Latin America from the time of the Aztecs to the present.

Kidron, Michael, and Ronald Segal. *The New State of the World Atlas.* New York: Simon and Schuster, 1987. Comparative maps show the distribution of natural resources, money, population, weapons, industries, and more.

Knight, Franklin W., and Colin A. Palmer, eds. *The Modern Caribbean.* Chapel Hill: University of North Carolina Press, 1989. A compilation of studies that approach the Caribbean from different disciplines and perspectives, examining the region's colonial past, its diverse racial heritage, and its complex relationship with the United States.

Oxford Analytica. *Latin America in Perspective.* Boston: Houghton Mifflin, 1991. Overview of society, economics, politics, and international relations.

Unit 2

Legacies of Empire:
From Conquest to Independence

The complex social structures of the Americas grew out of the existing native American cultures, and from those of the Spanish, Portuguese, English, Dutch, and French colonizers and the enslaved Africans they imported. © Abbas/Magnum

UNIT SUMMARY

Unit 2 summarizes the key features of the colonial period and the drive for independence in Latin America and the Caribbean. It illustrates the political, economic, social, religious, and cultural heritage of the new nations that achieved independence from the European imperial powers in the nineteenth and twentieth centuries.

The textbook chapter provides a history of the period from 1492 through the 1880s, including the conquest and consolidation of the Spanish and Portuguese empires, the realities of colonial rule, and the development and ultimate triumph of national independence movements. The text also illustrates some of the most important differences between Spanish and Portuguese America. Readings in the anthology describe the harsh reality of the conquest and colonial period for the indigenous and African American populations and describe the turmoil that accompanied the period immediately after independence. Unit 2 does not include a television program.

KEY ISSUES

· What factors have contributed to the multicultural nature of society in both colonial and contemporary Latin America and the Caribbean?

· What were the origins of divisions among races, classes, and ethnic groups in colonial society, and how did this stratification persist beyond the colonial period?

· What were the main characteristics of the economic systems of the Spanish and Portuguese colonies?

· What was the political legacy resulting from the Spanish and Portuguese administration of their American empires?

· What was the role of religion, especially of the Catholic Church, in the establishment and maintenance of the Spanish and Portuguese empires?

· How was independence from the colonial powers achieved, and what political, social, and economic changes resulted from independence?

GLOSSARY

cabildo (kah-BEEL-doh): a town council at the lowest administrative level in colonial Spanish America; some *cabildos* were centers of resistance to royal authority in the independence struggles.

cacao (kah-KAH-oh): cocoa; a major export product of the colonial period.

caudillo (kow-DEAL-yo): chief or leader; term applied to a "strong man" or dictator, often a military officer or ex-officer, who dominated local politics, sometimes gaining national prominence. The postindependence period was an era of *caudillos* throughout Spanish America.

corregidores (koh-rhey-hee-DOHR-es): regional administrators who collected taxes and tariffs and enforced royal decrees in Spanish America. *Corregidores* were replaced by intendants in the reforms of the late eighteenth century.

criollo (kree-OH-yoh): Spanish for Creole; in colonial Spanish America, a native-born white person as distinguished from one born in Spain. Usually *criollos* held a status superior to that of nonwhites, but inferior to that of whites born in Spain. In the eighteenth century, *criollos* became a focus of resistance to royal authority.

engenho (en-ZHANE-yo): from the Portuguese for "engine"; refers to a type of sugar cane plantation with an on-site mill that dominated the economy of northeastern Brazil during the colonial period. The Spanish word *engenio* refers to these plantations in the Spanish colonies.

fazenda (fah-ZEN-dah): the Portuguese term for a large agricultural estate (see *hacienda,* below).

hacienda (HAH-see-EN-dah): large agricultural estate in Spanish America. The *hacienda* system was sometimes semifeudal in nature, with the owner (which could be a family or an institution, such as a church or convent) controlling tracts of land of various sizes, sometimes substantial, along with entire villages of dependent laborers. The growth of *haciendas* throughout Spanish America led to the development of a native-born elite.

intendants: local governors responsible directly to the monarchy; part of a reformed system of colonial administration imposed by the Bourbon king Charles II in the late eighteenth century as a means of reasserting royal control over the colonies. Most intendants were born in Spain and sent to the Americas, rather than being chosen from among the *criollos*.

mercantilism: system of economic control imposed on the American colonies by Spain and Portugal; relied on exploiting wealth (including gold and silver) from the colonies and monopolizing trade in an attempt to maintain a continuing trade surplus for the mother countries. Trade among the colonies or with other European countries was discouraged, limiting local economic development.

mestizo (mess-TEE-soh): person of mixed European and indigenous ancestry. Although initially a small percentage of society, by 1825 *mestizos* constituted over one-quarter of Spanish American society and today form the majority in many of the former Spanish colonies.

mulatto (muh-LAH-toh): person of mixed European and African ancestry. In 1825, *mulattos* in combination with black descendants of Africans constituted over half of the population of Brazil.

peninsulares (pen-EEN-soo-LAH-rez): white persons born in Spain; from the Spanish word for "peninsula" referring to the Iberian peninsula. The colonial period was characterized by struggles for power and prestige between *criollos* and *peninsulares*.

Treaty of Tordesillas (tor-day-SEEL-yas): a negotiated agreement between Spain and Portugal in 1494, mediated by Pope Alexander VI, which divided the Americas between Spain and Portugal while guaranteeing a role for the Catholic Church in the new colonies.

OVERVIEW

When the Spanish and the Portuguese arrived in the Western Hemisphere at the end of the fifteenth and the beginning of the sixteenth centuries, they encountered many diverse peoples. Some, such as the tribes inhabiting the territory of present-day Brazil, were seminomadic and relatively few in number. Others, such as the Aztecs, who inhabited what is today Mexico, and the Incas, whose empire dominated an area 3,000 miles long on the Pacific coast of South America, had complex political, economic, social, cultural, and religious systems.

While the Spanish and Portuguese had tremendous impact on the indigenous populations, the reverse was also true. The early European societies absorbed many elements of the indigenous civilizations they attempted to dominate, which is reflected in the customs, languages, arts, and many other aspects of modern culture in Latin America and the Caribbean. After the initiation of the slave trade in Spanish America in 1518 and in Portuguese America after 1550, African cultural elements were also introduced, contributing to the development of complex, multicultural societies in which clear lines between the various racial and ethnic groups became blurred over time.

The fact that the Portuguese did not encounter as high concentrations of indigenous populations as the Spaniards did was an important contribution to the somewhat different socioeconomic development of Brazil. Unlike the economic system in most of Spanish America, which relied on forced labor from the indigenous peoples through the *encomienda* and *mita* systems, the economic system in Brazil was based on the massive importation of enslaved Africans. One result was that many Brazilians today have at least some African ancestry, while *mestizos,* those of mixed Indian and European parentage, predominate in most of the former Spanish colonies.

In both the Spanish and Portuguese colonies in the Americas, the economic system stressed the production of wealth through the exploitation and export of precious metals and agricultural products. Abuse of the indigenous labor force was rampant, as the Dominican friar Bartolomé de las Casas reported in his account of the colonization

TOLTECS
(about 700–1200 A.D.)

YUCATAN

Chichen Itza

MAYAS
(about 500 B.C.–1200 A.D.)

Tenochtitlan

AZTECS
(1200s–1520 A.D.)

CENTRAL
AMERICA

*A T L A N T I C
O C E A N*

CARIBBEAN SEA

SOUTH
AMERICA

Machu Picchu

Cuzco

Lake Titicaca

Tiahuanaco

INCAS
(1000s–1532 A.D.)

*P A C I F I C
O C E A N*

**The Americas
Before the Encounter**

of the Caribbean islands (see the anthology reading 2.1).

Indigenous people and African Americans did occasionally work as overseers or skilled workers on large landed estates known as plantations, *haciendas,* or *fazendas,* and as artisans in urban centers. A few succeeded in entering the small middle sector that emerged between the elite and the poor. For the vast majority, however, colonial life meant oppression and poverty. When the colonial period ended, it left Latin America and the Caribbean with a legacy of acute socioeconomic inequality based on class and race, with only limited social mobility.

For women, life in the colonial period varied a great deal depending on race and class. The status of indigenous women generally declined with the domination of their societies by the colonizing powers. A large number were treated violently and suffered from the destruction of their families; others entered into strategic marriage alliances, such as those between noble Inca women and Spaniards. Once European women began arriving in the Americas, the usefulness of such alliances diminished, although the children of mixed indigenous and European ancestry created a new group of people, the *mestizos,* who eventually became the majority population in some countries, such as Mexico and Peru.

European women also played an inferior role, even though a relatively high percentage were heads of their households. Limited opportunities for women, even among the elite, led some to enter convents to gain access to education and take greater control over their lives.

Colonial Administration

The imperial powers attempted to impose a high degree of political, economic, social and religious control over their American colonies, but they were not entirely successful. The limited resources of the monarchy, geographic factors such as the distance from Europe and difficult terrain in much of the Americas, as well as the emergence over time of powerful local interests, prevented the monarchies from exercising the degree of control they desired. The Spanish colonies were initially organized into two principal administrative units or viceroyalties—one based in Mexico City and the other in Lima, Peru. In the eighteenth century, Peru was subdivided into three viceroyalties, with capitals in Lima, Bogotá, and Buenos Aires. Viceroys, who represented royal authority, were assisted by colonial officials such as *corregidores,* or regional administrators, most of whom were concentrated in cities and towns.

In practice, the bulk of the population had little or no contact with royal officials, and distance and local circumstances made royal laws and regulations difficult to enforce. In Brazil, where the European population was smaller, control by the Portuguese was even more limited. Such circumstances contributed to the growth of ad-hoc arrangements for governing the colonies in which local elites had a much greater role than Spain or Portugal had intended.

A principal support of the Spanish and Portuguese empire in America was the Catholic Church. Priests and friars accompanied the explorers and conquistadors on their earliest expeditions, reflecting the strong religious motivation of the enterprise. In fact, the legal justification used by the Spanish and Portuguese for the conquest and colonization of the Americas was the 1494 Treaty of Tordesillas, by which Pope Alexander VI sanctioned the division of the Western Hemisphere between Spain and Portugal. In return for papal consent, these nations vowed to convert the indigenous populations to Catholicism and to provide financial and other support for the Catholic Church.

The Church's welfare thus became linked to the continuation of royal control, which later led most churchpeople to oppose the struggle for independence. There were some notable exceptions, however, such as in Mexico, where priests helped lead the independence forces. In general, though, the Catholic Church was conservative and closely linked to elite interests and the preservation of the prevailing socioeconomic order. The transformation of that historical role in the nineteenth and twentieth centuries has brought profound change to the Americas, as we shall see in Unit 8.

Economically, both Spain and Portugal attempted to impose a monopoly on the colonies and required that they trade only with the mother country. This system, known as mercantilism, limited the development of manufacturing and the growth of a significant middle sector in the Americas. At the outset of the colonial period the Spanish and Portuguese sought wealth primarily through the mining of precious metals. While rich deposits were found in such areas as Guanajuato in Mexico and Potosí in Bolivia, land and cheap labor were ultimately the two principal resources to be exploited. Agriculture became the chief economic mainstay of the colonies, with an emphasis on production for export. This stimulated the development of the sugar industry, particularly in the Caribbean and Brazil, cotton, in Mexico and Central America, as well as coffee, *cacao,* and indigo.

Neither Spain nor Portugal was ever able to enforce fully its economic monopoly, and the French, English, and Dutch all traded with a number of the American colonies. These economic relations contributed to the undercutting of Spanish and Portuguese control, particularly in the Caribbean, where the French, English, and Dutch succeeded in wresting away several of Spain's colonies. In Brazil, the Dutch were able to gain a toehold in the northeast in the seventeenth century.

The Route to Independence

By the mid- to late-eighteenth century, the principles of European Enlightenment thought—such as the illegitimacy of absolute monarchies, reliance on human reason, belief in democracy, and desire for greater social equality—were being spread in the Americas, reinforcing the pressures for greater self-rule and freer trade. The colonies were also affected by the successful revolution against England in North America. An important stimulus for the independence movements in Spanish America was the attempt by royal authorities to assert more control over the colonies in the second half of the eighteenth century, by limiting the power and prosperity of local elites.

Beginning in 1810, Spain's colonies began to rebel against the monarchy. Over the course of the next 15 years, numerous military campaigns were waged against royalist troops throughout the continent. Simón Bolívar, the most famous of Latin America's patriots, led a military force that ultimately liberated most of northern South America, while the forces in the south were led by José de San Martín. By the late 1820s, the former Spanish colonies were independent nations.

Brazil's independence movement was quite different, and the transition to independence was much less violent. In Brazil, independence meant the establishment of a local monarchy some 14 years after the Portuguese Court transferred to America in 1807. The idea of republicanism grew slowly in Brazil, which remained a monarchy until 1890.

The tradition of local autonomy inherited from the colonial period contributed to conflicts after independence between those who wanted a strong central government and those who preferred a weak one. The instability resulting from such conflicts contributed to the emergence of regional or national strongmen, known as *caudillos* in Spanish America and *coroneles* in Brazil, along with civil wars, frequent changes of government and constitutions, and shifting political alliances within the elites. The wars of independence had not been intended to democratize America fully, and socioeconomic disparities between the wealthy and the poor majority continued.

However, the social and political upheavals that accompanied the struggle for independence did have some unintended consequences and, in some cases, loosened the elites' hold on power. Several of the independence leaders were *mestizos* who through their military accomplishments achieved prominence and status. Mexican independence leader José Maria Morelos y Pavón was a *mestizo* who called for greater social justice, even advocating agrarian reform.

The struggles for independence throughout the Americas were motivated in part by a desire for an end to exploitation and oppression, goals that continue to be important today. Thus, although the colonial period left a powerful and, in many ways, restrictive legacy throughout the Americas, the seeds for new ways of thinking were taking root.

ASSIGNMENT

1. Read *Modern Latin America,* 3d ed., pp. 14–42.

   Chapter 1, "The Colonial Foundations, 1492–1880s," describes the arrival of the Spanish and Portuguese in America, their contact with and conquest of the indigenous peoples, and the subsequent domination and exploitation of the indigenous groups. The colonial experiences in Spanish and Portuguese America are compared and contrasted in terms of population, economics, and administrative patterns. Finally, the route to independence in the eighteenth and nineteenth centuries is discussed, as well as the legacy of the colonial period for the newly independent nations.

2. Read *Americas: An Anthology,* chapter 2, pp. 17–47.

The introduction and readings in the anthology present various perspectives on the expansion of European empires into the Western Hemisphere and the brutal nature of the conquest. The colonial systems for extracting labor from indigenous peoples and enslaved Africans are described, along with the contrast between the life-style of the elites and that of the workers who made their wealth possible. Final readings examine the drive for independence and the chaos of the postindependence period.

UNIT REVIEW

After reading the assignments you should be able to:

· Describe the intermingling of indigenous peoples, Africans, and Europeans which created new groups, such as *mestizos* and *mulattos,* and resulted over time in the complex, multicultural societies of modern Latin America and the Caribbean.

· Understand that colonial society in both Spanish and Portuguese America was characterized by hierarchies based on race and class: at the top was a small group of white elites; in the middle a somewhat larger group of whites, *mestizos,* and *mulattos*; and at the bottom, the vast majority, mainly indigenous and African populations.

· Realize that colonial economic systems were based on the production and export of raw materials, especially silver and cacao in Spanish America and sugar and gold in Brazil, and that these systems relied on the forced labor of indigenous populations and enslaved Africans.

· Recognize that the inability of Spain and Portugal to maintain tight control over their colonies allowed important administrative and legal matters to fall into the hands of powerful local elites.

· Understand the important role played by the Catholic Church in the establishment and maintenance of the Spanish and Portuguese empires.

· Describe the different means by which the former colonies in Spanish and Portuguese America and the Caribbean obtained their independence, and understand why the various independence movements generally did not seek the total transformation of political, economic, and social structures.

SELF-TEST QUESTIONS

Multiple Choice

*Mark the letter of the response that **best** answers the question or completes the statement.*

_____ 1. The empire that constructed Tenochtitlán on the site of present-day Mexico City was:
        a. the Inca.
        b. the Maya.
        c. the Aztec.
        d. the Spanish.

_____ 2. Which of the following accomplishments were attributed to the Incas? *(Mark all that apply.)*
        a. An intricate irrigation system.
        b. Terraced agriculture on mountainsides.

c. A system for treating head injuries.

d. Invention of the calendar.

_____ 3. Prior to the arrival of the Spanish, the religious beliefs of many native peoples of the Americas:
   a. had almost no similarities to Christian beliefs.
   b. included the concepts of an afterlife and a creator god.
   c. varied very little from one indigenous group to another.
   d. were virtually nonexistent.

_____ 4. Bartolomé de las Casas:
   a. witnessed and recounted the devastating conquest of the indigenous population in Hispaniola.
   b. led an important military wing under Hernán Cortés.
   c. was a poet who went on to lead the struggle for independence in Haiti.
   d. was a religious man who wholeheartedly supported the conquest of the indigenous groups by the Spaniards.

_____ 5. European colonizers who extended their empires into the Western Hemisphere were motivated by: *(Mark all that apply.)*
   a. the promise of wealth.
   b. the desire for power.
   c. missionary zeal to spread Christianity.
   d. the desire to preserve the New World's native civilizations.

_____ 6. The role of the Catholic Church in the American colonies of Spain and Portugal: *(Mark all that apply.)*
   a. only became important in the later colonial period, when Pope Alexander VI helped negotiate the Treaty of Tordesillas.
   b. was to win converts for Christianity.
   c. had an important social aspect that made it one of colonial America's most powerful social institutions.

   d. was restricted exclusively to religious aspects of the colonial societies.

_____ 7. In the hierarchical colonial societies of the Americas:
   a. *mestizos* tended to hold the highest positions in commerce and the Church.
   b. indigenous groups and enslaved Africans occupied the lowest positions in the social order.
   c. the intermediate positions of merchants and urban artisans were primarily held by freed slaves.
   d. *peninsulares* and *criollos* made up the majority of the population.

_____ 8. Which of the following statements are true of colonial economic systems in the Americas? *(Mark all that apply.)*
   a. They were based on the forced labor of indigenous groups and enslaved Africans.
   b. They were unable to generate much wealth for Spain and Portugal.
   c. They established free-trade patterns among the colonies and with numerous European countries.
   d. They emphasized the production of raw materials and agricultural goods for export.

_____ 9. People born in the Americas of exclusively European parentage were known as:
   a. *peninsulares.*
   b. *corregidores.*
   c. *criollos.*
   d. *mestizos.*

_____ 10. The term *engenho* refers to:
   a. a Portuguese landowner in Brazil.
   b. a representative of the Spanish monarchy who collected taxes and enforced royal decrees.
   c. a large cane sugar plantation with an on-site mill in northeast Brazil.
   d. a system for obtaining forced indigenous labor for the silver mines in Peru.

_____ 11. European women in the colonial system: *(Mark all that apply.)*
    a. were considered essential to keep the boundaries distinct between people of indigenous and/or African heritage and those of European descent.
    b. led a privileged life in which they had ample time to study, allowing them to achieve higher levels of education and a social position equal to that of men.
    c. found that entering the convent was virtually the only means of obtaining an education.
    d. were treated more harshly than their Indian and *mestizo* counterparts.

_____ 12. The independence movement of which country was an attempt to change the prevailing social order?
    a. Brazil
    b. Venezuela
    c. Chile
    d. Haiti

_____ 13. Independence movements in the Spanish and Portuguese colonies in the Americas:
    a. were in large part focused on the need to democratize Latin American societies.
    b. were inspired by European Enlightenment thought and the desire for dignity, along with a rejection of royal authority.
    c. were led by the intendants, who had been sent as Napoleon's emissaries to the Americas.
    d. brought about a lengthy period of political stability throughout the region.

_____ 14. Which of the following were important limitations on the growth of domestic industry in nineteenth-century Latin America? *(Mark all that apply.)*
    a. Latin American goverments' reliance on tariff revenues as an important source of income.
    b. The poor quality of machines, tools, and parts imported from Europe.
    c. European pressure on local elites to maintain free trade and reject protectionism.
    d. The large size and buying power of domestic markets in Latin America.

True or False

_____ 15. Winning converts to Catholicism was an important motivation for Spain and Portugal in their conquest of the New World.

_____ 16. Most of the European conquerors came from the ranks of the nobility.

_____ 17. In colonial Spanish America, the majority of the population was made up of *criollos.*

_____ 18. By the early nineteenth century, nearly two-thirds of the entire Brazilian population was of partial or total African ancestry.

_____ 19. The forced labor system known as the *mita* brought thousands of indigenous peoples to work in the silver mines of Peru under very harsh conditions.

_____ 20. The lack of large concentrations of indigenous people in Brazil led to the massive importation of slaves to provide the necessary labor.

_____ 21. The *caudillos* were religious leaders who accompanied the conquistadores to America in the early sixteenth century.

_____ 22. Because of the impact of mercantilism, England, France, and Holland were unable to carry out any direct trade with the Spanish and Portuguese colonies in the Americas.

_____ 23. The Treaty of Tordesillas gave papal consent to the division of America between Spain and Portugal.

Identification/Short Answer

Define and/or describe the following terms, concepts, or persons, or answer the following questions. Answers should be no longer than a few sentences.

24. Identify some of the factors that contributed to the ability of the Spanish to penetrate and conquer the Aztec and Inca empires.

25. Name three important differences between the Spanish and Portuguese empires in Latin America.

26. Identify the key exports during the colonial period for each of the following countries:

    Brazil:

    Cuba:

    Mexico:

    Peru:

27. Intendants:

28. *Mulattos:*

29. *Hacienda:*

30. What were some of the factors that made the *caudillos* especially important in the postindependence years?

QUESTIONS TO CONSIDER

1. In what ways did the movements for independence in Spanish and Portuguese America differ?

2. How has society and culture in the Americas been shaped by the various racial groups that live in the region?

3. The United States also experienced colonialism, yet its political and social development has been quite different from other countries in the Western Hemisphere. What are some of the differences in the colonial legacies of North and South America that may account for such divergent development patterns?

4. On balance, would you say the colonial period left a positive, negative, or neutral legacy in the Americas? Why?

RESOURCES

Nonfiction

Bedini, Silvio A., ed. *The Christopher Columbus Encyclopedia.* New York: Simon and Schuster, 1991. This two-volume reference encyclopedia contains more than 350 original articles by nearly 150 contributors from around the world.

Bowser, Frederick P. *The African Slave in Colonial Peru, 1524–1650*. Stanford, Calif.: Stanford University Press, 1974. A very well-written account of the impact of slavery on colonial society and individuals.

Bray, Warwick. "How Old Are the Americans?" *Américas* (May–June 1988). Explores the debate over when humans first reached the New World. Although most archaeologists once accepted the theory that America was first inhabited 12,000 years ago, artifacts recently discovered indicate that humans may have reached the area as long as 34,000 years ago.

Buarque, Cristobal. "A Lingering Legacy," *Américas* (May–June 1988). Examines the adverse impact of slavery on Brazilian society.

Clendinnen, Inga. *Ambivalent Conquests: Maya and Spaniards in the Yucatan, 1517–70*. New York: Cambridge University Press, 1987. Illuminating account of the religious role in the conquest and its ambiguities.

Columbus, Christopher. *The Log of Christopher Columbus*. Translated by Robert Fuson. Camden, Maine: International Maritime Publishing, 1987. The explorer's own account of his epochal journey and first encounters with the indigenous peoples of the New World.

Díaz del Castillo, Bernal. *The Conquest of New Spain*. Translated by J.M. Cohen. Baltimore: Penguin Books, 1963. A vivid, personal account by one of Cortés's soldiers of the conquest of the Aztec Empire.

Gutierrez, A. *When Jesus Came, the Corn Mothers Went Away*. Stanford, Calif.: Stanford University Press, 1990. This social history uses marriage as a case study to show the lasting impact of the Spanish conquest on the Pueblo Indians of New Mexico.

Hart, Richard. *Slaves Who Abolished Slavery: Blacks in Bondage*, vol. 1. University of the West Indies, Jamaica: Institute of Social and Economic Research, 1980. This volume deals with the origins of the slave trade and slavery in the West Indies. The conclusion focuses on the abolitionist movement in Britain and the successful revolt that ended slavery in Haiti.

Hemming, John. *Red Gold: The Conquest of the Brazilian Indians, 1500–1700*. Cambridge: Harvard University Press, 1978. Historical overview of the relations among the Portuguese monarchy, the Catholic Church, and the colonists and indigenous peoples of Brazil.

Hoetink, H. *Slavery and Race Relations in the Americas*. New York: Harper and Row, 1973. An insightful analysis of the realities and texture of slave societies and their consequences.

Knight, Franklin W. *Slave Society in Cuba during the Nineteenth Century*. Madison: University of Wisconsin Press, 1970. A socioeconomic analysis of the role of slavery in Cuban historical development.

Lavrín, Asuncion, ed. *Sexuality and Marriage in Colonial Latin America*. Lincoln: University of Nebraska Press, 1989. A pioneering collection of essays on the subject.

León-Portilla, Miguel, ed. *Broken Spears: The Aztec Account of the Conquest of Mexico*. Boston: Beacon Press, 1962. Excellent compilation of surviving Aztec views of the conquest.

Lynch, John. *The Spanish-American Revolutions, 1808–1826*. New York: Norton, 1973. Classic study of the origins and course of the wars of independence.

Milanich, J., and S. Milbrath, eds. *First Encounters: Spanish Explorations in the Caribbean and the United States, 1492–1570*. Gainesville: University of Florida Press, 1989. Using recent research, the period of early Spanish contact with the peoples of the New World is explored.

Padden, R. S. *The Hummingbird and the Hawk*. New York: Harper & Row, 1970. Classic account of the rise and fall of the Aztec Empire.

Poma de Ayala, Huamán. *Letter to a King: A Peruvian Chief's Account of Life Under the Incas and Under Spanish Rule*. Edited by Christopher Dilke. New York: Dutton, 1978. First-person account with drawings by the author depicting indigenous life before and after the conquest.

Queirós Mattozo, D. Katia. *To Be a Slave in Brazil, 1550–1888.* Translated by Arthur Goldhammer. New Brunswick, N.J.: Rutgers University Press, 1986. Illuminating and readable exploration of the topic.

Sale, Kirkpatrick. *Conquest of Paradise: Christopher Columbus and the Columbian Legacy.* New York: Knopf, 1990. Author examines the impact of the conquest, with special emphasis on ecological and environmental consequences.

Fiction and Poetry

Benitez-Rojo, Antonio. *Sea of Lentils.* Amherst: University of Massachusetts Press, 1990. This novel combines fact and fiction in portraying sixteenth-century Cuba, Puerto Rico, and the Dominican Republic. The novel's title comes from the misidentification of French cartographer Guillaume de Testu, who mistook the word *antilles* for *lentilles* (French for "lentils").

Galeano, Eduardo. *Memory of Fire.* New York: Pantheon, 1985. Loosely based on historical accounts of the conquest and colonization, this trilogy of vignettes ("Genesis," "Faces and Masks," and "Century of the Wind") offers a Latin American view of the New World in the making. The first and second volumes are most relevant to this unit.

Manzano, Juan Francisco. *The Life and Poems of a Cuban Slave.* Edited by Edward J. Mullen. Hamden, Conn.: Archon Books, 1981. Collection of creative writing by a Cuban slave (1797–1854). The reader has the opportunity to reflect on the effects of the transportation of enslaved Africans to the New World.

Rhys, Jean. *Wide Sargasso Sea.* New York: Norton, 1982. Written in a stream-of-consciousness manner, this novel tells the tale of women in early nineteenth-century Jamaica and Dominica. The concepts of race, gender, and class under slavery are dealt with from a woman's point of view.

Schwartz-Bart, Simone. *The Bridge of Beyond.* Translated by Barbara Bray. London: Heinemann, 1982. In this historical novel, a Guadaloupan woman recounts her life's story and reflects on her great-grandmother's life as a slave.

Zobel, Joseph. *Black Shack Alley.* Translated by Keith Q. Warner Washington, D.C.: Three Continents Press, 1980. This novel, set in French colonial Martinique, tells the story of José, a young boy being raised by his grandmother in a community of sugar-cane workers. (Filmed as "Sugar Cane Alley"; see "Films," below.)

Films

Unless otherwise indicated, all films listed are available in VHS video format.

Columbus and the Age of Discovery. Seven hours, 1991. Originally broadcast on public television, this documentary series is a balanced exploration of Columbus and the European conquest of America and its consequences. Available for purchase ($29.95 for each 60–minute program) from The WGBH Collection, P.O. Box 2053, Princeton, NJ 08543; (800) 828–WGBH.

Sugar Cane Alley. 107 minutes, 1984 (French, with English subtitles). Examines plantation life in colonial Martinique from the vantage point of José, an Afro-Caribbean boy whose grandmother is determined to free at least one of her grandchildren from the drudgery of life on a sugar cane plantation. Available for rental ($20) from Facets, 1517 West Fullerton, Chicago, IL 60614; (800) 331–6197.

Unit 3

The Garden of Forking Paths: Dilemmas of National Development

Juan Domingo Perón promoted Argentina's industrialization and, with the help of his wife, Evita, mobilized urban workers into a powerful social and political force. AP/Wide World Photos

UNIT SUMMARY

After achieving independence from Spain and Portugal, the new nations of the Americas faced three major challenges: developing a sense of national identity; building strong, viable states; and embarking on a path for economic development. Unit 3 examines the choices—and outcomes—that faced leaders in the Americas from the late nineteenth to the midtwentieth centuries. The decisions they made were neither easy nor clear-cut, and each choice had both benefits and costs.

The difficulties of pursuing particular paths to development are illustrated in the example of Argentina, a country whose combination of natural resources and political institutions made it one of the world's most prosperous nations in the early part of the twentieth century. The unit explains why particular policies were selected and, how internal and external forces combined to thwart the country's development plans. The unit also examines the importance of nationalism in Argentina and elsewhere in the region, especially how nationalist ideology and rhetoric has been used to enhance the popular appeal of political leaders both in and out of power.

KEY ISSUES

· What was the major economic strategy followed throughout Latin America in the first century after independence? What were the benefits and costs of that strategy? Were there any feasible alternatives?

· What prompted the decision by many Latin American nations to move toward a policy of import-substituting industrialization, and what were the political and social results of this choice?

· In what ways does Argentina's economic and political development differ from that of the rest of Latin America? How does Argentina resemble its neighbors?

· What role has nationalism played in the social and political history of Argentina in the twentieth century, and how was it used to support the leadership of Juan Perón and other political and military figures?

· What were the primary forces that led to the increasing involvement of the military in Argentine politics in the second half of the twentieth century?

· Why did the military ultimately leave power, and what challenges confront Argentina's democratically elected governments in the postmilitary period?

GLOSSARY

Austral Plan: Argentine president Raúl Alfonsín's 1985 monetary plan, which introduced a new currency (the austral) and set a wage-price freeze; the plan's objective was to end the hyperinflation that approached 700 percent annually in 1985. The Austral Plan was ultimately unsuccessful.

balance of payments: a record of the economic transactions between two countries, reflecting trade in goods, services, and capital. When there is a deficit in the balance of payments, more money is flowing out of the country than is coming into it.

comparative advantage: economic term for the lower costs and greater efficiency of producing certain products in one country rather than in another. According to the theory of economic liberalism (see below), Latin America had a comparative advantage in the production of raw materials. Therefore, it should have concentrated its efforts on exporting those products and used the revenue to import from Europe the manufactured goods it was not able to produce efficiently.

corporatism: political model in which broad-based parties are replaced by groups organized more narrowly by economic function—for example, industrialists, farmers, or workers. The corporatist model began in Europe and was adopted in modified fashion in Latin America by several populist leaders, including Brazil's Getúlio Vargas and Argentina's Juan Perón.

desaparecidos (des-ah-pah-reh-SEE-dos): literally, the "disappeared"; refers to those who were arrested and subsequently disappeared under repressive military governments. Most of the thousands who disappeared in Brazil, Argentina, and Chile are now presumed to have been killed by the military or the police. The issues of accountability and justice for the families of the disappeared have been very important in the transitions to civilian rule.

economic liberalism: set of economic theories imported from Europe that became well established among Latin America's elites in the nineteenth century, encouraging free trade and laissez-faire economic policies. Economic liberalism justified Latin America's integration into the world economy as the exporter of raw materials and the importer of manufactured goods.

exchange rate: the price of one country's currency in another currency, such as U.S. dollars; used to calculate prices of goods for trade purposes.

export-import growth: economic model followed throughout Latin America from independence through the 1930s; based on the export of raw materials and agricultural goods in exchange for imports of manufactured goods, luxury items, and capital from the industrial powers of North America and Europe.

foreign exchange: also known as "hard currency"; refers to the few internationally accepted currencies used for international trade (such as the U.S. dollar, the German mark, the British pound, and the Japanese yen). All countries need reserves of foreign exchange, obtained by selling exports, in order to pay for imports.

gauchos (GOW-choz): Argentine cowboys; legendary figures associated with romanticized tales of life on the *pampas* (see below), reminiscent of U.S. myths of the far West.

import-substituting industrialization (ISI): economic strategy of reducing economic dependence and vulnerability to external economic fluctuations by developing local industries. The strategy, which sought to substitute locally produced manufac-

tured goods for formerly imported goods, was adopted by many Latin American countries in the 1930s, 1940s, and 1950s.

nationalism: ideology of devotion to one's nation, especially its freedom and independence. Nationalism has been an important theme in Latin American political history, and has been used repeatedly by leaders of every political persuasion to enhance their legitimacy and popular appeal.

pampas (PAHM-pas): expanse of grassland in Argentina; wheat and beef raised on the *pampas* were the basis for Argentina's prosperity in the early twentieth century.

Perón, Eva (Evita): second wife of Juan Perón; charismatic and influential political leader in her own right who earned the fanatic loyalty of hundreds of thousands of Argentines with her personal compassion and state-financed handouts to the *descamisados*, the "shirtless ones." Evita's death in 1952 brought an outpouring of national grief, as she had come to symbolize the essence of Peronism (see below).

Perón, Juan Domingo: Argentine army colonel; political leader who founded Peronism and who exerted important influence over Argentine politics from the mid-1940s until his death in 1974. Perón served two consecutive terms as president (1946–55), was exiled by the military until 1973, then returned as president again from 1973 to 1974. His death left his third wife, Isabel, as president until a coup in 1976.

Peronism: political movement with populist tendencies named for its founder, Juan Perón. Based primarily among the organized urban working class, Peronism has been a major force in national politics since the mid-1940s.

populism: in Latin America, a political style that emerged in the 1930s and 1940s in response to the challenges and socioeconomic changes brought about by rapid industrialization. Populists based their power on multiclass coalitions of organized labor, the military, and nationalistic entrepreneurs. Nationalism and sovereignty were important themes to populists, who emphasized state involvement in promoting economic growth.

Roca-Runciman Pact: 1933 agreement between Argentina and England guaranteeing Argentine beef access to the English market in exchange for Argentina's purchase of British goods and an agreement to keep British industries in Argentina profitable. The pact's purpose was to protect the economies of both countries during the period of global economic recession after the crash of 1929.

Rosas, Juan Manuel de: Argentine dictator from 1829 to 1852; responsible for uniting the nation into a strong federalist union under Buenos Aires. Rosas later became an important patriotic symbol for Argentine nationalists.

tango (TAHN-go): Argentine dance, with immigrant and working-class roots, that originated in Buenos Aires in the 1880s and became enormously popular in Europe in the 1910s, especially through the work of singer/composer Carlos Gardel. The tango eventually became accepted in the upper circles of Argentine society and has become an important symbol of national culture and pride.

OVERVIEW

Unit 3 focuses on the postindependence experiences of countries in Latin America, and the policy decisions made by government leaders to bring the benefits of development and economic growth to their nations. Difficult choices had to be made at several critical points, and the outcomes of each option were neither obvious nor painless. The new leaders also had to assist in their countries' efforts to build a concept of themselves as nations. Nationalism, the ideology of devotion to one's nation, was a unifying theme that political leaders seized on to unite internal groups and to reinforce their own legitimacy and popular appeal.

The dilemmas of national development are illustrated in this unit with the example of Argentina. Although Argentina is the first country to be studied in detail in this course, it is in many ways atypical of Latin America as a whole. During the colonial period, Argentina received little attention from the conquerors, since, unlike Peru and Mexico, it did not have large deposits of gold and silver. Argentina's agricultural potential lay unde-

veloped as well; its nomadic indigenous peoples were never viewed as a potential source of indentured labor, nor did the country become a major slave destination. In fact, Argentina was virtually ignored by the colonial powers until well into the eighteenth century, when it began to grow as a trade center. The country's tremendous advantages in land, climate, and geographic location became evident in the late nineteenth century when it embarked on a sustained period of growth.

Argentina is an appropriate place to begin a detailed study of the region, however, because its nineteenth- and twentieth-century history and development highlight the choices and problems facing all of the Americas. Like other Latin American countries, Argentina followed a strategy of export-led growth. This strategy, based on the theory of economic liberalism then popular in Europe, encouraged free trade and laissez-faire economic policies.

The Export-Import Economy

Lacking technology, domestic industries, and capital, Latin American nations concentrated on accumulating wealth by exporting the products they did have—raw materials such as precious metals and agricultural products—to the growing industrial powers in Europe and North America. In return, they imported manufactured items, luxury goods, technology, and capital from European and North American countries.

Each nation began to develop its own particular speciality: guano in Peru, copper in Chile, *henequén* (hemp) in Mexico, coffee in Brazil. The Argentine *pampas* became the basis for a thriving industry in meat and grain production. Argentina's economy grew steadily from the 1860s into the early twentieth century, and its sophisticated capital, Buenos Aires, became known as the "Paris of the South."

Nevertheless, the export-import economic model had important limitations, which became more and more evident as time went by. Under this strategy, economic growth in Latin America was highly dependent on external forces: the growth of demand for exports; the stability of prices for both imports and exports; and the availability of foreign capital for investment. In addition, the

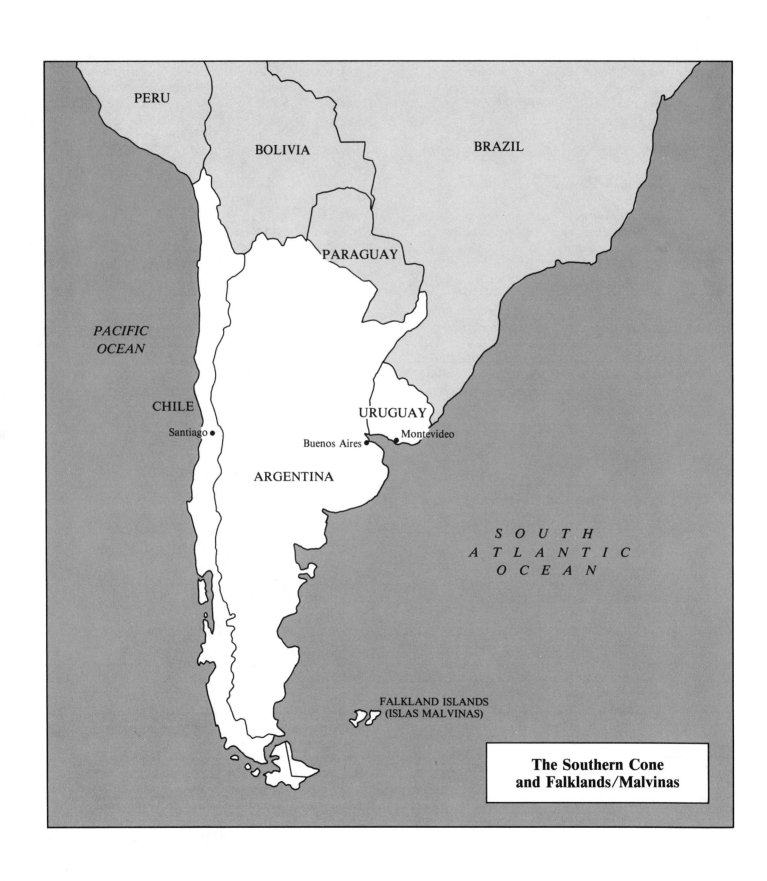

PERU

BOLIVIA

BRAZIL

PARAGUAY

PACIFIC OCEAN

CHILE

Santiago ●

URUGUAY

Buenos Aires ●   ● Montevideo

ARGENTINA

*S O U T H
A T L A N T I C
O C E A N*

FALKLAND ISLANDS
(ISLAS MALVINAS)

**The Southern Cone
and Falklands/Malvinas**

benefits of growth were restricted to small circles of elites, primarily the owners of land and other capital. Although a handful of economic nationalists, intellectuals, and even some political leaders argued that economic liberalism was undermining national sovereignty, it took a series of severe external pressures to convince the ruling elites to change their countries' path to economic development.

The Shift to Industrialization

The 1929 crash of the U.S. stock market and the subsequent worldwide depression was devastating for Latin America's economies, and highlighted the vulnerability of the export-import growth model. Larger countries, such as Argentina and Brazil, began to turn to a new strategy, import-substituting industrialization (ISI), to replace imported goods from Europe with domestically produced goods and to increase economic self-sufficiency. Their goal was to promote rapid industrialization by protecting local industries and creating jobs for the working class.

World War II brought a drop in available supplies from the Allied powers, which meant that Latin American industries either had to produce for themselves or do without. As a result, industrialization accelerated in Latin America, especially in Brazil, Argentina, and Mexico. The smaller countries of the region, such as those in Central America and the Caribbean, lacked the capital and technology to pursue ISI; their efforts to industrialize would come much later, typically during the 1960s and 1970s.

ISI's impact was not restricted to the economic sphere. The pursuit of ISI was a political as well as economic decision, cloaked in the mantle of nationalism. The political rhetoric that accompanied ISI policies tended to emphasize independence from foreign powers and enhanced national sovereignty.

Rapid industrialization led to an increasingly diverse society, in which economic power was distributed among several centers: organized labor; a growing group of middle-class professionals, merchants, and shopkeepers; and, at the top, entrepreneurs and industrialists. These newer sectors began to clamor for a greater share of political power, putting pressure on the export-import elites who had managed to contain most decision-making power among themselves for so long.

Thus, in many parts of Latin America, a new form of "populist" politics came into being. Populism was a response to the changing nature of Latin American societies, which were becoming increasingly urban and had greater numbers of competing social groups. In general, Latin American populism was characterized by an appeal to the working classes; leaders such as Argentina's Juan Perón and Brazil's Getúlio Vargas built their political base on organized labor (a labor force that was, however, controlled by the state). Populist leaders tended to be semiauthoritarian, highly nationalistic, and anti-imperialist, enhancing their popularity through such actions as expropriating foreign-owned industries.

Unit 4 will examine the limitations of the ISI model and the subsequent difficulties that Latin American countries faced in the midtwentieth century. For now, however, we shift to an examination of Argentina, which prospered earlier in the century but today finds itself confronting many of the same policy dilemmas as countries elsewhere in the region: chronic poverty, a stagnant economy burdened with both inflation and foreign debt, a fragile political system, and a contemporary legacy of injustice and inequity.

Argentina

Chapter 3 in the textbook traces the political and economic history of Argentina from the 1880s to the present. Four themes help describe this complex and unusual country. First, Argentina had no peasantry, and no long-standing struggles over land and its ownership. Its wealthy landowners raised cattle and wheat, products that did not require the heavy labor needed for crops elsewhere in the region, such as sugar or coffee.

Second, Argentine society became urbanized quite early, and the dominant influence was European. Enormous numbers of immigrants, especially from Italy and Spain, led to a conception of national identity in Argentina that differed markedly from that in other countries in Latin America. Argentine nationalists considered themselves more European than American, and believed their country to be innately superior to its neighbors in the region.

Third, organized labor became an active and influential force in Argentine society and politics beginning at the turn of the century. The importance of Juan Perón and the Peronist movement to Argentine politics was due largely to the strength in numbers and influence of his working-class base. Even when Peronism was banned and labor repressed, which happened repeatedly in the 1955–84 period, its strength as an ideology and nationalist symbol persisted.

Finally, the armed forces played a pivotal role in Argentine politics during the twentieth century. Contempt for politics, politicians, and the democratic process led the Argentine armed forces to interrupt repeatedly the course of electoral politics after 1930, and helped convince the military of its right and duty to lead the nation. The repeated cycles of economic and social chaos in the post–World War II period enhanced the country's desire for the political and social order represented by the military. We should not be surprised that the military, too, seized on the rhetoric of nationalism to justify its actions and solidify popular support.

When the armed forces led the coup against Isabel Perón in 1976, most of Argentine society approved. The military was determined not to return power to civilian government until political and economic stability was assured, even though that might mean prolonged military rule. A country that had prided itself on its sophisticated culture and educated population then suffered years of repression, torture, and disappearances engineered by the military regime. Public revulsion at this "dirty war," combined with frustration at the armed forces' failure to rescue the country's economy, eventually led to increased public demands that the generals leave office.

In 1982 the military government gambled that it could strengthen its domestic position by making a stand on the Malvinas, or Falkland Islands. In taking such a risky step, the military leaders made several miscalculations. They were correct in counting on the issues of national pride, sovereignty, and anticolonialism to unite Argentines behind their government. But patriotic appeals were no protection from the public's wrath after the disastrous military campaign against Great Britain, and the generals were ultimately forced to step down in disgrace.

Argentina's future as a democratic country is still not secure. Factions within the military continue to threaten the elected government with rebellion. The public remains dissatisfied with the lack of justice for the human rights offenders of the military regime. The president and legislature have been criticized for corruption and mismanagement. And Argentina's economic difficulties show few signs of abating. The country that thought of itself as more European than American is now seen as having much in common with its neighbors. Presidents Raúl Alfonsín (1983–89) and Carlos Menem (1989–) have used strong measures to turn the economy around, although Alfonsín found the task too difficult and, with the economy in disarray, had to resign from office six months early. Menem's ability to stick with the tough policies necessary to stabilize the economy has given some cause for hope that the country can regain its place as the showcase of Latin America. No doubt, Argentina's path to economic and political stability will remain a difficult one.

ASSIGNMENT

1. Before viewing the television program, read:

    Modern Latin America, 3d ed., pp. 43–56, 68–111.

    In chapter 2, "The Transformation of Modern Latin America, 1880s–1980s," the assigned section (pp. 43–56) examines four phases of economic and political change in the region. Phases 1 through 3, assigned in this unit, cover the initiation and expansion of export-import growth from the late nineteenth century to the 1929 depression, followed by the shift to import-substituting industrialization. Political and social trends that accompanied these economic strategies are also discussed. This chapter describes general patterns that were the case for most of the Americas, and helps the reader to situate the region within the context of global economic change.

Chapter 3, "Argentina: From Prosperity to Deadlock," (pp. 68–111) describes Argentina's economic prosperity at the turn of the century resulting from the country's successful application of the export-import economic model. The chapter goes on to explore the increasing complexity of Argentine society, the growth of a middle class, the rise of organized labor, and especially the role of Peronism. The increasing military interventions after 1930, culminating in the bureaucratic-authoritarian state of 1976–82, are also discussed, along with the challenges facing the country's contemporary civilian leadership.

2. View the program "The Garden of Forking Paths."

3. After viewing the program, read:

   Americas: An Anthology, chapter 3, pp. 48–71.

   The anthology readings give a sense of the commonalities among the countries of the Americas as they attempted to craft a successful development strategy. The anthology chapter provides an overview of the economic strategies of export-import growth and import-substituting industrialization, as well as a description of populism as practiced in Brazil, Mexico, Peru, and Argentina.

UNIT REVIEW

After viewing the program and reading the assignments, you should be able to:

· Understand why, in the first century after independence, most Latin American countries pursued the export-import economic model.

· Recognize that the export-import economy brought prosperity (although mostly to a small elite), vulnerability to external conditions, and overreliance on a few products for export.

· Explain why many of the larger Latin American governments chose to move toward a policy of

import-substituting industrialization (ISI) during the 1930s and 1940s, and describe the social and political trends that accompanied ISI.

· Name the factors that make Argentina different from the rest of Latin America, while also recognizing that Argentina faced the same constraints as other nations in the region in seeking to pursue independent economic development.

· Analyze Argentina's social and political history in the twentieth century, especially the importance of nationalism and its role in supporting the leadership of Juan Perón and other political and military figures.

· List the reasons for the Argentine military's increasing involvement in politics in the second half of the twentieth century.

· Explain how the Argentine military lost its domestic legitimacy and describe the challenges facing Argentina's democratically elected governments in the postmilitary period.

SELF-TEST QUESTIONS

Multiple Choice

*Mark the letter of the response that **best** answers the question or completes the statement.*

_____ 1. In the nineteenth century, the economic strategy of most Latin American nations was to:
   a. move toward rapid industrialization of their economies.
   b. continue to trade primarily with the former colonial powers—Spain and Portugal.
   c. develop new markets for their exports of luxury goods, especially in the United States.
   d. export raw materials and import manufactured goods, mostly from Europe.

_____ 2. Argentina focused on the export of beef and wheat because:
   a. its fertile grasslands were ideally suited to ranching and wheat production.
   b. the drop in U.S. supplies of beef and wheat had created an opening for Argentina in the world market.
   c. production of beef and wheat were ideal for using Argentina's surplus labor force.
   d. Argentina had exhausted its silver supplies and needed to find new products to export.

_____ 3. In order to expand the export-import economy in the early twentieth century, Latin American governments: *(Mark all that apply.)*
   a. sought foreign capital to develop transport systems.
   b. provided incentives for peasants to move to the cities.
   c. encouraged European immigration as a source of laborers.
   d. favored domestic industries while neglecting agriculture.

_____ 4. What did the guano trade in Peru and the beef and wheat trade in Argentina have in common? *(Mark all that apply.)*
   a. Foreigners controlled the production and subsequent profits of the export industries.
   b. Decisions made by external, industrial powers had a dramatic economic impact on Peru's and Argentina's economies.
   c. The benefits of economic growth were confined to a small circle of elites.
   d. Government receipts from the industries were used to fund limited social reforms aimed at the working class.

_____ 5. In 1914, approximately what percentage of Argentina's population was foreign-born?
   a. 10
   b. 20

   c. 30
   d. 40

_____ 6. Which of the following occurred in the export-import economies?
   a. Landowners were heavily involved in politics.
   b. Nationalists urged the continuation of unrestricted trade.
   c. Foreign investors had little access to Latin American markets.
   d. Industrialists allied with the military to take political control.

_____ 7. The turning point that prompted a shift in many of the larger Latin American countries from export-import growth to import-substituting industrialization was:
   a. World War I.
   b. the Great Depression.
   c. World War II.
   d. the Bretton Woods agreement.

_____ 8. As Latin American societies became more industrialized, which of the following occurred? *(Mark all that apply.)*
   a. Landowners retreated from politics.
   b. *Caudillos* dominated the political scene.
   c. The urban working class gained more political influence.
   d. Elites retained power while allowing very limited reform.

_____ 9. Import-substituting industrialization was deemed a solution for which of the following problems? *(Mark all that apply.)*
   a. Excessive Latin American dependence on economic conditions in industrial countries.
   b. The poor quality of imported technology and machinery needed to develop domestic industries.
   c. Insufficient agricultural production and the consequent need to import food.
   d. The unreliability of trade earnings due to fluctuations in export prices.

_____ 10. Import-substituting industrialization in Argentina was characterized by:

   a. a hands-off, or laissez-faire, attitude by the government toward the private sector.

   b. government incentives to increase agricultural productivity to feed the growing middle class.

   c. an aggressive search for foreign capital to develop local industrial and technological capacities.

   d. use of government subsidies and protective barriers to aid development of local industries.

_____ 11. Which of the following is true of populist leaders in Latin America? *(Mark all that apply.)*

   a. They were highly nationalistic.

   b. They aggressively promoted exports.

   c. They were strong supporters of free trade.

   d. They advocated a greater state role in economic policy.

_____ 12. In modern Argentina, the urban working class is closely associated with:

   a. the Radical party.

   b. Marxism.

   c. Peronism.

   d. fascism.

_____ 13. The tango is an unlikely symbol of Argentina's national pride because:

   a. it originated in Europe, not in Latin America.

   b. it was slow to gain acceptance within Argentine high society.

   c. its popularity in Argentina was confined to the working class.

   d. it was based on pre-Columbian cultural traditions.

_____ 14. Of the following political or economic ideologies, only one is not closely associated with nationalism. It is:

   a. economic liberalism.

   b. populism.

   c. Peronism.

   d. import-substituting industrialization.

_____ 15. The 1976 military coup in Argentina differed from earlier military interventions because:

   a. it provoked a high level of civilian resistance.

   b. it ushered in a "dirty war" against thousands of Argentine citizens.

   c. it prevented a popular sitting president from completing the term.

   d. it was urged on a reluctant military by the intensity of public outcry.

_____ 16. The "dirty war" refers to:

   a. the use of state-sanctioned terror against the civilian population.

   b. the dismal performance of the armed forces in the Malvinas conflict.

   c. terrorist acts by Argentina's revolutionary left in the mid-1970s.

   d. the severe austerity measures needed to eradicate hyperinflation.

_____ 17. Since returning to power in 1984, Argentina's civilian governments have faced which of the following problems? *(Mark all that apply.)*

   a. Continuing abuses of human rights by security forces.

   b. Public anger over the limitations on military trials.

   c. The refusal of the Peronist party to participate in politics.

   d. The need to impose unpopular economic austerity measures.

True or False

_____ 18. Argentina was one of the wealthiest and most important colonies in the Spanish Americas, due largely to its enormous silver deposits.

_____ 19. Export-import economies in Latin America in the late nineteenth century relied on imports of manufactured goods from Europe and North America and on exports of agricultural products and industrial raw materials from Latin America.

_____ 20. The United States was the primary source of investment capital for Latin America at the turn of the twentieth century.

_____ 21. Throughout its history, Argentina has tended to see itself as the most authentically Latin American of any country in the region.

_____ 22. General Onganía was most notable for his desire to reintegrate his Peronist opponents into Argentina's political system.

Identification/Short Answer

Define or describe the following terms, concepts, or persons, or answer the following questions. Answers should be no longer than a few sentences.

23. The Falkland/Malvinas Islands:

24. Raúl Alfonsín:

25. Juan Manuel de Rosas:

26. Soto-Keith Contract:

27. Economic liberalism:

28. Carlos Gardel:

29. Foreign exchange:

30. Name two characteristics that identify Lázaro Cárdenas, Juan Perón, Getúlio Vargas, and Victor Raúl Haya de la Torre as populists:

QUESTIONS TO CONSIDER

1. Argentina's early history (through the mid-twentieth century) is in many ways closer to the experience of the United States than to that of other countries in Latin America. Yet today Argentina and the United States are worlds apart in terms of political stability and economic development. What are some of the major similarities between the two countries, and what do you think are some of the reasons for their wide disparity today?

2. What were some of the miscalculations that Argentina's generals made when they decided to invade the Malvinas? How might Argentina's situation today be altered if they had won that war?

3. How has the legacy of the "dirty war" affected Argentine society in the 1980s and 1990s? How can a country such as Argentina recover from the effects of torture, repression, arbitrary arrest, and disappearances perpetrated by its own government? What will it take to renew Argentines' confidence in and loyalty to both their government and their armed forces?

RESOURCES

Nonfiction

Bergquist, Charles. *Labor in Latin America: Comparative Essays on Chile, Argentina, Venezuela, and Colombia.* Stanford: Stanford University Press, 1986.

Comparative review of the labor movement in Latin America which explores the implications of the labor movement for raw material export.

Brading, D. A. *The First America: The Spanish Monarchy, Creole Patriots, and the Liberal State, 1492–1867.* Cambridge: Cambridge University Press, 1991. Traces the origins of nation-states in Spanish America to the colonial period, and discusses the liberal ideology of the nineteenth century.

Fraser, Nicolas, and Marysa Navarro. *Eva Perón.* New York: Norton, 1980. The life of Juan Perón's controversial second wife, who rose from obscurity to a position of power second only to that of her husband.

Jacobsen, Nils, and Joseph L. Love, eds. *Guiding the Invisible Hand: Economic Liberalism and the State in Latin American History.* New York: Praeger, 1988. These essays explore the role of strong states in creating and guiding liberal economies. Especially relevant are "Argentina: Liberalism in a Country Born Liberal," by Tulio Halperín Donghi; "Structural Change and Conceptual Response in Latin America and Romania, 1860–1950," by Joseph L. Love, and "The Economic Role of the State in Liberal Regimes: Brazil and Mexico Compared, 1888–1910," by Steven Topik.

Martínez Estrada, Ezequill. *X-Ray of the Pampas.* Translated by Alain Swietlicki. Austin: University of Texas Press, 1971. A survey of the social conditions and national characteristics of Argentina.

Page, Joseph. *Perón: A Biography.* New York: Random House, 1983. This biography of Juan Perón also studies the enduring impact of his extraordinary political career on Argentina.

Partnoy, Alicia. *The Little School: Tales of Disappearance and Survival in Argentina.* San Francisco: Cleis Press, 1986. A nonfiction, autobiographical account of the author's experience of being one of the thousands of political detainees during the 1976–83 military regime in Argentina.

Shumway, Nicolas. *The Invention of Argentina.* Berkeley: University of California Press, 1991. An analysis of nineteenth century Latin American pol-itics, exploring the problems of national ideology and nation-building.

Smith, Peter H. "Crisis and Democracy in Latin America." *World Politics* 43:4 (July 1991): 608–34. Explores the paradox of how several Latin American countries became democracies during the economic crises of the 1980s.

Smith, Peter H. "The Failure of Democracy in Argentina, 1916–1930." In *The Breakdown of Democratic Regimes,* edited by Juan Linz and Alfred Stepan. Baltimore: Johns Hopkins University Press, 1978. Interpretation of factors that led to the overthrow of one of the first and apparently well-developed democracies in twentieth century Latin America.

Smith, Peter H. *Politics and Beef in Argentina: Patterns of Conflict and Change.* New York: Columbia University Press, 1969. A study of the political economy of a major export industry in Argentina and Latin America, from the midnineteenth century to the rise of Juan Perón.

Smith, Peter H. "The State and Development in Historical Perspective." In *Americas: New Interpretive Essays,* edited by Alfred Stepan. New York: Oxford University Press, 1992. A revisionist reinterpretation of the history of Latin American states and their development projects, written by a member of the *Americas* academic advisory board as an optional addition to this unit.

Timerman, Jacobo. *Prisoner Without a Name, Cell Without a Number.* New York: Knopf, 1981. Testimony of a Jewish Argentine journalist imprisoned by the military regime of the 1970s.

Fiction

Borges, Jorge Luis. *Labyrinths.* New York: New Directions, 1964. A collection of essays and fiction by Argentina's foremost literary figure, including the story "The Garden of Forking Paths," from which the program title was taken.

Cortázar, Julio. *Hopscotch*. New York: Pantheon, 1987. A complex and sometimes whimsical novel heavily influenced by the French surrealists. Explores the dilemma of the "overeducated" and the bankruptcy of the Western cultural tradition.

Hernandez, José. *The Gaucho Martin Fierro*. Binghamton: State University of New York Press, 1974. An epic poem depicting gaucho life in its twilight hours in the late nineteenth century.

Puig, Manuel. *Betrayed by Rita Hayworth*. New York: Random House, 1981. Puig's first novel portrays a sensitive middle-class boy growing up in provincial Argentina in the 1930s and 1940s. As in all of Puig's books, themes and techniques are borrowed from popular culture, especially film.

Films

Unless otherwise indicated, all films listed are available in VHS video format.

Camila. 105 minutes, 1984 (Spanish, with English subtitles). True story of a young socialist in Buenos Aires who runs away with a priest. They marry and live happily until they are discovered and condemned to death without a trial. Available in most video-rental outlets.

The Official Story. 112 minutes, 1985. A film about a woman's political awakening and the legacy of the *desaparecidos* in Argentina. Winner of the 1985 Academy Award for best foreign film. Directed by Luis Puenzo. Available in most video-rental outlets.

Unit 4

Capital Sins: Authoritarianism and Democratization

The squalor of huge shantytowns contrasts sharply with the sophistication of modern skyscrapers in Rio de Janeiro and many other Latin American cities. © Rick Reinhard/Impact Visuals

UNIT SUMMARY

Unit 4 examines key economic and political experiences shared by several Latin American countries over the last 30 years: the rise of military regimes, the push for rapid economic development, the crippling debt crisis, and the eventual return to democratic government. The unit concentrates on the example of Brazil.

During the past three decades, Brazil experienced tremendous economic growth under a bureaucratic-authoritarian regime, followed by a gradual transition toward democracy marked by rising levels of external debt and inflation. Since the country returned to civilian government in 1985, it has been in a deep and prolonged recession with only brief interludes of recovery. In the aftermath of the military period, the civilian leadership faces enormous difficulties in addressing the political, social, and economic issues that continue to prevent Brazil from achieving its promise of greatness.

While the television program and text focus exclusively on Brazil, the anthology also includes some information on two other bureaucratic-authoritarian regimes, in Chile and in Argentina, as well as on the Alliance for Progress, the basis for U.S. policy toward the region during the early 1960s.

KEY ISSUES

- What were some of the problems with the economic strategy of import-substituting industrialization, and how did Brazil's leaders change their economic policies in response to those problems?

- How were economic and social issues linked to the rise of military governments in Brazil and other Latin American countries during the mid-twentieth century?

- What are the central characteristics of bureaucratic-authoritarian regimes? How were the bureaucratic-authoritarian regimes in Brazil and elsewhere in Latin America different from earlier military dictatorships in those countries?

- What were some of the benefits and costs of the period known as Brazil's "economic miracle?"

- How did Brazil's military leadership eventually come to be discredited, and what was the process of transition to civilian government?

- What are some of the lingering problems that confront elected governments in Brazil and other former military dictatorships?

GLOSSARY

abertura (ah-bear-TOO-rah): literally, "opening"; refers to the post-1973 period in Brazil, when the military allowed a gradual political opening and began the transition toward democracy.

Alliance for Progress: economic and social development program for Latin America promoted and funded by the U.S. government; created by the Kennedy administration as a response to the Cuban Revolution and social unrest elsewhere in Latin America.

Brazil's "economic miracle": refers to the years 1968–74, when Brazil's economy grew at a rate exceeding 10 percent per year, industry boomed, inflation remained low, and prospects for the future seemed excellent.

bureaucratic-authoritarian regimes: new form of military government that first emerged in Brazil after 1964 and was established in Chile and Uruguay in 1973, and in Argentina in 1976. Although the regimes differed from one another, key shared features are the role of the military as a governing institution and the exclusion from power of all popular sectors.

capital-intensive technologies: technologies that substitute expensive machinery for human labor, eliminating jobs; typically these technologies in Latin America relied on imported parts and equipment.

Cruzado (croo-ZAH-doh) **Plan**: President José Sarney's economic plan, announced in early 1986, which introduced a new currency and strict wage and price controls to fight runaway inflation in Brazil.

"Direitas, Já" (dgee-RAY-tas zha): literally, "Direct elections, now"; popular call for direct presidential elections in Brazil heard at strikes and rallies toward the end of the military's rule.

Estado Nôvo (es-TAH-doh NO-voh): literally, "new state"; an authoritarian state model created by Getúlio Vargas from 1937 to 1945; period of direct government intervention and management of the economy, including control over labor unions.

export diversification: effort made by many Latin American countries to expand their economic growth through production of nontraditional exports.

favelas (fah-VELL-ahs): shantytowns surrounding major Brazilian cities, usually lacking in basic services such as water, sewers, and electricity.

grandeza (grahn-DAY-za): literally, "greatness"; term used frequently during the 1970s to express Brazil's potential to become a great power.

International Monetary Fund (IMF): international financial institution that provides emergency economic assistance to countries facing balance of payments problems, with particular conditions attached (see "structural adjustment policies," below).

Paulista (pah-oo-LEES-tah): person from São Paulo; many Paulistas felt that São Paulo's economic development would enable Brazil to rise to world prominence in the twentieth century.

petrodollars: refers to the large dollar deposits held in U.S. and European bank accounts of oil exporting countries. The rapid growth of these cash deposits after the 1973 oil price increase led to an increase in international lending by private banks.

pharaonic projects: huge development schemes launched by Brazil's military government in the 1970s, financed primarily by foreign loans. While some led to major improvements in infrastructure and energy (for example, the Itaipú Dam), the projects are generally seen as symbols of waste and corruption, and misplaced notions of *grandeza*.

structural adjustment policies: economic stabilization measures required by the IMF and World Bank as a condition of extending new loans; typically involve the sale of state enterprises, elimination of government subsidies, free exchange of the national currency, promotion of exports, reducing the barriers to foreign investment, and emphasizing free market economic policies.

OVERVIEW

By the early 1960s, the import-substituting industrialization (ISI) policies followed by many governments in Latin America in the post–World War II period were proving problematic. Under ISI policies, countries worked toward greater economic independence by manufacturing goods that had previously been imported from Europe and the United States. The newly created industries relied heavily on imported materials and machinery, and created few new jobs. High costs of production and tariff barriers weakened the industries' ability to export, but individual countries' domestic markets were not large enough to support the industries, since relatively few citizens could afford to purchase the new goods. Protected from outside competition, industries grew inefficient, producing low-quality goods at high prices.

Because ISI policies typically neglected the agricultural sector, more food had to be imported. Governments of the region faced a choice of whether to open the door to foreign goods, or to continue to shelter the domestic economy in the hope that the ISI strategy would eventually work.

In Brazil, as in the rest of Latin America, these economic policy choices were especially difficult because of their political and social implications. Throughout the postwar period, Brazil's leaders were determined to achieve economic development worthy of the country's great resources and potential. In fact, economic growth in Brazil reached remarkable levels in the late 1950s, and again ten years later in the 1968–74 period known as Brazil's "economic miracle."

Nevertheless, in the course of reaching for the elusive goal of *grandeza*, or greatness, Brazilians

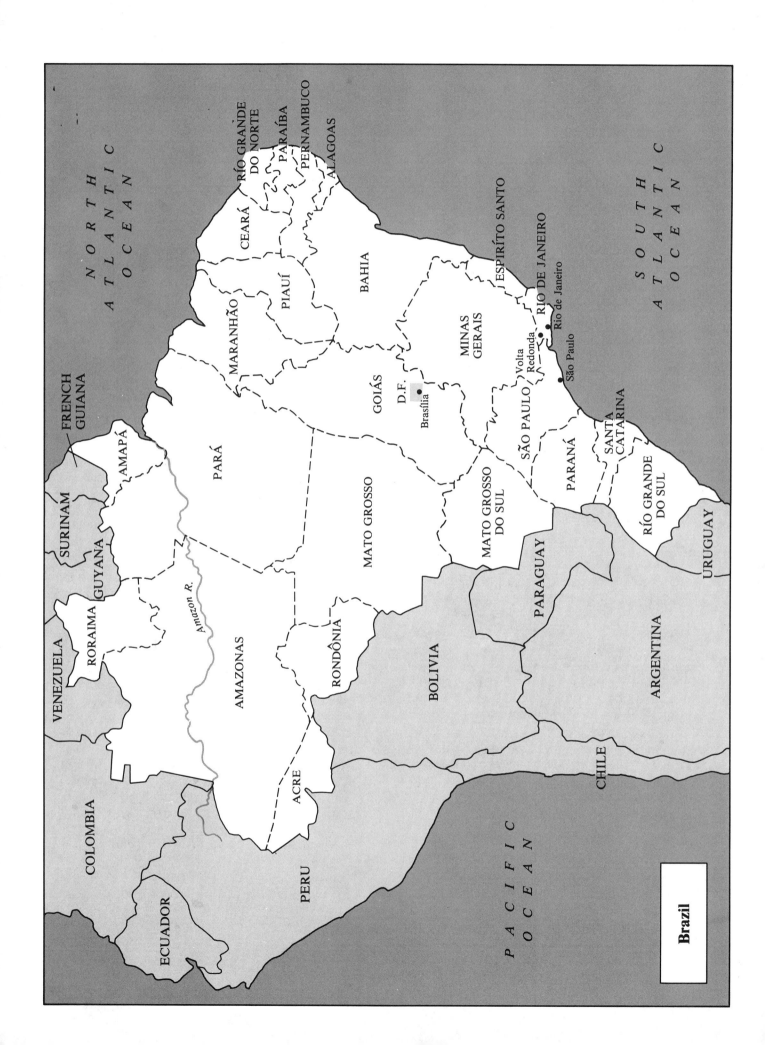

NORTH ATLANTIC OCEAN

SOUTH ATLANTIC OCEAN

PACIFIC OCEAN

VENEZUELA

SURINAM

FRENCH GUIANA

GUYANA

COLOMBIA

ECUADOR

PERU

BOLIVIA

PARAGUAY

CHILE

ARGENTINA

URUGUAY

RORAIMA

AMAPÁ

PARÁ

AMAZONAS

ACRE

RONDÔNIA

MATO GROSSO

MATO GROSSO DO SUL

MARANHÃO

PIAUÍ

CEARÁ

RÍO GRANDE DO NORTE

PARAÍBA

PERNAMBUCO

ALAGOAS

BAHIA

GOIÁS

D.F.

Brasília

MINAS GERAIS

ESPÍRITO SANTO

RIO DE JANEIRO

Rio de Janeiro

Volta Redonda

São Paulo

SÃO PAULO

PARANÁ

SANTA CATARINA

RÍO GRANDE DO SUL

Amazon R.

Brazil

experienced an extended period of authoritarian government, acquired a crippling external debt burden, and adopted a pattern of economic growth and industrialization that worsened what was already one of the world's most unequal distributions of income. Brazil today has sophisticated entrepreneurs and a well-educated middle class, but also an enormous underclass living in desperate poverty.

Brazil, 1930–1964

Getúlio Vargas, who first came to power in a military-sponsored coup in 1930, led the country until 1954 with only one five-year interruption. The *Estado Nôvo* created by Vargas in 1937–45 was a period of aggressive intervention by the Brazilian government in the country's economic development. The state-established unions kept labor firmly controlled while also creating a strong popular following for Vargas. Vargas promoted foreign investment, especially from the United States, which funded a large steel complex at Volta Redonda in return for Brazil's aiding the Allies during World War II.

By late 1945, when Vargas was deposed in a military-supported coup, the style of one-man rule he had imposed was seen as out of step with the worldwide trend toward democracy. However, after the *Estado Nôvo* was replaced with a constitutional government, Vargas was returned to power by popular vote in 1951.

Three years later, confronted with severe internal economic pressures, Vargas found himself unable to restore economic growth. He committed suicide rather than agree to his own resignation, ending a pivotal era in Brazilian politics.

Under the leadership of President Juscelino Kubitschek (1956–1960), Brazil made important steps toward industrialization. It was during this period that the automobile industry became firmly established as the engine for Brazil's economic development. Gross national product (GNP) growth was close to 10 percent in 1960 and 1961, and averaged 8.3 percent for the entire period from 1957 to 1961. Kubitschek also captured the world's imagination with his ambitious and daring plan to construct a new capital for Brazil on a previously undeveloped plateau 600 miles into the interior. When the futuristic city of Brasília was completed in just four years, it seemed a perfect symbol of Brazil's hopes for the future.

From 1961 to 1964, though, the country experienced a new recession, with the return of inflation and balance of payments deficits. Presidents Janio Quadros (1961) and João Goulart (1961–1964) found it increasingly difficult to balance the demands of Brazil's middle and working classes with the calls for economic stabilization from business and military leaders. By early 1964, increased activism by organized labor, the growth of peasant mobilization, and the rise of inflation to unprecedented heights of over 100 percent triggered fears among Brazil's elites of the breakdown of the prevailing social order.

In 1964, the Brazilian military once again intervened in domestic politics, with widespread upper- and middle-class support. This time, the military was to remain the governing institution for 21 years.

Bureaucratic-Authoritarianism and the Economic Miracle

Brazil was the first of several countries in Latin America to experiment with a new form of military government that came to be called the "bureaucratic-authoritarian regime." Bureaucratic-authoritarianism differed significantly from military dictatorships of the past. In Brazil, Argentina, and Uruguay, it was not tied to a dictator but instead relied on a coalition between the institution of the military and the "technocrats," economists and other professionals who designed and implemented policies in their areas of expertise.

This alliance was made possible by the willingness of the elites to accept a loss of political freedoms in their country in order to ensure social order, and to impose the stability they thought was essential for rapid economic growth. In Brazil, aided by favorable international economic trends, the military regime's promotion of industrialization and export production led to a period of sustained, rapid growth known as the "economic miracle." From 1968 to 1974, annual growth averaged 10 percent—even reaching 14 percent in 1973—and exports more than quadrupled. It seemed Brazil was fulfilling its destiny as a modern, urban, and industrial giant on the continent, and hopes ran high for continued prosperity.

But the prosperity of the miracle years was not shared by all Brazilians. The military's supporters ignored the high social and political costs of the "miracle": a dramatic increase in the gap between the rich and the poor; a flood of migrants into the *favelas,* or slums, which expanded around the country's major cities; and human rights abuses, including torture and execution, justified by "national security" and the need to preserve internal stability for continued growth.

In order to continue growing even as the cost of oil skyrocketed after 1973, Brazil's leaders chose to continue massive investment in industry and export promotion. They financed their plans with loans of "petrodollars" offered at favorable terms by U.S. and European banks. In the mid-1970s few questioned the wisdom of that choice. Money was abundant, interest rates were low, and both GNP and per capita income continued to grow until the end of the 1970s.

The inherent problem with Brazil's "debt-led development model" only became apparent later, when new oil price hikes eventually caused a global recession and interest rates on Brazil's loans soared. From real interest rates (interest minus inflation) that had been close to zero when the loans were first taken out, Brazil was paying close to 15 percent by 1980. New loans were then needed just to cover interest payments.

By 1982, Brazil's economy was close to ruin, and the estimated $100 billion the country owed to foreign lenders was the largest national debt in the world. From 1981 to 1983, per capita GNP declined by more than 12 percent and GNP overall fell by 5 percent. Brazil had to seek help from the International Monetary Fund and agree to severe terms, including a drastic reduction in imports. Efforts to revive the economy and increase exports generated triple-digit inflation in 1984.

Abertura *and Redemocratization*

As military governments throughout the region learned in the 1980s, the change from steady growth to stagnation and spiraling inflation, coupled with the burden of massive foreign debt, eventually destroyed the civilian support that had allowed

them to rule. Economic crisis hastened Brazil's redemocratization in the early 1980s, and the pattern was later repeated in neighboring Uruguay and Argentina.

Brazil's military leaders had begun to talk of a return to democratic rule during the presidency of General Ernesto Geisel (1974–79), after elections in 1974 showed substantial gains for the opposition, and the Church began to publicly question the regime's legitimacy. The process of political opening (or *abertura*) was supposed to be very gradual, but the impact of the slowdown in growth, combined with pent-up public demands for greater political freedom, raised the level of social and political activism.

Social unrest mounted along with the country's economic difficulties after 1980. Metalworkers, headed by the dynamic union organizer Luis Ignacio da Silva ("Lula"), began striking for higher wages, and workers in other industries soon followed. The price of having neglected for years such basic needs as housing, health care, and education now became clear as students, church leaders, and others criticized the military's management of the growth period and demanded a return to civilian government. In 1985, after more than 20 years in power, the Brazilian military returned to the barracks.

Brazil's first civilian president, José Sarney, took office amid a general euphoria at the end of military rule. Sarney's "Cruzado Plan," a set of wage and price controls designed to attack runaway inflation, was embraced enthusiastically by the public. When inflation slowed dramatically and growth temporarily resumed, it seemed that the plan had worked, but by late 1986 inflation was worse than ever, reaching 1,000 percent per year. Sarney's early popularity rapidly diminished in the face of widespread dissatisfaction at his failure to restore economic stability or implement promised social and labor reforms.

In 1989, Fernando Collor de Mello was narrowly chosen over labor leader Lula in Brazil's first direct presidential elections since 1960. Collor's stated mission was to rescue the country from bankruptcy. He also promised to pay greater attention to Brazil's environmental problems and do more to protect the rights of the country's indigenous people. However, the economic shock program that Collor instituted, which began with the freezing of bank accounts as well as wages and prices, plunged the country even deeper into recession without delivering the stability and return to prosperity that he had promised.

Like his predecessors, Collor was forced to continue a precarious balancing act, trying to restore the possibilities for growth and respond to the concerns of Brazil's industrialists while also holding off popular demands for social and labor reforms. Despite its dreams of *grandeza,* Brazil today remains a frustrated giant.

ASSIGNMENT

1. Before viewing the program, read:

    Modern Latin America, 3d ed., pp. 56–62, 60–67, 144–84.

    In chapter 2, "The Transformation of Modern Latin America, 1880s–1990s," the assigned sections (pp. 56–62, 60–67) cover the following issues:

    Phase 4: Stagnation in Import-Substituting Growth (1960s–1980s) discusses the failures of ISI and the emergence of bureaucratic-authoritari-\anism.

    Phase 5: Crisis, Debt, and Democracy (1980s–1990s) outlines the origins of the debt crisis, the plunge into recession, the impact of structural-adjustment policies, and the return to electoral government.

    A Framework for Comparison outlines the key questions to consider when comparing social, economic, and political structures in different Latin American countries.

    Chapter 5, "Brazil: Development for Whom?" (pp. 144–84) traces Brazil's history since independence from Portugal in 1822 and provides a summary of the most important political and economic developments in the country during the twentieth century.

2. View the program "Capital Sins."

3. After viewing the program, read:
    Americas: An Anthology, chapter 4, pp. 72–103.

The anthology readings provide various perspectives on Brazil's economic growth and the experience of bureaucratic-authoritarianism, including testimony on human rights violations under the military regime.

UNIT REVIEW

After viewing the program and reading the assignments, you should be able to:

·   Understand the inherent problems with import-substituting industrialization policies, and the various measures Brazil's leaders used to respond to those problems.

·   Recognize the links between economic and social issues and the rise of military governments in Brazil and other Latin American countries during the midtwentieth century.

·   Identify the central characteristics of bureaucratic-authoritarian regimes and understand how these governments in Brazil and elsewhere in Latin America differed from earlier military dictatorships.

·   Identify the benefits and costs of Brazil's "economic miracle."

·   Understand the process by which Brazil's military government left power.

·   Explain some of the lingering problems that confront elected governments in Brazil and other former military dictatorships.

SELF-TEST QUESTIONS

Multiple Choice

*Mark the letter of the response that **best** answers the question or completes the statement.*

_____   1. Which of the following statements are true about the political climate in late

nineteenth-century Brazil? *(Mark all that apply.)*
a. Civil war over the question of slavery was only narrowly averted.
b. Debates on the future of slavery and the monarchy dominated the political agenda.
c. A convergence occurred between republicans and abolitionists.
d. Republicanism became increasingly popular, especially among the young, university-educated sons of the elites.

_____ 2. The Estado Nôvo from 1937 to 1945:
a. was a military dictatorship under General Ernesto Geisel.
b. was a constitutional democracy led by President Joâo Goulart.
c. was a corporatist, authoritarian state created by Getúlio Vargas.
d. was the first republic in Brazil after the end of the monarchy.

_____ 3. Which of the following are generally consequences of the import-substituting industrialization strategy? *(Mark all that apply.)*
a. the creation of capital-intensive industries
b. inefficient firms unable to compete internationally
c. the neglect of agriculture
d. full employment

_____ 4. Why did President Kennedy propose the Alliance for Progress? *(Mark all that apply.)*
a. The United States had massive deposits of petrodollars to invest in Latin America.
b. Kennedy wanted to help Cuba and other Latin American countries develop economically.
c. Latin American governments wanted U.S. assistance to address poverty in their countries.
d. Kennedy believed that economic growth and social and political reforms would prevent revolutionary upheavals, such as that in Cuba.

_____ 5. The bureaucratic-authoritarian regime that assumed power in Brazil in 1964 defined its mission as: *(Mark all that apply.)*
a. promoting economic development.
b. fighting the slide toward Communism.
c. increasing social justice.
d. assuring national security.

_____ 6. Organized labor became a target of government repression under bureaucratic-authoritarian regimes because: *(Mark all that apply.)*
a. unions were seen as linked to international Communism.
b. unions encouraged their members not to buy consumer goods.
c. strikes and protests were believed to disrupt social order.
d. unions demanded higher wages that businesses said they couldn't afford.

_____ 7. Workers in which Brazilian industry were leaders in the attempt to organize labor and undertake strikes?
a. Auto
b. Silver
c. Rubber
d. Oil

_____ 8. "Social debt" refers to:
a. the money owed by governments to domestic banks.
b. the legacy of neglect of social services by military governments.
c. the aggregate debt owed by individuals in any one country.
d. the expensive projects undertaken by military governments.

_____ 9. Which statements are true of Latin America's bureaucratic-authoritarian regimes? *(Mark all that apply.)*
a. They adopted conciliatory policies toward social organizations.
b. The military controlled executive power.
c. They sought to break all ties with

international economic players, such as multinational corporations.

d. They differed in the degree to which they used political repression.

_____ 10. Which of the following statements are true about postauthoritarian politics in most Latin American countries? *(Mark all that apply.)*

a. The elected governments are civilian but the military still has considerable behind-the-scenes power.

b. The new democratic regimes are fragile and incomplete and face a wide variety of economic problems.

c. Economic and political power continue to be unequally distributed.

d. Political institutions, such as the judiciary, the congress, and political parties, remain very strong.

True or False

_____ 11. Brazil's economic miracle afforded its citizens a range of social programs as well as economic growth.

_____ 12. Bureaucratic-authoritarian regimes tended to use an import-substituting strategy for industrial development.

_____ 13. In Brazil's first direct presidential elections in almost 30 years, Fernando Collor de Mello won a narrow margin of victory over labor leader Lula in 1989.

_____ 14. During Brazil's first century of independence, sugar was the export crop that yielded the most profit for the country.

_____ 15. Brazil is the fifth largest country in the world, constituting nearly half the land mass of South America.

_____ 16. Brazil's move to military rule with the coup against President Goulart in 1964 was the first time the country had ever been led by a nonelectoral government.

_____ 17. The rise of Brazil's debt meant that during most of the 1980s more capital flowed out of the country in interest payments than into the country in aid, investments, and loans.

_____ 18. During the economic boom in Brazil in the late 1960s and the 1970s, the gap between the rich and the poor grew wider.

Identification/Short Answer

Define or describe the following terms, concepts, or persons, or answer the following questions. Answers should be no longer than a few sentences.

19. What are the central characteristics of bureaucratic-authoritarian regimes?

20. Brasília:

21. Explain some of the consequences military rule had on political institutions in Brazil and other countries in Latin America.

22. Lula:

23. *Favelas:*

24. Benedita da Silva:

25. What were some of the costs associated with Brazil's "economic miracle"?

QUESTIONS TO CONSIDER

1. In his speech announcing the Alliance for Progress, U.S. president John F. Kennedy acknowledged the extent of Latin America's social and economic problems and spoke of the historic ties binding North and South America. How has this situation changed since 1961? How is it the same?

2. How might Brazil's current policies be different if Lula had won the 1989 election? Where might Lula have made the most dramatic changes?

3. There continues to be a debate within Brazil about the costs and benefits to the country of the bureaucratic-authoritarian regime. Would you say that the military government was justified in its approaches, given the country's economic needs, or do you think the human rights abuses and Brazil's continuing economic and social difficulties prove it was a detrimental period in Brazilian history?

4. The problems of the Brazilian Amazon have received international attention. Why does exploitation of the rain forest continue? What should the Brazilian government's reaction be? Do you think that international organizations and the United States are right to criticize the rain forest destruction? Why or why not?

RESOURCES

Nonfiction

Dassin, Joan, trans. *Torture in Brazil: A Report.* New York: Vintage Books, 1986. This report, prepared by the Archdiocese of São Paulo, details human rights abuses and torture during the Brazilian military governments from 1964 to 1979. It is based on *Brasil: Nunca Mais* ("Brazil: Never Again"), the findings of a five-year research project documenting human rights abuses.

Davis, Shelton. *Victims of the Miracle: Development and the Indians in Brazil.* New York: Cambridge University Press, 1977. In this highly critical view of Brazil's "economic miracle," the author claims that the suffering of the indigenous Brazilian peoples and the devastation of the rain forest resulted directly from the economic development policies of the military government.

de Jesus, Carolina Maria. *Child of the Dark.* New York: Mentor Books, 1964. True story of daily life in a *favela* written by a poor Brazilian woman.

Diamond, Larry, Juan Linz, and Seymour Martin Lipse, eds. *Democracy in Developing Countries: Latin America.* Vol. 4. Boulder, Colo.: Lynne Rienner, 1989. Compares the perspectives of leading scholars on the issue of democracy in Latin America.

Evans, P. E. Liedke, and E. Liedke Filho. *Political Economy of Contemporary Brazil: A Study Guide.* Albuquerque: Latin American Institute, University of New Mexico, 1985. Includes a brief background on the political economy of contemporary Brazil and an annotated bibliography.

Fishlow, Albert. "The State of Economics in Brazil and Latin America: Is the Past Prologue to the Future?" In *Americas: New Interpretive Essays,* edited by Alfred Stepan. New York: Oxford University Press, 1992. An examination of how Latin American states need to restructure their economies in the face of a changing world market, written by a member of the *Americas* academic advisory board as an optional addition to this unit.

Golden, Tim. "Brazil's Gold Rush Brings a Brutal Clash of Cultures." *Miami Herald,* July 25, 1989. Describes how many of the indigenous groups in the Amazon are threatened by mining.

Linz, Juan, and Alfred Stepan, eds. *The Breakdown of Democratic Regimes: Latin America.* Baltimore: Johns Hopkins University Press, 1978. This collection of essays explains how and why democratic regimes failed and authoritarian rule emerged in Latin America.

Mendes, Chico. *Fight for the Forest.* London: Latin American Bureau, 1989. In this extended interview conducted weeks before his murder in 1988, Chico Mendes talks about the rubber tappers' life, their political struggle and alliances with local indigenous groups and the environmental lobby, and their campaign to save the rain forest. (Available from Monthly Review Press, 122 West St, New York, NY 10001.)

Skidmore, Thomas. *Politics in Brazil, 1930–1964.* New York: Oxford University Press, 1967. This book examines the political, economic, and social forces at work in Brazil since the 1930s which led to the breakdown of democracy and the overthrow of Brazilian president João Goulart in 1964.

Skidmore, Thomas. *The Politics of Military Rule in Brazil, 1964–1985.* Princeton: Princeton University Press, 1988. This comprehensive study of different military governments since 1964 highlights the role of internal divisions of the military in the movement toward a return to democratic rule.

Stallings, Barbara, and Robert Kaufman, eds. *Debt and Democracy in Latin America.* Boulder, Colo.: Westview Press, 1989. A collection of general articles and case studies that focus on how various types of regimes have dealt with foreign debt.

Stepan, Alfred. *Rethinking Military Politics: Brazil and the Southern Cone.* Princeton: Princeton University Press, 1988. A study of the military's role in the transition from authoritarian rule in the Southern Cone and the continued presence and role of the military in the new democracies.

Stepan, Alfred, ed. *Authoritarian Brazil.* New Haven: Yale University Press, 1973. Book of essays by leading scholars examining the origins of military rule in Brazil from a historical and comparative perspective, highlighting the role of economic-structural factors, political factors, and shifts in military control.

Stepan, Alfred, ed. *Democratizing Brazil: Problems of Transition and Consolidation.* New York: Oxford University Press, 1989. These essays focus on Brazil's transition to a democratic government and chronicle the first years of the new democracy. Articles discuss such topics as trade unionism, women in politics, the role of the Brazilian church, the economics of *abertura,* the debt crisis, and grassroots popular movements in the *favelas.*

Vesilind, Priit. "Brazil: Moment of Promise and Pain." *National Geographic* 171:3 (March 1987). An overall view of Brazilian people and culture, and of the impact of economic development on the poor.

Wirth, John L. *The Politics of Brazilian Development, 1930–1954.* Stanford, Calif.: Stanford University Press, 1970. Three case studies—foreign trade, the steel industry, and the oil industry—are used to analyze the way policy decisions were made in the Vargas era.

Fiction

Amado, Jorge. *Gabriela, Clove and Cinnamon.* New York: Avon Books, 1968. This is the story of Gabriela, who comes from the backlands of Brazil and is hired by the owner of the town's most popular café to replace his cook. The café owner soon finds himself with the most prosperous business—and the most sought-after woman—in town.

Machado de Assis, Joaquim M. *The Devil's Church and Other Stories.* Translated by Jack Schmit and Lorie Ishimatsu. Austin: University of Texas Press, 1977. Brazilian writer Machado de Assis (1839–1908) is considered to be an early modernist and the father of modern Brazilian fiction. This collection of 19 stories is set in Brazil in the second half of the nineteenth century.

Films

Unless otherwise indicated, all films listed are available in VHS video format.

Bye Bye Brazil. 105 minutes, 1980 (Portuguese, with English subtitles). In the words of director Carlos Diegues, this film, set in northeast Brazil, is "about a country which is about to come to an end in order to make way for another which is about to begin." Released on Warner Home Video and available in most video-rental outlets.

How Nice to See You Alive. 100 minutes, 1989. Film by Lucia Murat about the suspension of civil rights in Brazil after the 1964 military coup. Using a mix of fiction and documentary, the film interviews eight women who were political prisoners. Available from Women Make Movies, 225 Lafayette Street, New York, NY 10012; (212) 925–0606.

In the Name of Progress. 60 minutes, 1991. This fourth episode of the 10–part environmental television course *Race to Save the Planet* investigates the consequences of Western-style industrial development in India and Brazil, and profiles slain activist Chico Mendes and his work to help preserve Brazil's rain forest and ensure a sustainable living for the rubber tappers who live in it. Available for purchase ($29.95) from The Annenberg/CPB Project, P.O. Box 2345, S. Burlington, VT 05407–2345; (800) LEARNER.

Pixote. 127 minutes, 1981. This film is a poignant, blunt portrait of the lives of a group of street children in Brazil. Director Hector Babenco based the script on life stories, and uses real street children to play the main characters. Educational institutions may purchase the film on VHS video for $250 through New Yorker Films, 16 W. 61st Street, New York, NY 10023; (212) 247–6110. Available in some video-rental outlets.

Unit 5

Continent on the Move: Migration and Urbanization

The majority of Latin American and Caribbean migrants move within their own countries, from rural to urban areas, in search of better opportunities. © Robert Frerck/Odyssey Productions

UNIT SUMMARY

Unit 5 explores the causes and effects of migration, one of the most important forces transforming Latin America and the Caribbean in the twentieth century. In particular, the unit considers migration in Mexico, where domestic and international forces have caused millions of people to move out of rural villages in search of jobs, whether in Mexico City, the world's largest urban area, in new industrial cities along the United States–Mexico border, or across the border in the United States. The anthology readings and the television program concentrate on the perspectives of those who migrate, their motivations, and experiences, while the textbook provides important historical information on social, political, and economical change in twentieth century Mexico. Readings in the anthology also illustrate the widespread nature of the migration phenomenon and its effect throughout Latin America and the Caribbean.

KEY ISSUES

·   What causes migration?

·   How has political and economic development in Mexico affected migration?

·   How is land, especially land ownership, tied to migration patterns in Mexico and other countries in the Americas?

·   What are the benefits and costs of rural-to-urban migration for migrants?

·   What has been the impact of migration on Mexico's largest cities?

·   How is migration in Latin America and the Caribbean linked to the larger processes of economic and social change in the hemisphere?

GLOSSARY

barrios (BAH-ree-os):   literally "neighborhoods"; the Asamblea de Barrios (Assembly of Neighborhoods) in Mexico City is an organization of the city's poor residents pressing for better services from city government.

braceros (brah-SEH-ros):   Mexican manual laborers who were allowed to work in temporary agricultural and industrial jobs in the United States under a legal agreement between the U.S. and Mexican governments dating back to World War II.

campesino (kahm-peh-SEE-no):   literally, country person. Throughout Latin America, a *campesino* is a poor rural farmer or farm laborer; a peasant.

colonias proletarias (koh-LO-nee-ahs pro-le-TAHY-ree-as):   usually refers to poor communities, frequently lacking in basic municipal services, which have grown around the outskirts of major cities, including Mexico City, Tijuana, Ciudad Juárez, and others. Squatter communities of Mexicans and Mexican-Americans in poor areas on the U.S. side of the border have also become known as *colonias*. In Mexico City, however, even wealthy residential neighborhoods are called *colonias*.

compadrazgo (kom-pah-DRAHS-ko):   system of close friendships and relationships; from the Spanish *compadre,* for "godfather," or, more generally, a friend or close companion. *Compadrazgo* systems facilitate relocation, migration, and employment throughout the Americas.

coyote (koh-YO-teh):   slang term for someone who engages in the profitable and dangerous business of crossing illegal immigrants into the United States.

devaluation: government action to lower the value of a country's currency relative to the internationally recognized "hard" currencies such as the U.S. dollar, German mark, and Japanese yen. Devaluing a currency makes imported goods more expensive and exported goods cheaper, but usually causes great hardship within the country due to higher costs and inflation. In 1976 the Mexican government was forced to abandon its policy of a fixed rate of exchange between the Mexican peso and the U.S. dollar, devaluing the peso in two successive instances by a total of 100 percent.

ejidos (eh-HEE-dos): groups of peasant families who are communal owners of land distributed by the Mexican government in various waves of agrarian reform since the Mexican Revolution (1910–17). The small farmers who work the land are called *ejidatarios*.

informal economy: refers to economic activities that are not regulated and are often not taxed. Includes domestic workers, small businesses, home workers such as seamstresses, street vegetable vendors, and trash pickers. Much of the work is characterized by unstable and unsafe working conditions and no access to legal rights, social security, or union benefits. The informal economy is an important source of employment in Mexico and throughout the Americas.

latifundios (lah-tee-FOON-dee-ohs): large farms or estates, frequently thousands of acres in size. Many of Mexico's *latifundios* were divided and parceled out to peasants during President Lázaro Cárdenas's agrarian reform program in the 1930s and in subsequent redistributions by other Mexican presidents.

maquiladora (mah-kee-lah-DOH-rah): assembly plant usually located along the United States–Mexico border, often a subsidiary of a multinational corporation, where parts are imported from the United States, assembled, and re-exported. The *maquiladora* industry was created in a joint U.S.–Mexican agreement that established a duty-free zone along the Mexican side of the border to take advantage of the plentiful supply of cheap labor and easier regulatory environment. Although *maquiladoras* have been criticized for worker exploitation and disregard for environmental standards, they have also created thousands of jobs and drawn a new wave of migration from the center and south of Mexico to the border area.

North American Free Trade Agreement: the agreement proposed by U.S. president George Bush and Mexican president Carlos Salinas de Gortari in 1990 which would link the economies of the United States, Canada, and Mexico by lifting all trade barriers and allowing the free movement of capital, goods, and agricultural products within these three countries.

pepenadores (peh-peh-nah-DOHR-ehs): garbage pickers; people who make their livings, and sometimes their homes, in Mexico City's public garbage sites.

PRI (PREE): Spanish acronym for Mexico's Partido Revolucionario Institucional, or Institutional Revolutionary Party. The PRI replaced earlier versions of an official revolutionary party; its establishment after World War II was intended to signal pragmatism and a long-term institutional commitment to the goals of the Mexican revolution. The PRI has historically owned significant state enterprises; organized professional, labor, and peasant sectors; and controlled the presidency and legislature. Its dominant position in Mexican politics and society has only recently been challenged.

remittances: money migrants send back to families and friends in their place of origin. Remittances have been a significant source of income, particularly of foreign exchange, in many Latin American and Caribbean countries.

OVERVIEW

Understanding modern Latin America and the Caribbean requires an appreciation of the powerful impact of migration, the movement of millions of individuals and families within countries and from one country to another. Although the Americas absorbed successive waves of European and African immigrants from the colonial period into the early part of the twentieth century, those patterns have been transformed by the more rapid pace of industrialization, the growth of cities, and the increasing role of Latin America and the Caribbean in the world economy.

Most migration in the region today is from rural to urban areas, although that is by no means the only migratory pattern. Migrants come from

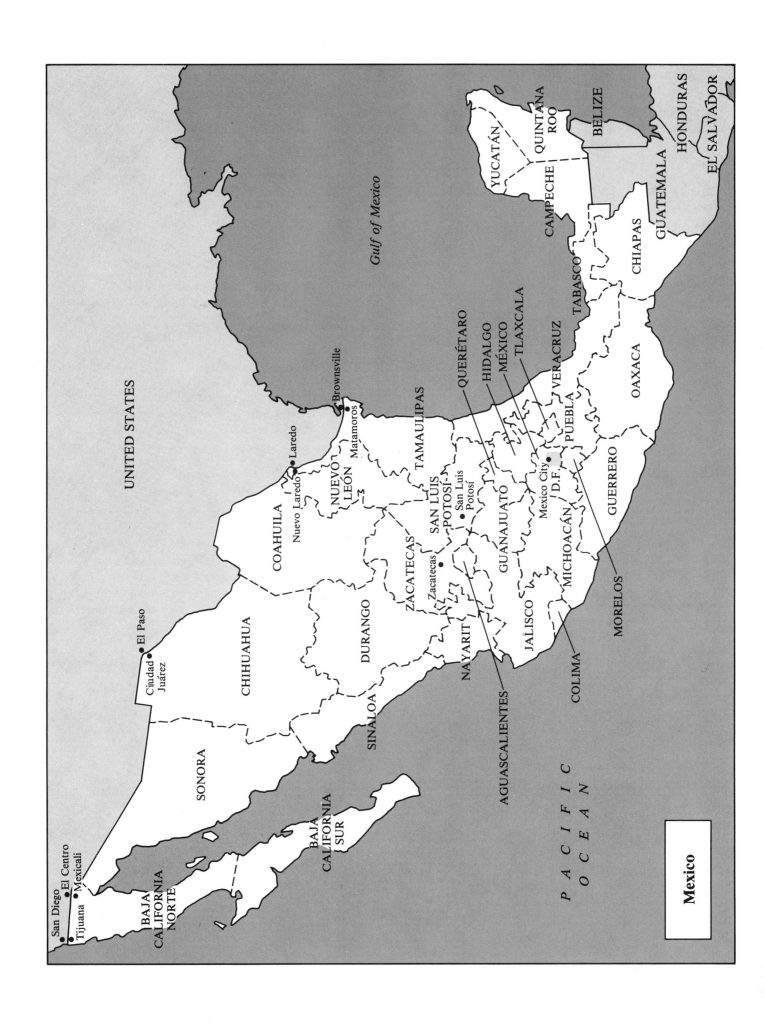

Mexico

every social class and move for a variety of reasons. Some of these reasons have been referred to as "push" and "pull" factors. The "push" factors that prompt people to abandon their homes may be lack of jobs, poor quality of land, boredom with rural life, hopes for a better future, the desire to be free of political and intellectual constraints, and the need to escape violence and war.

"Pull" factors, on the other hand, are those conditions that tend to draw people to particular locations. These include, for example, government policies that concentrate new industrial jobs in particular regions; the availability of housing, health care, education, and other services; networks of families and friends which ease the transition to a new environment; and international agreements that allow people to migrate from one country to another for political or economic reasons.

Migration in Twentieth-Century Mexico

The program "Continent on the Move" is set in Mexico, where extensive internal migration has emptied many rural villages and swelled major cities at a rapid pace. The example of Mexico shows clearly the linkages between migration patterns and economic development, especially the effect of policies that emphasize particular patterns of industrialization and investment.

Migration has benefits and costs for individuals and families who choose to move, as well as for society as a whole. On the positive side, most migrants from rural areas have, until recently, been successful in achieving better lives for themselves in the cities. Especially during Mexico's import-substituting industrialization phase, from the 1940s through the early 1960s, jobs were plentiful and new migrants were able to establish themselves quickly. During much of the 1950s and 1960s—the years of the "Mexican Miracle"—Mexico's national economic growth averaged more than 6 percent per year and was double that in the capital, where much of the new industry was located.

At the same time, the pace of agrarian reform, which started under Mexican president Lázaro Cárdenas in the 1930s, began to slow. Much of the land that had already been distributed was poor, and government promises to provide the necessary credit, fertilizer, and technology needed to make

it profitable did not materialize. What money was put into the rural economy went to promote agro-export industries, not peasant production systems. The *ejido* system was a political success but an economic failure, and the production of basic foods such as corn and beans declined steadily.

The result was a massive movement of people. Some migrated to the United States under the *braceros* program, the U.S.-Mexican agreement made during World War II. Under this agreement, which lasted until 1964, certain categories of agricultural and other manual laborers were allowed entry to the U.S. market to fill temporary jobs.

Most migration, however, occurred within Mexico from rural areas to the cities, especially Mexico City. The migrants' initial squatter settlements eventually obtained municipal services and became legally recognized; their children had access to public education and health care; and they had a degree of social mobility impossible in the more confining social structure of the countryside. The success of these migrants tended to reinforce the same rural-to-urban migration pattern: as word spread back to the countryside of the better opportunities migrants had found in the cities, others decided to follow. They found invaluable assistance in making the transition, including temporary housing and information on job opportunities, through the informal social contacts with relatives, friends, and neighbors already in the cities (known as kinship or *compadrazgo* networks).

Those who were not able to find factory work made their living in the dynamic informal sector, in the small businesses established to service the many needs of the new arrivals. Jobs in the informal economy could range from shoemaking to print production, for example, from car and bike repair to tailoring, from vegetable vending to sales of prepared food.

However, the costs of rapid migration within Mexico have also been high. Uncontrolled urban expansion, especially in Mexico City, has strained public services far beyond their capacity. As continual waves of migrants flooded in, their numbers overwhelmed the ability of the urban economy to provide adequate jobs, housing, and other basic needs. By the early 1990s Mexico City, with close to 19 million inhabitants, had deteriorated into a city known for its overcrowding, lack of adequate employment, terrible pollution, and tremendous extremes of wealth and poverty. It no longer offered new migrants hope for a better future, although conditions in the countryside and the scarcity of jobs continued to push people off the land and into the cities.

From the Mexican Miracle to Economic Crisis

The crash of the Mexican economy in the early 1980s added to the migratory pressures already in place. The discovery of major oil reserves in the late 1970s had temporarily provided the country with a reliable source of income and had raised hopes for a stable economic future. However, the spurt of growth in oil revenues between 1976 and 1981 fell off dramatically once world oil prices stagnated.

Oil had become the principal export, and the country's manufactured goods, developed under a mantle of protectionism, were not competitive in the international market. Meanwhile, the government had mortgaged the country's future by extensive foreign borrowing against income that was not to materialize, and international interest rates rose due to U.S. policy shifts. By the end of 1982, Mexico's enormous debt was over $80 billion. The country found it harder and harder to earn the foreign exchange it needed to buy necessary imports as well as to make payments on the debt.

When in late 1982 Mexico ran out of money to make interest payments on its debt, the U.S. government and the international financial institutions rushed in with an emergency rescue package of new loans. The price, however, was an agreement to abide by IMF rules, which plunged the Mexican economy into a deep recession. Over the next decade, Mexico suffered the effects of severe austerity, including dramatic cutbacks in public subsidies and services, negative GNP growth, and a precipitous drop in the standard of living of most Mexicans. Per capita income by the early 1990s was 10 percent less than it had been a decade earlier, and prospects for recovery appeared slim.

The Mexican government's new focus on manufacturing for export led to the creation of the so-called *maquiladora* industries, located primarily along the United States–Mexico border, which have become the newest magnet for migrants within Mexico. The *maquiladoras* resulted from a joint Mexican-

U.S. program that established tax-free manufacturing zones. New industries in these zones would be able to import parts, assemble them in Mexico (taking advantage of the cheaper labor and less constrictive regulatory environment), and re-export them for eventual sale—usually in the U.S. market. The *maquiladoras* have made Tijuana, across the border from San Diego, the fastest-growing city in Mexico today. Other border cities such as Ciudad Juárez and Mexicali have also boomed. The same social networks that played an important role in the growth of Mexico City are having a similar impact on current migratory patterns toward the border. In some cases, entire rural villages have relocated to Tijuana and other rapidly growing factory cities.

There are now about 1,500 *maquiladora* plants in northern Mexico, offering close to 500,000 jobs. Although they have proved to be one of the most dynamic sectors in the Mexican economy, the *maquiladoras* have also drawn intense criticism. Their bias toward hiring young women, the low wages that force workers to live in substandard housing (typically lacking sewers and running water), allegations of unsafe work environments, and a record of poor to dangerous environmental practices have angered Mexican and U.S. critics alike. At the same time, their success in creating jobs in a stagnant economy has prompted some Mexicans to see the *maquiladoras* as a model for the future, including under the proposed North American Free Trade Agreement.

The draw of jobs to the north does not stop at the border. Nowhere else in the world does a developing country share such a long and relatively open border with one of the world's foremost industrial powers. Migration has always been an important issue in U.S.–Mexican relations, and policies have ranged from limited encouragement of temporary migrants (such as the *braceros* program) to forceful attempts to stem the flow. In an important indicator of growing U.S. concern, Congress passed the Immigration Reform and Control (Simpson-Rodino) Act in 1986, establishing tough—although sometimes unenforced—sanctions for employers hiring undocumented workers. The legislation's impact on actual migration flows has been minimal, but its passage has enhanced the climate of fear and distrust on both sides.

The attempt by presidents Bush and Salinas

to unite Mexico with the United States and Canada in the North American Free Trade Agreement has sparked controversy on both sides of the border. U.S. critics complain of a continued flight of U.S. jobs to Mexico and environmental hazards that are already affecting border communities in the United States. They also fear the continued impact of cross-border migration, which has brought millions of Mexicans into the United States as temporary and permanent residents.

Proponents of the agreement on both sides of the border expect it to help diversify the Mexican economy, creating new jobs in a wide range of industries. Many Mexicans are concerned, however, that their country will continue an unhealthy dependence on the U.S. economy. The new jobs that will result from the agreement, they argue, are likely to perpetuate a low-wage, low-skill labor force without bringing the necessary technology and investment for broader-based economic development.

Salinas also stirred controversy with a 1991 package of agrarian measures. In a move that reversed decades of official policy, Salinas said he would halt any further land distribution to the *ejidos,* and that *ejidatarios* were free to sell or rent their own plots of land. The move was welcomed by some as an opportunity to modernize Mexico's rural economy and increase agricultural productivity, perhaps encouraging more peasants to remain in the countryside. Many peasants, however, reacted angrily and marched on the capital to demand continued government protection for their right to farm their own land.

The Many Faces of Migration

While the issues discussed here do not cover the entire spectrum of migration in the region as a whole, the anthology readings for this and other units provide insight into some of the many other motivations and causes for migration in Latin America and the Caribbean. These include, among others, the movement of political dissidents; flight of refugees from civil war and other violence; the "brain drain" of technical and professional classes in search of better opportunities; and seasonal migration to follow crop-harvesting patterns.

Economic and political developments are at the heart of migratory flows in the Americas. In the case of international migration, policies of both sending and receiving countries affect migratory patterns. For example, Cubans fleeing Fidel Castro found ready political asylum in the United States, and this encouraged further migration, amounting to 1 million since 1960. Puerto Rico's commonwealth status, which allows for the free movement of Puerto Ricans from the island to the mainland, has brought 2.5 million Puerto Ricans to the United States. At the same time, revolutionary upheavals in Central America and state-sponsored repression in the Southern Cone countries in the 1970s and 1980s resulted in new sources of migration to the United States.

One thing is clear: those who make the choice to leave their homes, families, and everything familiar to them do so with a great deal of courage and determination. They are not the poorest of the poor but rather people of at least minimal means—they have enough resources, knowledge, and ambition to make the move. The costs and benefits of migration are not easy to untangle, yet one cannot help but admire the migrants' deep desire to improve their lives, and the tremendous efforts they make to realize their dreams.

ASSIGNMENT

1. Before viewing the program, read:
   Modern Latin America, 3d ed., pp. 221–53.

   Chapter 7, "Mexico: The Taming of a Revolution," provides a concise history of Mexico since independence from Spain, including the factors that led to the Mexican Revolution of 1910–17 (covered in greater depth in Unit 11, "Fire in the Mind: Revolutions and Revolutionaries"). The chapter pays particular attention to the economic policies that affected the course of Mexico's development and which are at the heart of migratory patterns in the country.

2. View the program "Continent on the Move."

3. After viewing the program, read:
    Americas: An Anthology, chapter 5, pp. 104–36.

    The introduction and readings in the anthology provide a variety of perspectives on migration within and from Latin America. Examples from Brazil, Guatemala, Nicaragua, Mexico, and the Caribbean illustrate the range of motives for migration, the harsh conditions that many migrants confront, and the impact that massive rural-to-urban migration has had on the world's largest city, Mexico City.

UNIT REVIEW

After viewing the program and reading the assignments, you should be able to:

·   Recognize that migration is caused by a variety of political, economic, and social factors, and is affected by both domestic and international policies.

·   Describe the impact of Mexico's political and economic development on domestic and international migration patterns.

·   Understand that lack of access to land and the inability to make a living by farming are important underlying reasons for much of the rural-to-urban migration in Mexico and elsewhere in the Americas.

·   Identify some of the benefits and costs of rural-to-urban migration for migrants.

·   Describe the impact of migration on Mexico's largest cities.

·   Draw connections between migration in Latin America and the Caribbean and the larger processes of economic and social change in the hemisphere.

SELF-TEST QUESTIONS

Multiple Choice

*Mark the letter of the response that **best** answers the question or completes the statement.*

_____ 1. What were the terms of the Treaty of Guadalupe Hidalgo?
          a. The United States agreed to allow a certain quota of Mexicans into the U.S. market as temporary workers.
          b. Mexico and the United States announced their intentions to form a free trade union.
          c. Mexico withdrew from U.S. lands it had occupied during the Mexican-American War.
          d. The United States paid Mexico $15 million and obtained nearly one-half of the country's former territory.

_____ 2. The "Mexican Miracle" refers to:
          a. the success of untrained rebel leaders in carrying out the Mexican Revolution.
          b. the thousands of jobs created by *maquiladora* industries.
          c. Mexico's high economic growth rate during the 1950s and 1960s.
          d. the potential for economic growth represented by the North American Free Trade Agreement.

_____ 3. The *colonias* that have sprung up on the outskirts of Mexico City:
          a. are government-subsidized housing projects for new migrants.
          b. are working-class communities funded by *maquiladora* industries.
          c. are squatter communities frequently lacking basic municipal services.
          d. have been nearly eliminated due to government antipoverty programs.

_____ 4. Agrarian reform in Mexico:
   a. is no longer an important issue despite its association with the Mexican revolution.
   b. was accomplished by distributing land from former *latifundios* to the *ejidos*.
   c. helped to make the *ejido* system a highly efficient means of producing basic foods.
   d. included the provision of credit, tools, and equipment, along with land, to peasant farmers.

_____ 5. The *braceros* program:
   a. encouraged internal rural-to-urban migration.
   b. brought Mexican professionals to underserved areas of the United States.
   c. was replaced in 1986 by the Simpson-Rodino Act.
   d. allowed limited temporary Mexican migration to the United States.

_____ 6. Which of the following is true of migration patterns in Latin America and the Caribbean in the twentieth century?
   a. Latin America and the Caribbean have experienced significant internal migration.
   b. Migration to the region from Europe and Africa has increased.
   c. Overall migratory flows have declined.
   d. There has been a decrease in migration from Latin America to the United States.

_____ 7. Rural-to-urban migration:
   a. is the least common form of migration in Latin America.
   b. usually takes place between two countries, such as from Mexican rural villages to U.S. cities.
   c. is usually prompted by the desire for greater political freedom.
   d. has led to a growth of the metropolitan areas around most major Latin American cities.

_____ 8. Which of the following is true of migrants in Latin America and the Caribbean? *(Mark all that apply.)*
   a. They have a variety of motives, including social, political, and economic reasons.
   b. Their remittances are a major source of foreign exchange in many countries.
   c. Only the poorest citizens tend to migrate out of their countries.
   d. They are typically unaffected by government policy initiatives.

_____ 9. How is *compadrazgo* related to migration? *(Mark all that apply.)*
   a. People tend to migrate more readily when relatives and friends have preceded them.
   b. Fear of the *compadres* has driven many refugees from their homes.
   c. *Compadrazgo* networks serve as information referrals for jobs and housing.
   d. *Compadrazgo* networks enable the family members left behind to receive government assistance.

_____ 10. The discovery of large deposits of which resource in the late 1970s led Mexicans to believe their economic future was assured?
   a. Bauxite
   b. Oil
   c. Silver
   d. Gold

_____ 11. Which of the following occurred when Mexico was forced to devalue the peso in 1976?
   a. Its exported goods became more expensive in the world market.
   b. Imported goods became more affordable for ordinary Mexicans.
   c. Its exported goods became cheaper in the world market.
   d. Inflation declined and the economy had a robust recovery.

_____ 12. The 1986 Immigration Reform and Control Act:
a. indicated that the United States would continue to welcome Mexican migrants as long as their skills were needed in the U.S. market.
b. signaled a harsher U.S. policy line on immigration, including the imposition of employer sanctions.
c. made a significant reduction in the flow of illegal migrants across the border.
d. was responsible for the growth of *maquiladoras* as a "safety valve" for migrants pushing northward in search of jobs.

_____ 13. The PRI is significant because:
a. its leaders have been too weak to maintain political stability in the postrevolution era.
b. it brought multiparty politics to Mexico after years of authoritarian rule.
c. it lost the support of workers and peasants when President Lázaro Cárdenas abandoned the *ejido* system.
d. it has dominated Mexican politics and society during the post–World War II era.

_____ 14. Which of the following is true of the *maquiladora* industries? *(Mark all that apply.)*
a. They tend to employ young, single women with low levels of education.
b. They have created thousands of high-paying jobs for skilled Mexican workers.
c. The repetitive work, long hours, and low wages do not seem to deter hundreds of hopeful applicants.
d. They are best established along the Mexican-Guatemalan border.

_____ 15. How have migration patterns shifted within Mexico due to the economic crisis? *(Mark all that apply.)*
a. More migrants than ever are abandoning their rural homes and moving their families to Mexico City.
b. President Salinas's decision to reinvigorate agrarian reform has brought thousands of former migrants back to their homes of origin.
c. The focus of migration has moved from Mexico City to the border region.
d. More migrants are looking for temporary work rather than moving their entire families.

_____ 16. Which of the following is an example of the "informal" economy?
a. Factory jobs producing manufactured goods for the domestic market.
b. Work in the oil refineries and other state-owned industries.
c. Three- to five-year job stints in the *maquiladora* industries.
d. Independent, unregulated small businesses in the colonias of Mexico City.

_____ 17. The Mexican and Brazilian "miracles" share which of the following characteristics?
a. Both resulted from government policies of nonintervention in the private market.
b. Both increased the gap between the rich and the poor in their countries.
c. Both were based on industrial policies of export-led growth.
d. Both were the expected outcome of import-substituting industrialization policies.

True or False

_____ 18. The movement of refugees escaping civil wars is the most common form of migration in Latin America.

_____ 19. Urban areas have expanded faster than the total population growth rate in almost every Latin American country.

_____ 20. Remittances often exceed or match large foreign assistance programs, such as U.S. development aid.

_____ 21. Latin America remains a primarily rural region, with about three-quarters of its population living in small farming communities.

_____ 22. A rationale used to justify employing women in low-paying assembly work in *maquiladoras* is that women have greater manual dexterity and are less likely to find the work tedious.

_____ 23. The island nations of the Caribbean have experienced little migration due to their isolation from the rest of the region.

_____ 24. The North American Free Trade Agreement would unite all of Latin America into one economic union led by the United States and Canada.

_____ 25. Mexicans refer to the war with the United States between 1845 and 1848 as the War of the North American Invasion.

Identification/Short Answer

Define or describe the following terms, concepts, or persons, or answer the following questions. Answers should be no longer than a few sentences.

26. List some of the "pull" factors that encouraged the migration of rural dwellers into Mexico City.

27. What was the most important force shaping migratory flows in the Caribbean in the early twentieth century?

28. *Braceros:*

29. Who are *pepenadores* and why are they a powerful symbol of the costs of migration?

30. North American Free Trade Agreement:

QUESTIONS TO CONSIDER

1. What responsibility, if any, does the U.S. government have for the working conditions, salaries, and environmental practices of the *maquiladora* industries? Should there be a greater awareness in this country of the *maquiladoras?* Do students feel that the industries are generally positive or negative for Mexican economic development?

2. Starting in 1991, the Caribbean faced a new migration crisis when thousands of impoverished Haitians fled their country after the overthrow of popular president Jean-Bertrand Aristide. Close to 30,000 Haitian boat people were intercepted at sea by the U.S. Navy and subsequently housed at Guantanamo Bay, Cuba; others were turned back to Haiti. The U.S. government, supported by the Supreme Court, decided to repatriate the Haitians despite criticism that the Haitians who were sent back might face violence and repression in their homeland. The State Department argued that

allowing the Haitians temporary protective status would send a signal to others and would encourage a massive flight from the country. What do you think about the U.S. repatriation policy in this case? What other solutions to the crisis can you suggest?

3. How is the movement of international capital and investment tied to migration patterns in the Caribbean, Mexico, and elsewhere? Should there be "migration analyses" similar to environmental analyses prior to any major new foreign investment? Who should take responsibility for the migrants attracted to the promise of new jobs?

RESOURCES

Nonfiction

Calderon de la Barca, Fanny. *Life in Mexico: The Letters of Fanny Calderon de la Barca.* Edited by Howard T. Fisher and Marion Hall Fisher. Garden City, N.Y.: Doubleday, 1966. Originally published in 1843, the letters and journal entries of Fanny Calderon de la Barca provide a detailed and descriptive account of life in nineteenth-century Mexico. The author, a Scot, was married to a Spanish diplomat who served as Spain's first minister to Mexico.

Fernández Kelly, M. Patricia and Alejandro Portes. "Continent on the Move: Immigrants and Refugees in the Americas." In *Americas: New Interpretive Essays,* edited by Alfred Stepan. New York: Oxford University Press, 1992. An examination of the causes and consequences of the migration of more than 5 million people per year across national borders within the Americas, written by two members of the *Americas* academic advisory board as an optional addition to this unit.

Fernández Kelly, María Patricia. *For We Are Sold, I and My People: Women and Industry in Mexico's Frontier.* Albany: State University of New York Press, 1983. The hidden human dimensions of present-day multinational manufacturing procedures are revealed in this examination of *maqui-*

ladoras, the hundreds of assembly plants that since the 1960s have been part of the Mexican government's development strategy.

Friedrich, Otto. "A Proud Capital's Distress." *Time,* August 6, 1984, 26–30, 33–35. This article provides a description of Mexico City's plight—overcrowding, poverty, pollution, and corruption—and discusses the Mexican and U.S. governments' attempts at political reform and economic development.

Helper, Susan, and Philip Mirowski. "Mexico's Desperate Experiment." *Dollars and Sense* (September 1989). Critically asks the question, will *maquiladoras* save the economy? Examines the role of multinational corporations, the benefits for employees, and political linkages.

Mangin, William. "Young Towns of Lima." *The World and I* (June 1989). Examines the hundreds of permanent squatter settlements in the environs of Lima, Peru, and dispels many myths about these "young towns."

Oster, Patrick. *The Mexicans.* New York: Morrow, 1989. Brief descriptions of the different Mexican social classes by a journalist.

Reavis, Dick J. *Conversations with Moctezuma.* New York: Morrow, 1990. After immersing himself in Mexico for a year, the author provides a vivid description of Mexico's past and a glimpse of its troubled future.

Richardson, Bonham C. "Caribbean Migrations, 1838–1985." In *The Modern Caribbean,* edited by Franklin W. Knight and Colin A. Palmer. Chapel Hill: University of North Carolina Press, 1989. From the colonial period to the present, Richardson discusses the variety of people, destinations, and reasons for migrating, and the results in the Caribbean and new communities where Caribbean emigrants settle.

"The World's Urban Explosion." *The Unesco Courier* (March 1985) 24–29. General survey of the four themes addressed at the international symposium "Metropolis 84": demography and town planning; economic and technological change; transport; and culture and the environment.

Fiction

Castellanos, Rosario. *Another Way To Be: Selected Works of Rosario Castellanos*. Athens: University of Georgia Press, 1990. Poetry and fiction that examines the role of women in modern Mexico.

Cisneros, Sandra. *Woman Hollering Creek*. New York: Random House, 1990. Collection of 20 short stories, including "Eyes of Zapata," the tale of the Mexican Revolution as told by the mistress of General Zapata.

Fuentes, Carlos. *A Change of Skin*. Translated by Sam Hileman. New York: Farrar Straus Giroux, 1968. As four people drive from Mexico City to Veracruz, the narrator exposes the object of each one's search: redemption for ex-Nazi Franz; experience for his Mexican lover, Isabel; success for the poet Javier; and love for Javier's wife, Elizabeth.

Fuentes, Carlos. *The Death of Artemio Cruz*. Translated by Sam Hileman. New York: Farrar Straus Giroux, 1988. This novel conveys the sweep of modern Mexican history through the eyes of one man.

Rulfo, Juan. *Pedro Paramo*. New York: Grove/Weidenfeld, 1990. A young man searches for his father, who he discovers is the corrupt political boss of an impoverished town in southern Mexico.

Sainz, Gustavo. *The Princess of the Iron Palace*. New York: Grove Press, 1985. Gustavo Sainz is a leader of a group of Mexican writers known as "The Wave" who gained notice in the 1960s. The teenage protagonist of this novel is exuberant, cynical, and ambitious.

Yáñez, Agustin. *The Edge of the Storm*. Arlington: University of Texas Press, 1963. The saga of an isolated village in Mexico in 1909 and 1910, just before the revolution.

Films

Unless otherwise indicated, all films listed are available in VHS video format.

Hour of the Star. 96 minutes, 1986. This film tells the story of a young woman who migrates from the countryside of northeast Brazil to São Paulo. Multi–award winner at the Brazilian Film Festival. Available for rental ($20) from: Facets, 1517 West Fullerton, Chicago, IL 60614; (800) 331–6197.

El Norte. 139 minutes, 1984. This movie chronicles the illegal immigration of a Guatemalan brother and sister through Mexico into the United States. Available in most video-rental outlets.

Three short films on population issues in Latin America are available from the Population Reference Bureau for a $10 rental fee. They may be ordered by writing: Film Librarian, Population Reference Bureau, 777 14th Street N.W., Suite 800, Washington, DC 20005.

Immigration: What We Promised, Where to Draw the Line. 15 minutes, 1986. (3/4" or 1/2" videocassette.) Addresses the United States' attraction for immigrants and the effects of immigration on U.S. society.

Lessons for the Future. 17 minutes, 1980. This 16–mm. film presents the case studies of three teachers as they discuss family planning with their students.

Mexico in the Year 2000. 12 minutes, 1979. (16 mm.) This film, produced in cooperation with the Mexican government, describes the rapid increase in Mexico's population and the difficulties Mexico will face in providing social and economic services to its people.

Unit 6

Mirrors of the Heart:
Color, Class, and Identity

These Bolivian women, dressed in the traditional Andean *polleras,* sell
high-tech audio equipment at an urban market. © 1989 Vera Lentz/
Black Star

UNIT SUMMARY

"Mirrors of the Heart" examines the complex issue of racial and ethnic identity in Latin America. The television program, set in the Bolivian Andes and in the Afro-Caribbean countries of Haiti and the Dominican Republic, explores how race and ethnicity interact with gender, class, occupation, family, and generational factors. It also considers how identity has been affected by urban growth, changing occupations, the international media, and the modern consumer culture in contemporary Latin America. The text and anthology readings complement the program by establishing the historical context and by extending the examination of race, class, and ethnicity to other countries in the region: Peru, Guatemala, and the English-speaking Caribbean.

KEY ISSUES

· How important are racial and ethnic factors in defining the identities of various peoples in contemporary Latin America?

· How are race and ethnicity shaped by history, class, culture, gender, age, and politics to define identity?

· To what extent do individuals view race and ethnicity as static and unchanging, and to what extent are they seen as fluid and adaptable?

· How have race and ethnicity in Latin America and the Caribbean been used by people in and out of power to define themselves and others?

· How have social changes affected racial and ethnic identities in contemporary Latin America and the Caribbean?

· How are concerns for self-determination by ethnic and race-based cultural movements shaping complex definitions of identity for peoples throughout the region?

GLOSSARY

altiplano (al-tee-PLAH-no): arid, high plateau in the Andes where indigenous populations flourished before the conquest, and where haciendas and resistance communities were established during the colonial period; still home to large numbers of indigenous people.

Aristide, Jean-Bertrand: Haitian priest elected to the presidency in 1990 in a landslide victory. Aristide's commitment to Haiti's poor majority raised fears among the military and the elite, who removed him from office in a coup nine months after he took office.

Aymara (eye-MAHR-ah): one of the major indigenous languages in South America and the name of a major indigenous group in the Andean countries.

bateys (bah-TAYS): workers' camps, typically with substandard living conditions, set up as temporary housing for sugar cane cutters in the Dominican Republic.

Bosch, Juan: social reformer elected president of the Dominican Republic in 1962, removed in a coup in 1963. The resulting conflict between Bosch's supporters and opponents was cited by U.S. president Johnson as the justification for sending 22,000 U.S. Marines to the D.R. in April 1965.

Césaire, Aimé: Poet, native of Martinique, considered one of the founders and foremost exponents of Negritude. He served as Mayor of Fort-de-France, President of the Provincial Council, and delegate to the National Assembly in Paris.

chuño (CHOON-yo): freeze-dried potatoes for long-term storage, developed centuries ago by Andean peoples, prepared by compressing the potatoes with bare feet at altitudes above the frostline.

derecho de pernada (deh-REH-choh deh pear-NAH-da): term for the hacienda owner's sexual rights to the women on his estate. The landowners' rape of indigenous women, which they justified by the *derecho de pernada*, was partly responsible for the growth of the mestizo population in countries with large indigenous populations. Carried out against the wishes of local populations, the derecho de pernada epitomizes the brutal nature of colonial domination of indigenous groups by elites of European descent.

Duvalier, François ("Papa Doc"):   Haitian dictator from 1957 to 1971 whose dynasty continued until 1986 through his son, Jean-Claude ("Baby Doc"). The Duvaliers used the terror of their personal paramilitary force, the Tonton Macoutes, along with *noirisme* (celebration of Haiti's African heritage) and Haitian popular religion, *vodún* (or voodoo), to intimidate and dominate the general population.

Hispanidad (ees-pah-nee-DOD):   official policy promoted by Dominican Republic dictator Rafael Trujillo (1930–61) emphasizing the country's cultural connection with Spain.

K'ara (CAH-rah):   literally, "peeled ones." Aymara term for persons who resist or deny their indigenous identity. Usually applied to Aymara who have changed their names, given up ethnic for Western dress, or otherwise attempted to become "Westernized," leaving behind markers of their Aymara identity in the process.

ladino (lah-DEE-noh):   term used in Guatemala to refer to nonindigenous, Spanish-speaking nationals. Indigenous Mayas can pass as *ladinos* if they shed Maya ethnic markers, such as traditional dress or use of indigenous language. Today, a Maya rights movement is helping to give educated young people the option of being simultaneously indigenous, urban, and professional.

negritude: Similar to *noirisme,* this term refers to the ideology common throughout the French-speaking Caribbean which asserts the common African rootedness and history of Caribbean peoples.

Pachamama: Aymara name for the omnipresent Mother Earth deity.

patois (pah-TWAH):   a regional dialect that differs from the parent language in vocabulary, grammar, and pronunciation; used most often to refer to various versions of French Creole spoken in the Caribbean.

pongo (POHN-go):   term for workers forced to stay at the haciendas in Bolivia under the debt peonage system, who often were required to provide personal services as well as field labor to the landowners.

pollera (pohl-YEH-rah):   full, layered skirts traditionally worn by Bolivian indigenous women; originally a style of clothing imposed by the Spanish to differentiate the peasant population that over time became a distinctive marker of indigenous identity. The *pollera* today is a source of pride to many Aymara and Quechua women, who mark their family's economic position by the fullness and opulence of the skirts.

Tontons Macoutes (tone-tone mah-KOOT):   literally, "bogey men." Powerful, violent paramilitary force created by Haitian dictator François Duvalier; source of great fear among the general population for their well-known brutality.

Trujillo, Rafael Leonidas: dictator in the Dominican Republic from 1930 to 1961 who used his power base in the country's national guard to maintain power. As with the Duvaliers, Trujillo's regime was identified with corruption and brutality.

vodún (voh-DOON):   also known as voodoo, Haitian religion with African roots in combination with Christian beliefs and practices.

OVERVIEW

As we have already learned, Latin America is a region of many different cultures. The conquest of indigenous civilizations by Europeans, along with the importation of huge numbers of enslaved Africans, had a profound and enduring impact on racial and ethnic relations in the region, and continue to affect Latin American and Caribbean societies today. With the European "invasion"—as indigenous people call colonization—indigenous, African, and European peoples began to change and adapt as a consequence of their social, political, and economic relations with one another. This contact, however, took place within a system that made individuals into commodities, deprived indigenous communities of their agricultural lands, and obtained forced labor for the colonizers.

Contemporary Americans are descendants of the constant interplay of these cultures. They may be biologically indigenous, European, or African, but, like most North Americans, the vast majority have ancestors from more than one ethnic group. Subsequent migrations from other Latin American, European, and African countries have continued the process of cultural and biological intermingling.

Although North Americans tend to think in mutually exclusive categories of black/white or indigenous/European, people throughout Latin America and the Caribbean recognize that reality is far more complex. The use of *mulatto* (a person with mixed African and European ancestry), *mestizo* (mixed indigenous and European ancestry, used to refer to those in the national, urban culture), and other terms for a racially mixed person are indications of this more complex color consciousness, but such categories do not begin to capture the intricacies of modern Latin American society. Labels such as these point to the continued blurring of cultural and biological issues and the different understandings of color, family, genealogy, culture, and social status in the Americas.

"Mirrors of the Heart" concentrates on the issue of identity in three different countries: Bolivia, Haiti, and the Dominican Republic. In Bolivia, the program focuses on indigenous people whose original cultures predate the European conquest and who today continue to make up approximately three-quarters of the country's population. In Haiti and the Dominican Republic, the key issue has been the birth of Afro-Caribbean cultures and races, since both countries experienced massive importation of slaves after the virtual elimination of their original indigenous populations.

Most important, perhaps, is the fact that for people of all colors, races, and ethnic backgrounds, culture and identity are neither fixed nor unchanging. Individual identity is crafted not only from the changing meanings of race and ethnic background, but also from such factors as age, sex, occupation, class, family, religion, political affiliation, migratory experience, and whether a person lives in a rural village or major industrial city. Identity can also change for people depending on where they are or how they dress at any particular moment.

The program and anthology readings highlight the many different interpretations of what it means to call oneself Aymara, black, *mulatto*, *ladino*, or any other name in modern Latin America and the Caribbean. Such terminology has been used to dominate and discriminate in work, housing, education, and politics, but also to express group pride, struggle for equity, and political goals. In the highly urban, industrial, and rapidly changing societies of contemporary Latin America and the Caribbean, identity is continually being redefined.

Bolivia

When the conquering Spanish arrived in Bolivia, they encountered indigenous people from different cultures, each with their own histories: Quechua, Aymara, Guaraní, Calcha, and others. They also discovered silver, and used their political domination over the indigenous peoples, to whom they gave the universal name *indio* (Indian), to impose a system of forced labor for the mines and other colonial projects. Many native Bolivians also were forced to give up their lands and become indentured laborers, or *pongos,* on the great haciendas.

As was the case throughout the Americas, the indigenous peoples of Bolivia used many measures to resist European domination. Their efforts ranged from flight to remote areas, to refusal to share their knowledge or work productively, to revolts and armed rebellions. Colonial domination brought tremendous indignities, persecution, and cultural displacement. Indigenous women on the haciendas were treated as the equivalent of the landowner's property, and were exposed by the *derecho de pernada* to rape and sexual abuse by the landowner and his relatives. Women were also obliged to abandon their traditional dress to wear the *pollera,* a full skirt worn by Spanish peasant women, as a means of social identification and subjugation. Thus, some of the characteristics we see today as "Indian" are actually cultural impositions that have been transformed and given new significance by indigenous populations.

Independence for Bolivia did not bring de-

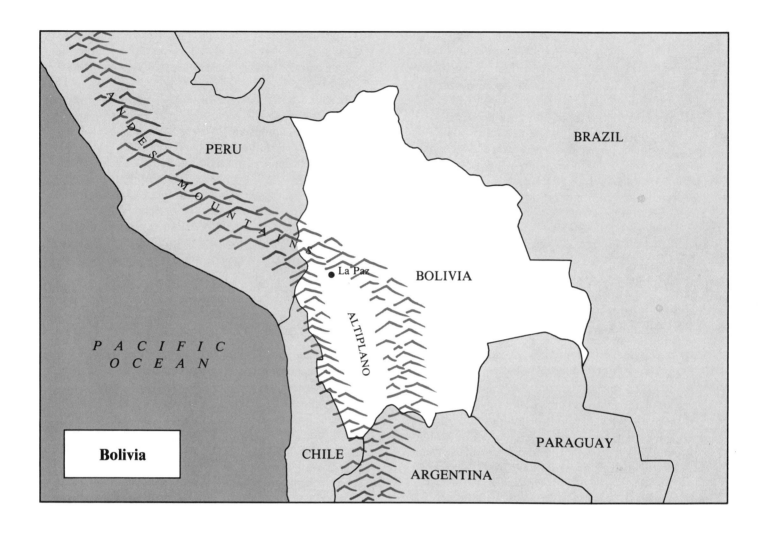

Bolivia

monstrable improvements to the country's indigenous people. Most remained in the *altiplano,* leading a life of poverty, illiteracy, hunger, disease, and hardship. Yet their identities as Aymara, Calcha, and other groups remained important, their religion and sense of community serving as a cultural buffer against the full effects of social marginalization.

In 1952 the Bolivian Revolution shook the foundations of the country's social, political, and economic systems. The haciendas were broken up and distributed as small landholdings to the *pongos,* the mines nationalized, and indigenous people granted full citizenship. Many migrated to the cities in search of a better life. There, their lives began to change very rapidly. Some obtained higher levels of education and created a small indigenous middle class. Others made their living in new oc-

cupations as bus drivers, street vendors, and shopkeepers. Many young people switched to Western clothing and made a wide range of social contacts at work.

As indicated in the program, Aymara speakers today blend rural, urban, and international cultures in their daily lives. They must make important decisions about the connections between their urban residence and older markers of identity such as their linkages with the land, the deity Pachamama, and practices such as making *chuño.*

The questions raised in this unit for the Aymara of Bolivia and for all of the Americas' indigenous peoples are complex: What are the personal and spiritual costs of assimilation in societies where racial and cultural prejudice are such a part of daily life? How do individuals and generations meet the challenges of discrimination, economic mobility, and political participation in different ways because of their different experiences and opportunities?

Although the program illustrates how the Mamani family members retained pride in their unique heritage, resisted prejudice, and worked to improve their class status, there is also reference to others who have abandoned their names and other ethnic markers in an effort to participate more freely in modern Bolivian society. Those who criticize this process call those who assimilate *K'aras*, or "peeled ones," just as some African-Americans in this country have used terms such as *Uncle Toms*, or *Oreos*.

Some conservative elites, including Peruvian author Mario Vargas Llosa, argue that it is inevitable, even essential, that indigenous Andean peoples lose their distinct identity in order for national development to provide equitable benefits for all citizens. But for those indigenous peoples who choose to assimilate, acceptance is not assured, since the ingrained social discrimination bred of 500 years of oppression is not easily eliminated.

In many countries of the region, indigenous rights groups are forging new options and defining cultural pride in new ways. Like multiculturalists in the United States, they criticize school textbooks and official histories for portraying indigenous people as outside the flow of history. They advocate the teaching of alternative histories that document indigenous peoples' political struggles against domination, and attempt to create new possibilities for cultural self-determination. They also want to show that national life is multicultural, much more complex and layered than would be suggested by the dominant mestizo culture of modernity. These groups hope to give their children the option of being indigenous, modern, *and* economically successful.

Haiti

Haiti was the world's first black nation, established in 1804 after nearly 15 years of fighting by Haitian slaves. About 90 percent of Haiti's population is black, and many aspects of popular culture, including music, dance, language, and religious practices, exhibit the distinctive influence of African culture in the country. Haiti's identification with its African heritage has inspired blacks in North America and throughout the region, but racism still impedes the country's acceptance by its neighbors, as is shown in the program's interviews with Dominicans.

Since its proud beginning as the second independent country in the Western Hemisphere, Haiti's history has been affected by a succession of corrupt, self-serving, and brutal governments. Perhaps most infamous is the Duvalier dynasty, which ruled the country for close to 30 years, from 1957 to 1986. The culture of fear, repression, and violence created by François ("Papa Doc") Duvalier still haunts the country today. Ironically, Duvalier used Haitians' pride in their African heritage to help consolidate his own position, expelling mulattos from public office and identifying himself with Haiti's popular religion, *vodún*. He wielded a mystically based power over the general population, enhanced also by the terror tactics of his personal police force, the Tontons Macoutes.

In the years since the Duvaliers, Haiti has barely had a respite from political violence and upheaval. While a tiny elite (many with lighter-colored skin), pursue high-salary professions and live in considerable luxury, most Haitians are desperately poor. The legacy of the rule of force and the failure of the country to diminish inequality and remedy conditions of poverty have prevented any government from bringing much-needed stability and recovery, and there have been repeated occurrences of widespread repression.

In September 1991 a coup forced from office Father Jean-Bertrand Aristide, a popularly elected president who promised radical changes to improve the lives of Haiti's poor. Race and color were again intertwined with politics when the U.S. government was criticized for refusing entry and repatriating the tens of thousands of boat people who fled Haiti after the coup.

The Dominican Republic

Haiti shares the island of Hispaniola with the Dominican Republic, a country with its own distinct colonial legacy. Despite a long association with Africans and slavery, the Dominican Republic self-definition has been European rather than African. Centuries of racial intermingling have produced a

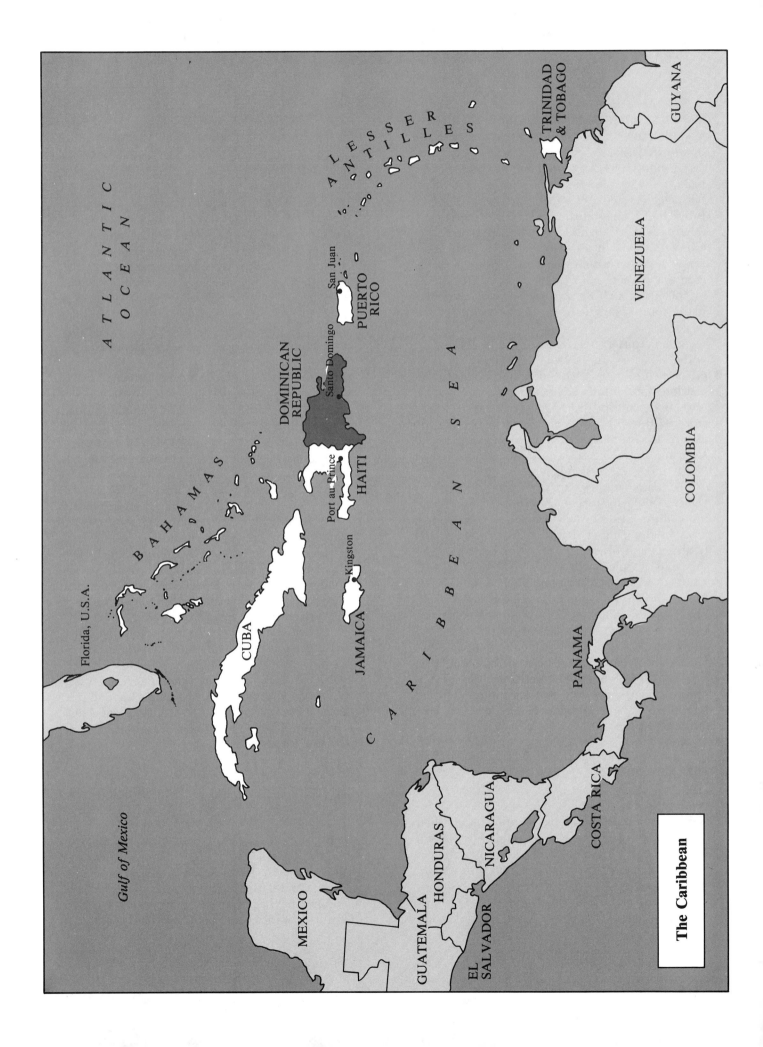

ATLANTIC OCEAN

Gulf of Mexico

Florida, U.S.A.

BAHAMAS

CUBA

MEXICO

GUATEMALA

HONDURAS

EL SALVADOR

NICARAGUA

COSTA RICA

PANAMA

JAMAICA

Kingston

HAITI

Port au Prince

DOMINICAN REPUBLIC

Santo Domingo

San Juan

PUERTO RICO

A LESSER ANTILLES

CARIBBEAN SEA

TRINIDAD & TOBAGO

GUYANA

VENEZUELA

COLOMBIA

The Caribbean

population in which three of four people are mulattos, and in which the cultural aspects of identity appear to stem as much from class as from racial or ethnic differences.

A good part of the antipathy within the Dominican Republic's toward its African heritage may in fact derive from its history of antagonism toward Haiti, a conflict that has taken on racial overtones. After Haiti won its independence in 1804, Haitian forces invaded and occupied the Spanish colony to its east from 1822 to 1844. It is symbolic that the Dominican independence day marks the end of Haitian occupation rather than liberation from Spain. Relations during the twentieth century between the neighboring states have remained tense, erupting at times into violence. For example, in October 1937, General Rafael Leonidas Trujillo, who ruled the Dominican Republic from 1930 to 1961, carried out a massacre in 1937 of approximately 20,000 Haitians living in the country.

Trujillo, himself a mulatto, emphasized an official policy of *Hispanidad*, the veneration of Spanish culture. *Hispanidad* was a means for Trujillo to associate himself with modern Western Europe, enhance his own prestige and power, and manipulate racial issues by focusing domestic attention on the country's superiority to its neighbor, Haiti. Trujillo was assassinated in 1961, but the social cleavages he reinforced within Dominican society, phrased in the language of racism, remain powerful.

The Dominican Republic segment of the program provides some insight into the internalized nature of racism in the Caribbean, described in the anthology selection by Eric Williams. The very fact that races have intermingled to such a degree makes it impossible to practice physical and legal segregation. However, conversations with several Dominicans reveal the depth and persistence of racist attitudes and prejudices. A Dominican cab driver, himself a mulatto, describes the physical characteristics of Haitian blacks in derogatory terms; a young mother complains of her friend's disappointment when her child's hair loses its baby straightness; Blas Jiménez talks of the official reluctance he encountered when he sought to list his race as "black" on his Dominican passport. Although there is a negritude movement within the Dominican Republic that asserts the common African heritage of Dominicans and other Caribbean

peoples, it remains unclear whether the movement's efforts or the example of biracial couples such as Enrique and Narcisa Frias can succeed in eliminating stereotypes and prejudice based on skin color.

ASSIGNMENT

1. Before viewing the program, read:
    Modern Latin America, 3d ed., pp. 185–87, 290–97, 308–11, 403–4.

    The introduction to chapter 6, "Peru: Soldiers, Oligarchs, and Indians" (pp. 185–87), discusses the ethnic heritage of Peru, a country, like Bolivia, in which, a large percentage of the population is directly descended from the Aymara and Quechua-speaking pre-Columbian peoples.

    Haiti: Slave Republic, Voodoo Dictatorship (pp. 290–94), and *The Dominican Republic: Unfinished Experiment* (pp. 295–97), in chapter 9, "The Caribbean: Colonies and Mini-States," offer a brief history of the two countries that share the island of Hispaniola.

    The introduction to chapter 10, "Central America: Colonialism, Dictatorship, and Revolution" (pp. 208–11) considers the impact of conquest and colonialism on the region's indigenous groups, particularly the Maya. Descendents of the Maya continue to live in Guatemala, while other indigenous peoples are present in southern Mexico and the other countries of Central America.

    What Will Happen to the Non-European Cultures in Latin America (pp. 403–04) in the epilogue, "What Future for Latin America?" discusses the possible future for the numerous non-European cultures throughout the region.

2. View the program "Mirrors of the Heart."

3. After viewing the program, read:
    Americas: An Anthology, chapter 6, pp. 137–72.

The introduction and readings in the anthology expand the consideration of racial and ethnic identities in the region, including selections from Peru, Guatemala, and the English-speaking Caribbean, along with Bolivia, Haiti, and the Dominican Republic.

UNIT REVIEW

After viewing the program and reading the assignments, you should be able to:

· Explain the historical and contemporary role of racial and ethnic factors in defining the identities of various peoples in Latin America.

· Recognize that identity is not static and is never defined by just one factor but instead by a combination that includes, but is not limited to, race, ethnicity, and class.

· Understand that racial and ethnic identities are continually in flux, adapting to new social realities and interacting with other factors such as class, gender, age, religion, occupation, and political affiliation.

· Describe how race and ethnicity in Latin America and the Caribbean have been used to define particular groups as a means of consolidating power and exerting control, as well as to defend against conquest, exploitation, and marginalization.

· Recognize that processes of social change have had an ongoing impact on racial and ethnic identities in contemporary Latin America and the Caribbean.

· Understand how concerns for self-determination by ethnic and race-based cultural movements continue to shape complex definitions of identity for peoples throughout the region.

SELF-TEST QUESTIONS

Multiple Choice

*Mark the letter of the response that **best** answers the question or completes the statement.*

_____ 1. The conquest of the Caribbean differs from that of Mexico and Peru because:
a. there was only a tiny indigenous population in the Caribbean islands.
b. the Spaniards used alliances and treaties, not military force, to subdue the native peoples in the Caribbean.
c. the destruction of the indigenous Caribbean civilizations was nearly complete.
d. the indigenous societies of the Caribbean were highly centralized and militaristic.

_____ 2. The importation of Africans as slave labor in the Caribbean was mainly tied to the production of:
a. sugar cane.
b. rice.
c. silver.
d. gold.

_____ 3. The historic tension between Haiti and the Dominican Republic stems at least in part from the fact that: *(Mark all that apply.)*
a. the Dominican Republic is mostly white while Haiti is mostly black.
b. Spain attempted to incorporate Haiti into Hispaniola after Haiti gained its independence from France in 1804.
c. Haiti invaded and occupied the Dominican Republic between 1822 and 1844.
d. the two countries have different languages and religious traditions, although both share an African heritage.

_____ 4. The Haitian leader elected in 1990 who sought to carry out significant social and political reform was:
  a. Prosper Avril.
  b. Jean-Bertrand Aristide.
  c. Baby Doc Duvalier.
  d. René Depestre.

_____ 5. Negritude:
  a. is an artistic and cultural movement that celebrates the African roots of Caribbean peoples and traditions.
  b. has been especially influential in the Dominican Republic, where more than 80 percent of the population is at least partially black.
  c. developed as a Caribbean parallel to the U.S. civil rights movement.
  d. advocates racial assimilation as the most likely means of achieving a society free of racial discrimination.

_____ 6. According to Aimé Césaire in reading 6.6 in the anthology, the negritude movement was inspired by his encounter with a multinational group of black artists living in:
  a. Martinique.
  b. France.
  c. Haiti.
  d. the United States.

_____ 7. According to Eric Williams in reading 6.5 in the anthology, race relations in the Caribbean:
  a. are very similar to those in the United States.
  b. are characterized by an apartheid-like system of racial separation in public facilities.
  c. have a legacy of laws similar to the "Jim Crow" laws in the United States, but lack the U.S. experience of the civil rights movement.
  d. are not burdened with any overt legal discrimination.

_____ 8. Peruvian author José Maria Arguedas's novel *Yawar Fiesta* (excerpted in anthology reading 6.1) describes indigenous resistance to colonial domination through control over which of the following resources?
  a. Land
  b. Water
  c. Corn
  d. Livestock

_____ 9. Which of the following characteristics does merengue in the Dominican Republic share with the tango in Argentina? *(Mark all that apply.)*
  a. It began among the industrial working class.
  b. It was slow to gain acceptance among the national elite.
  c. It has become a symbol of national identity and a famous export.
  d. It has become associated in particular with dictatorship and authoritarian government.

_____ 10. Which statement is true of the majority of the Caribbean states today?
  a. After close to two centuries as independent states they remain dependent on the former colonial powers.
  b. Independence has arrived only recently or partially for many countries.
  c. Independence has brought increased employment opportunities, enough virtually to end out-migration from the islands.
  d. The military has played a critical role in the postindependence governments of most countries.

_____ 11. In the anthology reading 6.4, Peruvian author Mario Vargas Llosa argues that the European conquest of the Americas:
  a. brought the important concept of self-determination and individualism to the region.

b. introduced barbaric, violent practices to a largely peaceful land.

c. was inspired by lofty principles and ideals, although in practice the ideals were not always followed.

d. was for the most part a disastrous event in Peru's history and development.

_____ 12. Contemporary, urban Aymara dress: *(Mark all that apply.)*
a. has remained unchanged since pre-Columbian times.
b. continues to be made almost entirely by hand.
c. marks wealth as well as ethnic distinctiveness.
d. incorporates elements from different cultures and periods.

_____ 13. In both the Andean *altiplano* and the highlands of Central America, indigenous people have:
a. largely rejected the "benefits" of modernization by refusing to become urban residents.
b. retained access to the most productive agricultural lands by a combination of resistance and legal battles.
c. been forced onto smaller, less productive lands by European and mestizo groups.
d. in most cases received generous financial compensation for the lands sold to Europeans and mestizos.

_____ 14. Cloth woven by Calcha women of southern Bolivia:
a. continues to provide clothing for the majority of the community.
b. is still used as daily dress because it is less expensive than Western manufactured clothing.
c. is no longer used as daily wear but now brings in a significant amount of income through sales to tourists.
d. is reserved for ceremonial wear.

_____ 15. Among the important changes that have affected the lives of Aymara in Bolivia are:
a. They are no longer free to migrate within and outside the country.
b. They have become an urban as well as a rural people.
c. They no longer believe in the deity Pachamama.
d. Women are no longer the primary income earners in the family.

True or False

_____ 16. The multicultural societies of Latin America and the Caribbean have developed as a result of different colonial experiences, migration, and patterns of economic development.

_____ 17. The Tontons Macoutes were created as a personal paramilitary force by François ("Papa Doc") Duvalier.

_____ 18. The Spanish managed to retain all their Caribbean possessions despite pressures from other European colonial powers.

_____ 19. Cuba and Haiti are the only Caribbean countries whose independence was achieved by long wars with the colonial power.

_____ 20. Although Haiti was once the wealthiest colony in the Americas, it is the poorest country in the Western Hemisphere today.

_____ 21. Unlike most of the other island nations of the Caribbean, both Haiti and the Dominican Republic have experienced significant military interventions in their government.

_____ 22. Both indigenous peoples and Africans brought as slaves to the Americas resisted their subjugation by a variety of measures.

_____ 23. During the colonial period and later, many of Bolivia's indigenous people were forced to labor in the mines and on haciendas.

_____ 24. Migration by the Aymara to Bolivia's cities has almost destroyed their identity as a unique culture.

_____ 25. Most Aymara women no longer wear the *pollera* because it is considered a symbol of colonial domination over their culture.

Identification/Short Answer

Define or describe the following terms, concepts, or persons, or answer the following questions. Answers should be no longer than a few sentences.

26. The Revolution of '52:

27. *Hispanidad:*

28. How is the *pollera* both a symbol of pride and a source of discrimination in Bolivia?

29. What does Eric Williams mean when he says that there is no overt legal discrimination against race in the Caribbean but that it exists in "radical form" on the social level?

30. What is significant about the choice of February 27 as the Dominican Republic's independence day?

QUESTIONS TO CONSIDER

1. Many issues are raised by the story of the Dominican couple portrayed in the program, Enrique and Narcisa Frias. Why did she choose to reject her family's traditions and marry Enrique? How would your interpretation of their situation be affected if she were black and he were white? How might class issues affect their relationship?

2. In the program, taxi driver Carlos Perez discusses his experience of racism in the United States after bluntly describing his and other Dominicans' aversion to blackness. Eric Williams, in the anthology, examines some of the differences in how racial divisions are played out in the United States and in the Caribbean. In which society do you consider racism to be more prevalent? Why?

3. Members of the Mamani family are leaders of the Aymara community in La Paz, and they also maintain close ties to their original highland community. Yet the Mamanis are urban, educated, professional people, and Señor Mamani was once a high official in the government; in the program they are shown speaking Spanish among themselves. Are the Mamanis an example of the assimilation of Aymara and the loss of their identity? Are they an illustration of the ways in which the Aymara people continue to adapt their culture to new realities, incorporating new elements without ceasing to be Aymara?

RESOURCES

Nonfiction

Allen, Catherine J. *The Hold Life Has: Coca and Cultural Identity in an Andean Community*. Washington, D.C.: Smithsonian Institution Press, 1988. Ethnographic study of the social, ceremonial, and spiritual uses of coca leaves in a Quechua community in Peru. Contrasts the white elite perception of coca leaves with that of the indigenous peoples.

Barrios de Chungara, Domitila with Moema Viezzer. *Let Me Speak! Testimony of Domitila, a Woman of the Bolivian Mines.* New York: Monthly Review Press, 1978. A very readable autobiographical account of the family life and political struggles of today's miners.

Bastien, Joseph W. *Healers of the Andes: Kallawaya Herbalists and Their Medicinal Plants.* Salt Lake City: University of Utah Press, 1987. Survey of the ancient medical tradition *Kallawaya,* which still survives in the Andes; explores the social and cultural contexts of this medical tradition as well as the efficacy of some of the cures.

Bourque, Susan C., and Kay Barbara Warren. *Women of the Andes: Patriarchy and Social Change in Two Peruvian Towns.* Ann Arbor: Univ. of Michigan Press, 1981. Shows the interplay of gender, class, and ethnic identity in agrarian and conventional settlements, with a focus on community political debates, and economic and family dynamics.

Crandon-Malamud, Libbet. *From the Fat of Our Souls: Social Change, Political Process, and Medical Pluralism in Bolivia.* Berkeley: University of California Press, 1991. Examines the medical care options in a village in highland Bolivia. The choices people make are influenced by their social and political significance, in addition to health considerations. Social status and ethnic identity can be negotiated or reinforced by choosing one practitioner over another.

Harrison, Regina. *Signs, Songs, and Memory in the Andes: Translating Quechua Language and Culture.* Austin: Univ. of Texas Press, 1989. An important study of the linguistic and cultural richness of the indigenous culture and world view in the Andes.

Hill, Jonathan D., ed. *Rethinking History and Myth: Indigenous South American Perspectives on the Past.* Urbana: Univ. of Illinois Press, 1988. A collection of essays on indigenous constructions of culture and history.

Isbell, Billie Jean. *To Defend Ourselves: Ecology and Ritual in an Andean Village.* Prospect Heights, Ill.:

Waveland Press, 1978. A classic view of Andean religion in everyday life that considers how Andean people transform their understandings of the world as they migrate to urban culture.

Maingot, Anthony P., "Race, Color, and Class in the Caribbean." In *Americas: New Interpretive Essays,* edited by Alfred Stepan. New York: Oxford University Press, 1992. An exploration of the numerous permutations of race, color, and class in the Caribbean, written by a member of the *Americas* academic advisory board as an optional addition to this unit.

Mamami Condori, Carlos. "History and Pre-history in Bolivia: What About the Indians?" In *Conflict in the Archaeology of Living Tradition,* edited by Robert Layton, pp. 46–59. Boston: Unwin Hyman, 1989. An important analysis of indigenous identity by an Aymara anthropologist that considers the indigenous view of Bolivian history, archaeology, and the struggle for indigenous rights in the face of Bolivian nationalism.

Meyerson, Julia. *Tambo: Life in an Andean Village.* Austin: Univ. of Texas Press, 1990. An accessible source on community culture and social life in an Andean community that describes rural life.

Moody, Roger, ed. *The Indigenous Voice: Visions and Realities,* vols 1 and 2. London: Zed Books, 1988. Short statements from a variety of sources that reflect indigenous politics and critique social change.

Nichols, David. *From Dessalines to Duvalier: Race, Colour and National Independence in Haiti.* Cambridge: Cambridge Univ. Press, 1979.

Rappaport, Joanne. *The Politics of Memory: Native Historical Interpretations in the Colombian Andes.* Cambridge: Cambridge University Press, 1990. How Andean individuals and culture have shaped local history, identity, and social change. This book looks at how the concerns of the present shape understandings of the past and create history.

Spalding, Karen. *Huarochirt: An Andean Society Under Inca and Spanish Rule.* Stanford: Stanford Univ. Press, 1984. An excellent study of Andean politics before and after the Spanish conquest, which shows

Andean adaptation, resistance, and transformation.

Stein, William W., ed. *Peruvian Contexts of Change.* New Brunswick, N.J.: Transaction Books, 1985. Essays by North American and Peruvian authors on social conditions in modern Peru. Includes studies of slum living in Lima, class stratification in peasant communities, and the social standing of men and women.

Stern, Steve J., ed. *Resistance, Rebellion, and Consciousness in the Andean Peasant World, 18th to 20th Centuries.* Madison: Univ. of Wisconsin Press, 1987. A well-known collection of articles on the responses of Andean peoples to the economic and political transformation of their lives that occurred with the Spanish conquest, colonization, and the formation of New World Latin American national culture.

Warren, Kay Barbara. "Transforming Memories and Histories: The Resurgence of Indian Identity." In *Americas: New Interpretive Essays,* edited by Alfred Stepan. New York: Oxford University Press, 1992. An analysis of how contemporary Mayan communities are exploring, redefining, and reasserting their identities, written by a member of the *Americas* academic advisory board as an optional addition to this unit.

Weiner, Annette B. and Jean Schneider (eds.) *Cloth and Human Experience.* Washington, D.C.: Smithsonian Institution Press, 1989. A classic analysis of the cultural importance of cloth in Incan rule, expansion, and control over indigenous populations long before the conquest.

Fiction

Alegría, Ciro. *Broad and Alien is the World.* Chester Springs: Dufour, 1987. A deeply sympathetic por-trayal of Peru's highland Indians and their struggles against exploitation.

Astorias, Miguel Angel. *Men of Maize.* New York: Delacorte Press, 1975. Mythic, magical novel of an Indian rebellion in Guatemala. Much of this book is a reworking of Mayan legends. Astorias won the Nobel Prize for literature in 1967.

Vargas Llosa, Mario. *Aunt Julia and the Scriptwriter.* New York: Avon, 1985. Semiautobiographical novel from Peru's most famous author.

Films

Unless otherwise indicated, all films listed are available in VHS video format.

Burn. 1969. 112 minutes, 1969. Political drama about Sir William Walker who is sent by the British to instigate a slave revolt on a Portuguese-controlled, sugar-producing Caribbean island, based in part on Haiti. Available in most video-rental outlets.

Bye Bye Brazil. Directed by Carlos Diegues. 110 minutes, 1980. This comedy drama about traveling entertainers functions as a travelogue of Brazil, exploring jungles and port towns. Available in most video-rental outlets.

Los Olivados. Directed by Luis Buñuel. 88 minutes, 1950. Story of juvenile delinquency among the slums of Mexico, enforced with surreal dream sequences. Available in most video-rental outlets.

Xica da Silva. Directed by Carlos Diegues. 107 minutes, 1978. The story of the strong-willed black slave Motta who seduces the new Royal Diamond Contractor in corrupt, repressive, colonial Brazil. Available in most video-rental outlets.

Unit 7

In Women's Hands:
The Changing Roles of Women

In Santiago, Chile, women led many of the protests against human rights violations committed by the Pinochet government, which held power between 1973 and 1990. © Steve Rubin/JB Pictures

UNIT SUMMARY

Unit 7 is primarily concerned with the changes that have occurred in the lives of women in the Americas in the late twentieth century. The unit traces the transformation of women's roles from the colonial period, when women were confined to the spheres of home, family, and church, to the recent past, when women have become much more active in public life. The unit focuses on Chile, a country in which women have been especially active in the political and social developments of the past 20 years. The anthology broadens this focus by providing glimpses of the experiences of women from different ethnic and class backgrounds in Guatemala, El Salvador, Honduras, Mexico, Brazil, Bolivia, and Argentina, as well as Chile.

Unit 7 also covers important political and economic events of the past few decades in Chile. The television program and textbook examine the forces that brought Salvador Allende to the presidency in 1970, his experiment with socialism, the economic and social turmoil of his administration, and the violent coup that ushered in one of Latin America's most repressive military governments under General Augusto Pinochet. The unit ends by raising questions on the likelihood of continued stable democracy in Chile, which returned to civilian government in 1990.

KEY ISSUES

· How do issues of class and race affect Latin American and Caribbean women both in the household and in the labor market?

· What have been the effects of economic, political, and social changes on different types of families, and what are some ways in which women's activities have adapted in order to contribute to family survival?

· What are some of the ways in which women in the Americas influence the political process in their countries?

· How have women's traditional roles been both a help and a hindrance to them as they seek to respond to current economic and political conditions?

· What are some of the factors that brought about the violent end to Chile's experiment with socialism under Salvador Allende, and how was Chilean society changed under the regime of General Augusto Pinochet?

· What are some of the issues that prompted Chilean women on both ends of the ideological spectrum to become politically active?

GLOSSARY

arpilleras (ahr-pee-YEH-rahs): appliquéd tapestries sewn by Chilean women illustrating their personal experiences of torture, hunger, unemployment, and the arrest and disappearance of their loved ones. This work, supported by the Chilean Catholic Church, not only created solidarity and relieved loneliness among the women, but also served as a source of income and a means of bringing international attention to human rights violations in Chile.

machismo (mah-CHEESE-mo): a cultural ideal that exalts male virility, superiority and control, especially over women; it has been the ideological basis of male-female relations in Latin America for centuries but is now widely questioned.

Madres de la Plaza de Mayo (mah-drays day la PLA-za day MY-oh): literally, mothers of May Plaza, a central location in Buenos Aires, Argentina. Women gathered weekly in the Plaza de Mayo to protest the arrest, disappearance, and execution of their family members under military rule.

marianismo (mah-ree-a-NEEZ-mo): a cultural norm that idealizes women as the custodians of virtue, piety, morality, and spirituality; from Maria, or Mary, the Virgin Mother of God in the Catholic tradition. Traditionally, this feminine code was linked with *machismo* and precluded women from independent life beyond their duties as wives and mothers.

ollas comunes (OH-yas koh-MOO-nez): communal kitchens, organized and run by poor and working-class women. With the support of the Catholic Church and international organizations, the *ollas* appeared all over Chile during the Pinochet years as a response to poverty, unemployment, inflation, and hunger.

patria potestad (PAH-tree-ah po-tess-TAHD): paternal authority; part of a legal framework derived from Roman law under which women were officially subordinated to the authority of their father or, if married, their husband. Women could not enter into contracts, own property, seek divorce or protection from domestic violence, or in general have any independent legal rights.

Popular Unity government: coalition government headed by Salvador Allende from 1970 to 1973; a controversial period of experimentation with democratic socialism. The government was ended by a brutal military coup in which Allende died along with thousands of others.

"Somos más" (so-mos MAHS): Literally, "We are more," or "There are more of us." Chant used by women's groups in angry street demonstrations against the authoritarian Pinochet regime in the mid-1980s.

OVERVIEW

Women in Latin America and the Caribbean have always been a vital part of family and national survival, although historically their contribution has often been overlooked. In addition to their roles as wives and mothers, women have frequently borne a large share of economic responsibility for their households. This is particularly true for poorer women, whose income is essential for providing food, clothing, school supplies, and other basic goods for their families.

Despite this critical contribution, it is only in the latter part of this century that women in the Americas have exercised much political influence. This has come about not only through women's gaining the right to vote (which came relatively

late, in the 1930s and 1940s, in most countries of the region), but especially through their participation in various social and popular movements. The social, economic, and political turmoil in many Latin American and Caribbean countries over the past 30 years has drawn many women from the sidelines into the streets, and contributed to the development of various feminist movements throughout the region.

Although women have been involved in support of issues at many different points on the political spectrum, they have usually been motivated by the common desire to protect their families. In this way, women have expanded upon the emphasis on home and family that has traditionally been their expectation in life.

Evolution of Women's Roles

In the pre-Columbian era, women's lives and roles were not as constricted as they later became under colonial rule, although what they were able to do varied markedly depending upon their culture and where they were in the social structure. As we saw in Unit 2, women's status declined with the domination of the indigenous civilizations by the colonizing powers. Most women were treated brutally and suffered sexual exploitation, although there were a few cases of strategic marriage alliances, such as those between noble Inca women and Spaniards.

One role of European women in the New World was to keep the lines between the conquerors and the conquered clear. The conquerors had also brought with them a strong ideology linking family honor with women's purity, which had to be protected by men. An elaborate social and legal code kept women's movements and activities under male control.

Economic factors during the three hundred years of colonialism did bring some changes; for example, the number of female-headed households grew as the economy shifted from subsistence agriculture to home-based crafts and industries. However, women's experiences varied a great deal depending on whether they were from land-owning or landless families, and were European, *mestizo*, indigenous, mulatto, or black. Differences based on social class and ethnicity have been of continuing importance in Latin America and the Caribbean and have precluded, until quite recently, the creation of broad-based solidarity movements among women.

The Family and Women's Political Activism

From the struggles for independence onward, small numbers of Latin American and Caribbean women have been involved in aspects of the political process, although they have largely been absent from formal positions of power. In general, despite this limited public role women never openly challenged their subordination to men whether in the home or in society at large. Even major female political figures such as Eva Perón in Argentina retained a distinctly feminine style, never seeming to question traditional roles and values. Although women did tend to be involved in various projects in their communities, these activities were typically seen as an extension of their mothering and household roles.

The increased political activism of recent decades, which has led many women to depart from traditions of semiseclusion within the confines of the home, has been prompted in large part by the powerful urge of women to defend their families. Particularly in countries with repressive regimes, women became important national political actors through an increasing number of grassroots and middle-class women's groups mobilized both in opposition to and in support of the regimes. In Chile, for example, women's groups were instrumental in the opposition to Salvador Allende (a socialist who was elected president in 1970 and overthrown by a military coup in 1973) and, later, to General Augusto Pinochet (military dictator between 1973 and 1990).

Today, women who played a vital part in the popular movements to bring down military governments in Brazil, Chile, and Argentina are questioning whether they must now return to prior ways of life, or whether democracy will be preserved for women in the public sphere as well as extended into the home and family. In Chile's first civilian government since 1973, for example, no women were appointed to cabinet-level positions in the first year, and women's issues did not initially receive much official attention. Despite the decline in their direct political impact, though, women remain organized at the local level. One example, shown in the program "In Women's Hands," is that of the *ollas comunes* (soup kitchens), which provide for the day-to-day needs of poor neighborhoods in many cities in Chile and elsewhere in the region.

Feminism in Modern Latin America and the Caribbean

Political developments are not the only, or even the primary, influences that affect women's lives. New economic and social realities at work since the 1960s are also prompting dramatic changes. More and more women have left the home to engage in economic activities, in part because of higher educational levels and in part because of the increasing economic squeeze on the household. In general, women throughout the Americas are also having fewer children through the use of modern contraceptive methods, although the ability to choose freely whether to have children, and how many, is still a function of women's economic and social status. Birth rates for poorer and rural women remain much higher than for those with better educations and a wider range of economic opportunities.

Today, women are making a significant contribution to daily economic activity in Latin America and the Caribbean. Women are represented in occupations that range from doctors and teachers to agricultural laborers and factory workers. The various crafts and other economic activities that women conduct from within the home have also expanded. Throughout the region, many women are actively employed in the informal sector as domestic workers, small business operators, seamstresses, street vegetable vendors, trash pickers, and others.

As a result of their experiences, the women of the Americas have developed their own distinct feminism, one that challenges the persistence of male and female stereotypes. As the anthology readings vividly illustrate, the act of organizing and sharing experiences has been a radicalizing one for some of the region's most underprivileged women. In most countries, the new feminist movements have crossed class and ethnic lines to embrace issues held in common by all women: reproductive rights, adequate health and child care, equal opportunities for employment, occupational safety, an end to domestic violence, and political representation. These movements are likely to have far-reaching effects on their families, communities, and nations.

Chile

The textbook assignment summarizes the political and economic history of Chile since independence from Spain in 1818. Compared with most other countries of the region, Chile has a particularly long history of civilian and democratic government. The evolution of a parliamentary, multi-party system led to a lengthy period of successively elected governments, with few (usually quite temporary) military interventions in the political process.

In the election of 1970, the Popular Unity coalition headed by Salvador Allende won a plurality and came to office with only 36 percent of the popular vote. The three years of Popular Unity government were among the most turbulent in Chile's history. In spite of his weak mandate, Allende pushed through radical economic and social reforms, raising high expectations among poor and working-class Chileans while provoking grave doubts among the military, the elite, and the middle class. The economy suffered from rising inflation, shortages of basic goods, and severe balance of payments problems aggravated by the United States' and international lending institutions' decisions to cut off Chile's access to credit.

By 1973, the country was being shaken by frequent mass demonstrations for and against Allende. The military, led by General Augusto Pinochet and supported by the United States, intervened to end Chile's brief experiment with socialism. In September 1973, Allende and at least 5,000 of his supporters were killed when he was overthrown in a violent coup.

The military regime that led Chile for the next 17 years was one of Latin America's most brutal and repressive. Thousands were arrested, imprisoned, tortured and killed, sent into exile, or simply disappeared.

Although the country earned widespread condemnation for its human rights abuses, the economic progress of the post-1983 period was a source of pride for many Chileans and helped shore up Pinochet's domestic support. During those years, inflation declined, foreign investment flooded in, exports expanded and were diversified, and the economy grew steadily at an annual rate of about 7 percent or better. At the same time, labor was repressed, real wages fell, and social services were significantly reduced. Many poor Chileans suffered from unemployment and hunger despite the wealth that accrued to the elite.

In 1988, Pinochet attempted to extend his government via an expression of popular will—the yes or no referendum—which resulted in a stunning 55 percent to 43 percent margin against him. In 1990, Chile returned to civilian government under the presidency of Patricio Aylwin, while Pinochet retained important influence as commander-in-chief of the armed forces, a position guaranteed to him under the constitution until 1998. Like other newly restored civilian governments in the region, Aylwin's administration confronted formidable challenges; it was unclear whether he would manage to revive internal democracy and enhance social equity while also maintaining economic growth and placating the military and other conservative sectors.

ASSIGNMENT

1. Before viewing the program, read:

    Modern Latin America, 3d ed., pp. 62–66, 112–43.

    The section entitled *Women and Society*, (pp. 62–66) in chapter 2, "The Transformation of Modern Latin America, 1880s–1990s," briefly describes the concepts of *machismo* and *marianismo* and explores the reasons for women's traditionally low level of participation in the public arena.

    Chapter 4, "Chile: Socialism, Repression, and Democracy," (pp. 112–43) examines some of the forces and developments that shaped and changed the country's economic, political, and social conditions. The authors trace the rise of

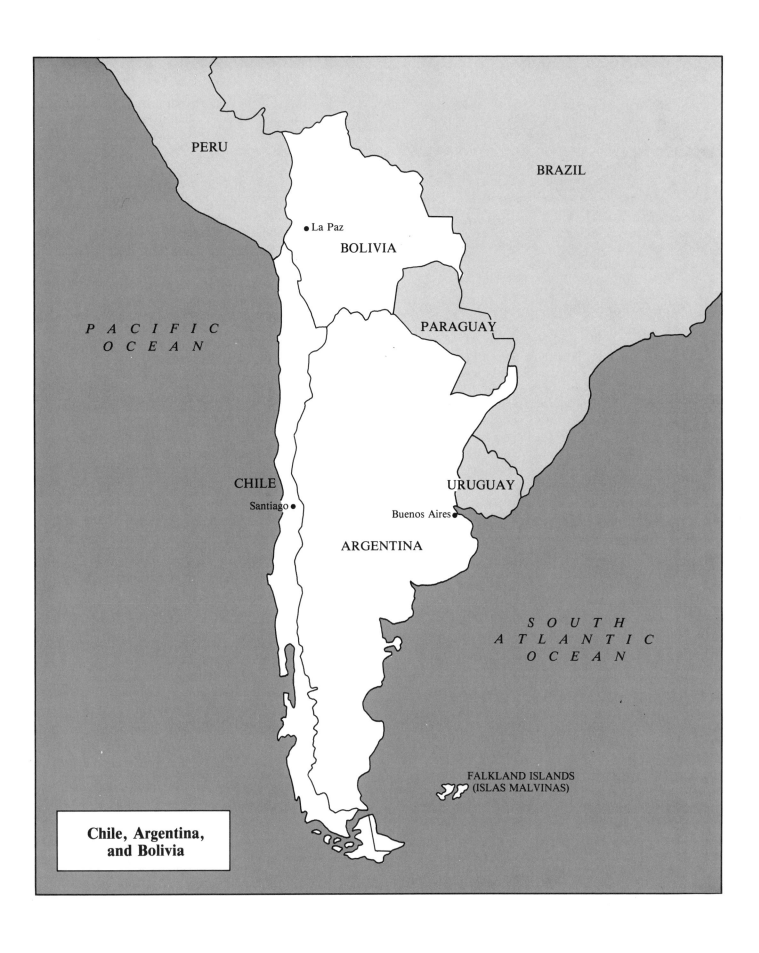

PERU

BRAZIL

BOLIVIA

• La Paz

*PACIFIC
OCEAN*

PARAGUAY

CHILE

URUGUAY

Santiago •

Buenos Aires •

ARGENTINA

*SOUTH
ATLANTIC
OCEAN*

FALKLAND ISLANDS
(ISLAS MALVINAS)

**Chile, Argentina,
and Bolivia**

modern multiparty politics, the experiments with reform under presidents Eduardo Frei and Salvador Allende, and the move to eliminate all political activity under General Augusto Pinochet's 17–year dictatorship. The restoration of civilian government and the challenges to democratic reform and consolidation are also discussed.

2. View the program "In Women's Hands."

3. After viewing the program, read:

Americas: An Anthology, chapter 7, pp. 173–207.

The anthology illustrates the effects of national, class, and ethnic differences on the experiences of Latin American and Caribbean women. The readings explore issues confronting women in different parts of the region and show how women, from the poorest peasants to the most well-educated elite, are beginning to question the validity of traditional female roles. The readings and introduction also provide different examples of women's economic and political activities.

UNIT REVIEW

After viewing the program and doing the assigned readings, you should be able to:

· Analyze how class and race influence what women do both inside the household and in the labor market in Latin America and the Caribbean.

· Understand the effects of economic, political, and social changes on different types of families, especially on what women must do to contribute to family survival.

· Describe various ways in which women in the Americas are involved in the political process.

· Understand the ways in which women's traditional roles have both helped and constituted their efforts to respond to economic and political situations in their countries.

· List some of the factors that brought about the coup against Salvador Allende, and the political and economic changes that military rule brought to Chilean society.

· Describe some of the issues that prompted Chilean women on both ends of the political spectrum to become politically active during the Allende and Pinochet years.

SELF-TEST QUESTIONS

Multiple Choice

*Mark the letter of the response that **best** answers the question or completes the statement.*

_____ 1. Historically, the contributions of women in Latin American and Caribbean society:
   a. were minimal because the cultural codes of *machismo* and *marianismo* prevented women from becoming active in politics, the arts, or their communities.
   b. increased after the European colonial powers introduced more equal relationships between women and men.
   c. have brought about important community and political changes, although they have received only limited public recognition.
   d. increased after independence from the colonial powers.

_____ 2. Sor Juana Inés de la Cruz:
   a. was encouraged by her family to develop her intellectual capacities.
   b. asked her mother to disguise her as a boy so that she might study at the university.
   c. entered the religious life because she wanted only to serve others.
   d. used her poetry to idealize traditional female roles.

_____ 3. Women's participation in nineteenth-century independence movements resulted in:
   a. greater respect and recognition for women.
   b. an end to women's status as legal minors.
   c. women's gaining the right to vote in most countries.
   d. a backlash against women, commonly characterized by the phrase *machismo*.

_____ 4. Women's organizations in the Americas: *(Mark all that apply.)*
   a. have existed in much of the region since the early twentieth century.
   b. gained the right to vote for women in the first two decades of the twentieth century.
   c. are often concerned with the exploitation of poor women by middle- and upper-class women.
   d. have concentrated all of their efforts on electing women to higher office and reforming marriage and property laws.

_____ 5. The election of Salvador Allende to the presidency in 1970 showed that Chileans:
   a. were firmly united behind the socialist goals he represented.
   b. were convinced that opening the economy to foreign investment would create more jobs and higher wages.
   c. were apathetic and uninterested in participating in national politics.
   d. were deeply divided in their ideologies and political beliefs.

_____ 6. The copper industry became a target for nationalization under Salvador Allende's Popular Unity government because: *(Mark all that apply.)*
   a. copper was an important source of revenue.
   b. foreign ownership of this important resource caused resentment in the country.

   c. Allende wanted to create many more jobs for Chilean workers.
   d. it was a symbol of Allende's commitment to changing Chilean society completely.

_____ 7. The September 1973 coup that overthrew Allende's socialist government:
   a. was relatively peaceful, and Allende's supporters quickly became involved in the new regime's plans for economic and political reform.
   b. killed at least 5,000 of Allende's supporters, and caused thousands more to be imprisoned and tortured.
   c. was followed by a temporary military government that brought democracy back to Chile by holding new elections.
   d. was halted, and peace was restored after an emergency meeting of the Organization of American States.

_____ 8. General Augusto Pinochet's regime:
   a. defended Chile's constitution and worked to restore the country to democracy.
   b. was opposed to foreign investment and sought greater national control over industries.
   c. plunged the country into economic crisis and a decade-long recession.
   d. repressed all political activity in the country, dismantling political parties, unions, and popular organizations.

_____ 9. Chilean appliquéd and embroidered wall hangings or *arpilleras: (Mark all that apply.)*
   a. were the basis of a state industry developed for women by the Popular Unity government.
   b. were produced in workshops sponsored by the Catholic Church.
   c. depicted personal stories of pain and the loss of loved ones under the military dictatorship.
   d. raised consciousness and exposed human rights violations to the international community.

_____ 10. Under the leadership of Chilean first lady Lucía de Pinochet: *(Mark all that apply.)*

    a. conservative Chilean women volunteered in programs to aid poor women.

    b. volunteers worked to increase support for the military.

    c. middle- and upper-class volunteers encouraged poor women to challenge their traditional roles.

    d. General Pinochet filled many new, high-level positions with women.

_____ 11. The legacies of the Pinochet dictatorship in Chile include: *(Mark all that apply.)*

    a. the development of new women's groups to protest human rights violations.

    b. the lingering effects of nearly two decades of high inflation and little to no economic growth.

    c. significant reductions in social services, even though hunger rates became higher.

    d. the nationalization of many industries and an increase in union support of the government.

_____ 12. According to Rigoberta Menchú of Guatemala and Carolina Maria de Jesus of Brazil, poor Latin Americans:

    a. are so isolated from the affluent that they don't have to interact with them.

    b. are ridiculed and scorned because of class, race, and ethnic differences.

    c. are appreciated for their quaint dress and rural life-styles.

    d. are seen as a vital link to traditional folkways currently being rediscovered by the affluent and educated classes.

_____ 13. Women work as agricultural producers and processors in Chile and El Salvador because: *(Mark all that apply.)*

    a. they do not have enough education to get factory jobs.

    b. they need to work, no matter how poor the employment conditions are.

    c. the work is easier than doing subsistence agriculture on peasant farms.

    d. their husbands are proud of the independence they gain through holding well-paying jobs.

_____ 14. The peasant women's federation in the Bolivian highlands: *(Mark all that apply.)*

    a. was organized as part of a men's peasant organization.

    b. worked only for issues that transcended class and ethnic differences, such as violence against women.

    c. made alliances with women in other sectors such as domestic workers and women from the mines.

    d. enabled women to address gender as well as economic issues.

_____ 15. Under the ideology of *machismo* it is socially acceptable for: *(Mark all that apply.)*

    a. men to consume large amounts of alcohol.

    b. women to have lovers outside of marriage.

    c. men to have lovers outside of marriage and sometimes even more than one family.

    d. men to use violence against those less powerful, such as women or lower-class people.

_____ 16. The current feminist movement in Argentina: *(Mark all that apply.)*

    a. worked to change laws that gave fathers rights over their offspring without obligations to look after them.

    b. worked successfully for liberal divorce laws.

    c. is similar to the women's movement in the United States.

    d. is the largest feminist movement in Latin America today because of its middle-class base.

True or False

_____ 17. In recent decades, external threats to home and family due to social, political, and economic turmoil helped propel many women in the Americas into political advocacy.

_____ 18. In the Americas upper-class women are free to work outside the home because they can hire poor domestic servants who will work long hours at low pay.

_____ 19. Before European women came to the New World, some indigenous women achieved privileged positions through strategic alliances with European men.

_____ 20. Recognizing their important role in the special election that ended the military dictatorship, Chilean president Patricio Aylwin appointed several women to his cabinet when he took office in 1990.

_____ 21. Women overwhelmingly supported the Popular Unity government of Salvador Allende in Chile.

_____ 22. In recent years, birth rates for Latin American women in all classes and social groups have declined equally.

_____ 23. Poor Latin American and Caribbean women have shown no interest in feminist issues that challenge the division of power and responsibility between women and men.

_____ 24. The women's movement in Chile grew out of a multiclass and politically diverse alliance.

Identification/Short Answer

Define or describe the following terms, concepts, or persons, or answer the following questions. Answers should be no longer than a few sentences.

25. *Patria potestad:*

26. How does the experience of Maria Antonietta Saa, profiled in the program, illustrate the changes in Latin American women's roles in recent decades?

27. *Marianismo:*

28. List three problems for women working in agro-export production in Chile.

29. Why did Chilean women pool food resources in communal kitchens?

30. How has the emphasis on home, family, and community helped propel women into political activism?

QUESTIONS TO CONSIDER

1. What are some of the issues that divide women in Latin America?

2. In what ways has the political activism of women in Latin America affected their traditional roles?

3. What issues for women seem to transcend class, race, ethnic, and national divisions? Why do you think this is so?

4. Why is it that Chile, long considered to be Latin America's most democratic country, endured one of the region's most brutal and violently repressive military dictatorships? How could this shift occur? Could it happen again?

RESOURCES

Nonfiction

Agosin, Marjorie. *Scraps of Life*. Trenton, N.J.: Red Sea Press, 1987. Moving account of the *arpillera* movement in Pinochet's Chile.

Alvarado, Elvia. *Don't Be Afraid, Gringo*. Translated by Medea Benjamin. New York: Harper and Row, 1987. This autobiography of a Honduran *campesina* outlines the dual pressures placed on women by rural poverty and *machismo*. It also illustrates ways rural women are organizing themselves to enact social change on the local level.

Bunster, Ximena, and Elsa M. Chaney. *Sellers and Servants: Working Women in Lima, Peru*. New York: Praeger, 1985. This book illustrates the development and interaction of the two main sources of employment for poor women in Lima, Peru: street selling and domestic service. In intensive interviews, working mothers describe their experiences in their own words.

Burkett, Elinor C. "In Dubious Sisterhood: Class and Sex in Spanish Colonial South America." In *Women in Latin America: An Anthology from Latin American Perspectives*. Riverside, Calif.: Latin American Perspectives, 1979. This essay illustrates how women from all classes shared ideas of what was expected of them by the male-imposed social standards. However, the women's social status determined what they were able to do.

Chaney, Elsa M. *Muchachas No More: Household Workers in Latin America and the Caribbean*. Philadelphia: Temple University Press, 1989. Presents the history of domestic service in Latin America and the Caribbean, the ideology and reality of domestic service today, the organization of women who work in domestic service, and their relation to the state. Includes testimonies of domestic workers from Brazil, Colombia, Peru, and Venezuela.

Chuchryk, Patricia M. "Subversive Mothers: The Women's Opposition to the Military Regime in Chile." In *Women, the State, and Development*, edited by Sue Ellen M. Charlton, Jana Everett, and Kathleen Staudt, 130–151. Albany: State University of New York Press, 1989. By tracing the growth of various mothers' organizations in Chile during the Pinochet military regime, this essay shows how women use their traditional roles to resist and subvert the political system.

Ehlers, Tracy Bachrach. *Silent Looms: Women and Production in a Guatemalan Town*. Boulder, Colo.: Westview Press, 1990. This intimate portrait of women in an entrepreneurial Indian town in highland Guatemala addresses issues of female subordination and power as the economy changes.

Ellis, Pat, ed. *Women of the Caribbean*. London: Zed Books, 1986. All of the essays included in this collection are written by Caribbean women. The introduction provides an overview of women's experiences in Caribbean society within the context of race, ethnicity, and class. Women's changing roles—within the formal and informal sectors—are described and explored.

Flora, Cornelia Butler. "Women in Latin American Fotonovelas: From Cinderella to Mata Hari." *Women's Studies: An International Quarterly* 3:1 (1980): 95–104. This article traces the shifting image of women in one of the most common forms of popular culture in Latin America.

Jaquette, Jane S., ed. *The Women's Movement in Latin America: Feminism and the Transition to Democracy*. Boston: Unwin Hyman, 1990. These essays illuminatingly describe the political roles and organizations of women in South America.

Levy, Marion Fennelly. "Reyna de Miralda: Organizing Peasant Women in Honduras." In *Each in Her Own Way: Five Women Leaders of the Developing World*. Boulder, Colo.: Lynne Rienner, 1988. A peasant woman leader tells how she used grassroots political organizing techniques to empower women first in her community, then in her region, to address their common needs.

Mcleod, Ruth. "The Kingston Women's Construction Collective: Building for the Future in Jamaica." In *Seeds: Supporting Women's Work in the Third World,* edited by Ann Leonard, 163–94. New York: Feminist Press, 1989. This essay describes a project to integrate low-income women into Jamaica's construction industry.

Miller, Beth, ed. *Women in Hispanic Literature: Icons and Fallen Idols.* Berkeley: University of California Press, 1983. A historic overview of the wide variety of portrayals of women in Hispanic fiction from the eleventh century to the 1970s.

Miller, Francesca. *Latin American Women and the Search for Social Justice.* Hanover, N.H.: University Press of New England, 1991. A pioneering synthesis of the experience of Latin American women and social and political change.

Navarro-Aranguren, Marysa. "Latin American Feminism." In *Americas: New Interpretive Essays,* edited by Alfred Stepan. New York: Oxford University Press, 1992. An analysis of the new feminist voice in Latin America, and its potential effect on the world feminist movement, written by a member of the *Americas* academic advisory board as an optional addition to this unit.

New American Press, ed. *A Dream Compels Us: Voices of Salvadoran Women.* Boston: South End Press, 1989. Salvadoran women speak of their experiences working for change in popular organizations, in women's organizations, with guerrilla groups, in liberated zones, and in exile. This collection of relatively short readings includes some very radical analysis of women's condition in El Salvador.

Partnoy, Alicia, ed. *You Can't Drown the Fire: Latin American Women Writing in Exile.* Pittsburgh: Cleis Press, 1988. Latin American women in exile write of their painful experience of exile, torture, and death through personal testimonies, letters, poems, and stories.

Patai, Daphne. *Brazilian Women Speak.* New Brunswick, N.J.: Rutgers University Press, 1988. Con-

temporary and historical views of women from various locales and classes.

Safa, Helen I. and Cornelia Butler Flora. "Production, Reproduction, and the Polity: Women's Strategic and Practical Interests." In *Americas: New Interpretive Essays,* edited by Alfred Stepan. New York: Oxford University Press, 1992. An exploration of the role of women in organizing the community to fulfill family survival needs, written by two members of the *Americas* academic advisory board as an optional addition to this unit.

Fiction

Allende, Isabel. *The House of the Spirits.* Translated by Magda Bogin. New York: Knopf, 1988. In her first novel, Allende traces the lives of three generations of Chilean women from the early to the late twentieth century. Written in the magic realism style, the novel skillfully weaves the family intrigues and the romantic relationships of these women with the general sociopolitical changes that the country experienced during those decades.

Cruz, Sor Juana Inés de la. *Dreams.* Mexico: Imprenta Universitaria, 1951. The author, one of the most important literary figures of colonial Latin America, epitomized the women who entered the convent in order to pursue intellectual and literary growth.

Cruz, Sor Juana Inés de la. *A Sor Juana Anthology.* Translated by Alan Trueblood. Cambridge: Harvard University Press, 1988. This anthology of the major poems and treatises of the Mexican nun includes a foreword by Octavio Paz and a complete translation of Sor Juana's famous poem, "First Dream."

Ferré, Rosario. "When Women Love Men." In *Contemporary Women Authors of Latin America,* edited by Doris Meyer and Margarite Fernandez Olmos. Brooklyn, N.Y.: Brooklyn College Press, 1983. This story by a Puerto Rican author explores the issues of women's traditional roles as wives and mothers.

Kincaid, Jamaica. *Lucy.* New York: Farrar Straus Giroux, 1990. This novel is a series of stories about a Caribbean woman's adaptation to her new home in the United States. She settles in a large metro-politan city as the governess for a wealthy family with four children. Through Lucy's unique per-spective, the reader learns about her life in the islands as well as her impressions of North American society.

Schwartz-Bart, Simone. *The Bridge of Beyond.* Translated by Barbara Bray. London: Heinemann, 1982. This historical novel, recounted in the first person, examines women's strength and empowerment through the matrilineage of one black family in Guadaloupe.

Vigil, Evangelina, ed. *Woman of Her Word: Hispanic Women Write.* Houston, Tex.: Arte Publico Press, 1983. Anthology of short stories that reflect a diverse selection of Latin American women writ-ers—Mexican, Puerto Rican, Cuban, Costa Rican, Chilean, and others.

Films

Unless otherwise indicated, all films listed are available in VHS video format.

The Official Story. 112 minutes, 1985. Chronicles a woman's political awakening and the legacy of the *desaparecidos* in Argentina. Winner of the Academy Award for best foreign film. Available in most video-rental outlets.

Unit 8

Miracles Are Not Enough: Continuity and Change in Religion

This Holy Week celebration in Nicaragua illustrates the enduring relevance of religion to people in the Americas. © Claude Constant/JB Pictures

UNIT SUMMARY

Unit 8 focuses on the importance of religion in Latin America and the Caribbean from both historical and contemporary perspectives. The anthology readings examine the roots of various religious traditions in the Americas, the evolving role of the Catholic Church, and the active commitment to social and economic justice that churches have increasingly promoted in the twentieth century. The anthology also considers the complex religious character of the region today. Although approximately 90 percent of Latin Americans continue to identify themselves as Catholics, many engage in non-Catholic religious practices. Protestant, Pentecostal, and Evangelical churches are all active throughout the region, while many people practice religions based on indigenous and African beliefs.

The program examines religion in Brazil and Nicaragua, showing the range of religious alternatives available, and how religion relates to the major social questions of the day. Readings in the textbook help set the context for examining the interaction of religion with revolutionary movements in Nicaragua and in El Salvador.

KEY ISSUES

· What accounts for the diversity of religions and religious beliefs in the Americas?

· How has the multicultural nature of Latin American and Caribbean society contributed to the role of religion?

· What is the historical and institutional basis for the decision by the Latin American Catholic Church in the late 1960s to take a more prominent role in support of profound political, economic, and social change?

· What is the role of the Catholic Church in the Americas today, and what are some of the tensions—within the Church and in society at large—that the Church's activist stance has produced?

· What are some of the reasons for the growth of Pentecostalism and spiritism over the last fifty years, and what features, if any, do they share with more traditional religious institutions?

GLOSSARY

Candomblé (kahn-dohm-BLEH): Afro-Brazilian religion practiced by many people in Bahia, in northeastern Brazil. Modern *Candomblé* reflects the intermingling of African belief systems with Catholicism.

comunidades eclesiales de base (**CEBs**) (koh-moo-nee-DAH-dehs ec-clee-zee-AHL-ehs deh BAH-zeh): base Christian communities; small base or grassroots groups of both Catholic and Protestant denominations that meet regularly to discuss the relevance of Scripture and church doctrine to their daily lives. Brazil has the largest number of CEBs in Latin America.

Conference of the Latin American Bishops (CELAM): organization of the Catholic bishops of Latin America. CELAM II, a meeting that took place in Medellín, Colombia, in 1968, was notable especially for the bishops' extensive critique of structural violence and repression of the poor. The bishops' advocacy of the need to eliminate socio-economic inequalities and to accompany the poor in their struggle for liberation from exploitation became known as the "preferential option for the poor."

crentes (KREN-chay): literally, "believers"; Portuguese term for members of the many Pentecostal groups.

guía (GHEE-ah): literally, "guide"; term used by believers in *Umbanda* (see below) to describe the spirits who act through human mediums.

Iemanjá (ee-ay-mahn-JAH): Portuguese name for the goddess of the sea; African deity who has assumed a co-identity with the Catholic Virgin Mary. Iemanjá's feast day, December 31, is celebrated widely throughout Brazil with ritual processions and ceremonies along beaches.

liberation theology: theology that equates the teachings of Christ with a call for liberation of the materially and spiritually poor. Gustavo Gutierrez, one of the earliest and most important liberation theologians, has argued since the 1960s that the Church has a responsibility to participate in class struggle, to take action against the various forms of oppression in society, and to work for greater socioeconomic justice. Some liberation theologians de-emphasize class struggle because of the conflict between their religious values and violence.

orixás (oh-ree-SHAHS): African deities worshipped in the Brazilian religions of *Umbanda* (see below) and *Candomblé*.

patronato real (pah-troh-NAH-toh ray-ALL): system of royal privileges in Catholic Church matters which emerged in the Iberian Peninsula prior to 1492 and was subsequently brought to the Americas. Under this system, the Spanish and Portuguese monarchs had certain rights in the areas of Church appointments, finances, and discipline in return for assuming some obligations for maintaining and spreading Catholicism.

Pentecostalism: term applied to a number of Protestant sects that emphasize direct connection between the believers and the Holy Spirit; from Pentecost, the Christian festival celebrating Christ's gift of the Holy Spirit to his followers. Pentecostals believe that the Holy Spirit gives powers of prophecy, vision, and healing. Pentecostal churches have drawn increasing participation throughout the Americas.

Popol Vuh (poh-pol VOO): the Holy Book of the Mayan religion, written in the early sixteenth century, which emphasizes the connection between humans and the natural world.

spiritism: general term for religions that rely on a spiritual connection between believers and the deities or spirits; includes many non-Western religions of indigenous and African roots, such as *Candomblé* and *Umbanda,* as well as spiritist traditions of European origin.

Umbanda (uhm-BAHN-da): Brazilian religion with roots in European spiritism and African beliefs,

adapted and modified by centuries of interaction with Catholic, indigenous, and other religious practices. *Umbanda* emphasizes the use of mediums who receive the spirits from the gods *(orixás)* and speak to the petitioner in answer to prayers and offerings. Among these spirits are *Petros Velhos* (the spirits of Africans enslaved in Brazil during colonial times) and *Caboclos* (the spirits of indigenous people from pre-Columbian times).

Vatican II: Second Vatican Council; important worldwide meeting of Roman Catholic bishops called by Pope John XXIII in 1962. The Council, which met from 1962 to 1965, brought major changes to Catholic practices and emphasized Church support for peace, justice, and human rights in an effort to make the Church more relevant to the daily lives of its members.

OVERVIEW

Religion has always played a vital role in Latin America and the Caribbean, and it continues to have great importance for millions of people in the region today. The multicultural complexity of the Americas, seen in culture, language, arts, and other areas, is clearly reflected in the diversity of religions and religious beliefs. While Catholicism predominates, there are numerous other religions being practiced today by people of all classes and races in the Americas, including many of the approximately 90 percent who consider themselves Catholics.

From the time of its introduction to the Americas during the Spanish and Portuguese conquests, Catholicism has adapted to local circumstances and pre-existing belief systems. Although much of the indigenous population of the Americas was nominally "converted," in fact they continued to practice their own religions. The beliefs and deities brought to the Americas by enslaved Africans added to the complexity of the religious beliefs in the region. More recently, evangelical Protestant religions have grown. Each new element has tended to be adapted to local circumstances and pre-existing traditions, leading to unique mixes of religious practices throughout a region that most of the world identifies only with the Catholic Church.

In Latin America and the Caribbean today, the intermingling of numerous religions is evident in Catholic masses, Protestant services, and popular religious feasts. The sacred hill dedicated to the Aztec goddess Tonantzín is the site of the basilica of the (Catholic) Virgin of Guadalupe, Mexico's most sacred Catholic shrine; processions in the Virgin's honor in modern Mexico continue to reflect elements of preconquest beliefs. Pentecostals in rural Nicaragua participate in an annual festival celebrating the Catholic feast of the Assumption of Mary which includes ceremonies to appease the indigenous deities of sun and water.

Similarly, African deities and religious practices have had a profound impact, especially in Brazil and the Caribbean. Catholic saints and African deities have become identified with one another in some cases, such as the Virgin Mary's identification in Brazil and the Caribbean with Iemanjá, goddess of the sea, or Yemaya, the Yoruba goddess of maternity. Such intermingling has infused religion in the Americas with a dynamism that has given it substantial influence.

The Catholic Church in the Americas

As we learned in Unit 2, the desire to win new converts to Catholicism was part of the motivation for the conquest, and the Catholic Church remained intimately connected with the state throughout the colonial period. After the wars of independence, church and state relations began to change in some Latin American countries. Mexico, for example, limited the amount of property that could be held by the Church. In general, though, the Catholic Church remained a powerful institution with a great deal of social and political influence.

This influence contrasted sharply with the practical limitations on the Church's reach and its impact at the local level. Catholic churches and schools were concentrated in the cities and were identified principally with the middle and upper classes. In some rural areas few people had ever seen a priest. Although individuals and groups within the Catholic Church had over the centuries worked on behalf of the poor and oppressed, the Church as an institution was widely regarded as a bulwark of the status quo.

It was not until the 1960s that the Catholic Church and its hierarchy became identified in the public mind with the poor. After World War II, the Church was challenged to respond as an institution to the Cold War, the nuclear arms race, totalitarianism, authoritarianism, socioeconomic inequality, and widespread human rights violations.

In the early 1960s, Pope John XXIII convoked the Second Vatican Council (1962–65) to rethink the mission of the Church in the modern world. Vatican II emphasized the need to reassert the Church's moral leadership through the promotion of peace, justice, and human rights. In light of the significant socioeconomic inequalities that characterized Latin America, such a mandate implied action by the Church to seek substantial changes in the distribution of political, economic, and social power.

Religious Activism, Liberation Theology, and Social Change

The new image of the Catholic Church was reinforced by the Latin American bishops in 1968 at their conference in Medellín, Colombia. There they proclaimed a preferential option for the poor—that is, a commitment to accompany the poor and the oppressed in their struggle for justice and dignity. This stimulated a considerable amount of activism among church people, many of whom became involved in such efforts as organizing squatters to demand public services; participating in land invasions, strikes, and other protests; and conducting literacy and health campaigns. Their actions, along with high-visibility statements by Church officials on the need for profound societal change, led to criticism that the Church was encouraging revolution, even leaning toward Marxism.

This impression was reinforced by the emergence of liberation theology, which emphasizes the believer's obligation to struggle for peace and justice in this world rather than focus exclusively on individual salvation. According to liberation theology, churches and individual believers should actively work to eliminate exploitative and oppressive societal structures.

When liberation theology first gained attention

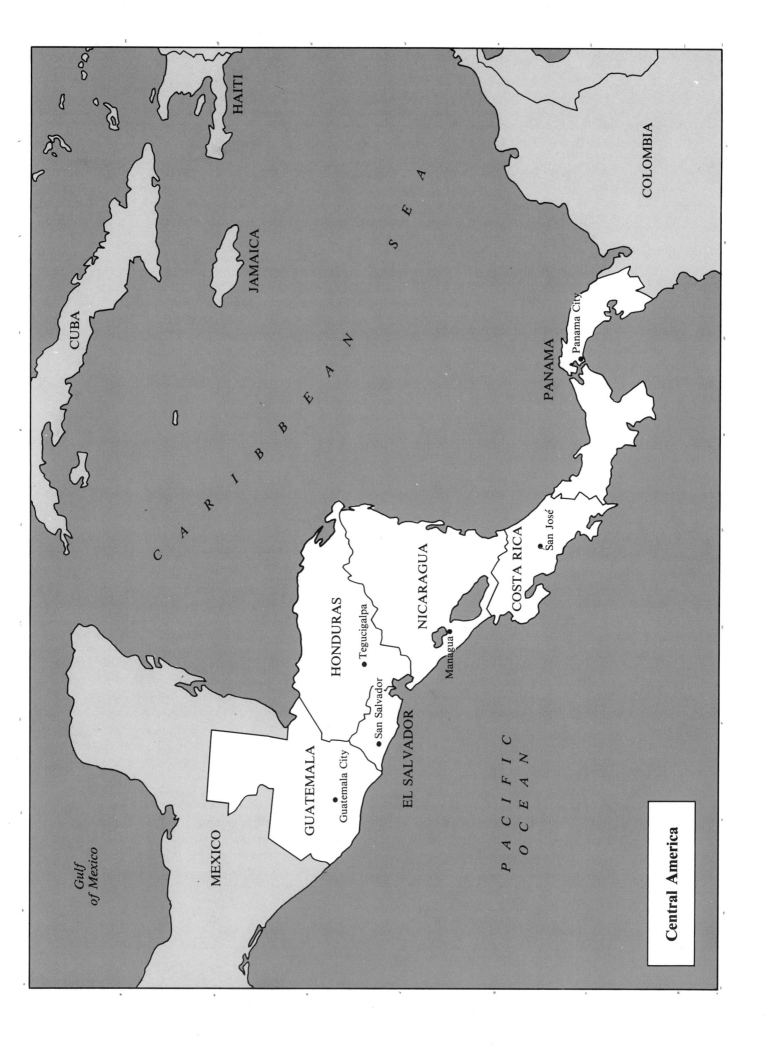

HAITI

COLOMBIA

CUBA

JAMAICA

CARIBBEAN SEA

PANAMA

Panama City

Gulf
of Mexico

MEXICO

GUATEMALA

Guatemala City

HONDURAS

Tegucigalpa

San Salvador

EL SALVADOR

NICARAGUA

Managua

COSTA RICA

San José

PACIFIC
OCEAN

Central America

in the 1960s—due in part to the work of Peruvian Franciscan priest Gustavo Gutierrez—it criticized the excesses of capitalism and argued for the introduction of a more just system—that is, socialism. Opponents charged that its justification of class warfare was contrary to the Christian ideals of nonviolence and community. More recently liberation theology has given greater importance to individual liberty along with social justice. Liberation theology continues to be an important aspect of current theological study and debate, and is most influential among Catholic and Protestant intellectuals and university students.

In many countries during the 1970s and 1980s, church people, who had long been immune to violence in their societies, became the targets of right-wing repression. Among the most notable cases were the 1980 assassinations of the Catholic archbishop of San Salvador, Oscar Romero, and four U.S. women missionaries in El Salvador. The assassinations of six Jesuits, their housekeeper, and her daughter at the Central American University in San Salvador in 1989 vividly illustrated the continuing hostility toward activist church people.

Elsewhere in the region, Catholic and Protestant churches also spoke out vigorously against abuses by military governments and, in Nicaragua, even supported the insurrection against Anastasio Somoza in the late 1970s as legitimate and moral. Many Catholics and Protestants participated in the Nicaraguan Revolution, and several priests went on to serve in the Sandinista government. This level of social and political activism caused tensions within the Catholic Church and prompted criticism from outside. In some countries, a split grew between the activities of the so-called popular church—those churchpeople actively working on behalf of the poor—and the hierarchy of the institution.

Mainline Protestant churches in this period were also rethinking and redefining their missions. Most were inclined to support substantial political, economic, and social change in order to promote greater peace and justice in Latin America. Like the Catholic hierarchy, they were also preoccupied with the tendency of some believers to interpret the churches' greater emphasis on justice as legitimation for armed revolution.

Overall, both the Catholic and the Protestant churches entered the 1990s much more directly involved in the political and ideological struggles of the region. The return to civilian government throughout most of the Americas in the 1980s coincided with a diminished need for churches to speak out against state-sponsored repression. Although grassroots efforts continue to involve churches in poor people's struggles, some church leaders appear to be refocusing their attention on individual spirituality and other more traditional concerns.

The Growth of Religious Alternatives

Over the past half century Pentecostal churches, funded initially by North American groups, have grown in Latin America. Their popularity stems, in part, from the badly needed resources they provide impoverished communities, as well as the sense of stability they offer in the midst of rapid social change and economic distress.

In some countries, such as Brazil, escalating societal tensions have increased the attractiveness not only of Pentecostalism but also of spiritism, particularly among the lower and middle classes. As a result, both *Candomblé,* based on African and Catholic beliefs, and *Umbanda,* with roots in African religions and nineteenth-century European spiritism, have expanded in Brazil. As shown by both the anthology readings and the program, many Brazilians practice more than one religion, finding that each has particular benefits to offer.

There have been other experimental religious responses to the challenges of the modern world. Base Christian communities (known as CEBs, from their Spanish and Portuguese acronyms) are an innovative means for making the institutional churches more open to individual and local needs. CEBs began to emerge prior to the 1960s but have spread widely since then. Each CEB is composed of approximately 15–30 people who meet regularly to discuss Scriptural passages or other religious materials and apply them to their daily lives.

CEBs grew out of the search for smaller, more meaningful and personal religious communities than those offered by many institutional churches. The involvement of lay people as CEB leaders also helped to compensate for the scarcity of priests and ministers. Although the popular image is that CEBs are universally progressive, even revolutionary, in reality they range across the political and ideological spectrum. As with Pentecostalism and spiritism, CEBs' popularity appears to spring in part from the desire of believers for a more direct connection between their daily struggles and their religious beliefs.

Despite the growth of these and other alternatives in contemporary Latin America and the Caribbean, Catholicism is not in imminent danger of losing its dominant position. A good number of the newer religious movements have not had very long life spans, despite their initial popularity. Nevertheless, they have contributed to the sense of religious ferment that permeates the Americas. The active involvement of various churches and denominations in addressing the daily concerns of their members has brought new vigor to long-standing religious institutions and has increased religious participation of all kinds, confirming the dynamic role that religion continues to play in the region.

ASSIGNMENT

1. Before viewing the program, read:

    Modern Latin America, 3d ed., pp. 326–30, 332–37; review pp. 179–84.

    These readings are intended to set the context for understanding the relationship between religion and society in a revolutionary setting. Most of the material contained in these two readings will be considered in greater depth in Unit 11, "Fire in the Mind: Revolutions and Revolutionaries."

    Nicaragua: From Dynasty to Revolution, (pp. 326–30) in chapter 10, "Central America: Colonialism, Dictatorship, and Revolution," is a brief look at the years of dictatorship under the Somozas and the triumph of the Sandinistas in 1979, with the support of church people throughout Nicaragua. The clash with the United States and the ultimate replacement of Daniel Ortega in the presidency are also discussed.

    El Salvador: From Stability to Insurgence, (pp. 332–37) in chapter 10, "Central America: Co-

lonialism, Dictatorship, and Revolution," covers the period from 1930 to 1991, focusing on the effect that brutal repression and increasing impoverishment of the rural peasantry had in encouraging revolution. It also examines the active role of the Catholic Church on behalf of El Salvador's poor during the 1970s and 1980s.

Review pp. 179–84, assigned in Unit 4, which describes Brazil's experience of military rule and the return to democracy, including the position of the Brazilian Catholic Church on human rights issues.

2. View the program "Miracles Are Not Enough."

3. After viewing the program, read:

    Americas: An Anthology, chapter 8, pp. 208–40.

    The anthology readings examine the roots of various religious traditions in the Americas, the evolving role of the Catholic Church, and the active commitment to social and economic justice that churches have increasingly promoted in the twentieth century. The anthology also explores the complex religious landscape that characterizes the region today, using the example of Catholicism, Pentecostalism, and spiritism in Brazil.

UNIT REVIEW

After viewing the program and reading the assignments, you should be able to:

·   Understand that the diversity of religions and religious beliefs in Latin America and the Caribbean is a reflection of the region's cultural complexity.

·   Recognize that adaptation to local conditions and beliefs has allowed religion to play an evolving and dynamic role in Latin American and Caribbean society.

·   Explain the historical and institutional basis for the decision by the Latin American Catholic

Church in the late 1960s to take a more prominent role in support of profound political, economic, and social change in the region.

- Be familiar with the role of the Catholic Church in the Americas today and recognize some of the tensions that the Church's activism has produced.

- List some of the reasons for the growth of Pentecostalism and spiritism over the last 50 years, and explain the principal ways in which these religions differ from Catholicism and mainline Protestantism.

SELF-TEST QUESTIONS

Multiple Choice

*Mark the letter of the response that **best** answers the question or completes the statement.*

_____ 1. The system of royal patronage that illustrates church/state linkages in the colonial period is known as:
    a. *patronato real.*
    b. *encomienda.*
    c. *Inter Caetera.*
    d. *latifundia.*

_____ 2. Which of the following is true of the religious beliefs of indigenous peoples in the Americas? *(Mark all that apply.)*
    a. No traces of former religions can be seen today due to the success of Catholic missionaries in converting the indigenous groups.
    b. Some indigenous beliefs corresponded with Christian beliefs and facilitated an intermingling of different religions.
    c. Indigenous peoples' holy sites and feast days may have a dual identity with contemporary Christian symbols.
    d. Christianity and African religions had virtually no impact on indigenous beliefs.

_____ 3. The Catholic Church in Latin America and the Caribbean: *(Mark all that apply.)*
    a. has been the dominant religious institution in the region since the colonial period.
    b. has been unable to respond to the profound changes in Latin American and Caribbean society, especially during the past 50 years.
    c. continues to be identified almost exclusively with the interests of the region's wealthy, as it has for centuries.
    d. has taken public stands challenging social injustice, state-sponsored repression, and economic inequalities in the region.

_____ 4. Which of the following is a source for the diversity of religious beliefs in contemporary Latin America and the Caribbean? *(Mark all that apply.)*
    a. Indigenous religions that predate the conquest
    b. Western religions introduced by the conquistadors and later missionaries
    c. Hindu and Buddhist influences, which arrived via trade patterns in the late seventeenth century
    d. spiritist religions stemming from both African and European sources

_____ 5. Which of the following is true of the relations between the Church and state in the colonial and early independence periods? *(Mark all that apply.)*
    a. Church relations with royal authorities were very difficult because of the monarchs' refusal to allow missionaries into the Americas for the first 50 years after the conquest.
    b. The Church was initially very close to the monarchies, but almost all of the Latin American hierarchy began to call for independence as early as the midseventeenth century.
    c. Church relations with the Spanish and Portuguese monarchies and the colonial authorities were solidified by negotiations and papal agreements.

d. The Church was seen as a bastion of support for the monarchies during the independence struggles and was therefore the subject of criticism and restrictive legislation by the republican governments.

____ 6. Both *Umbanda* and *Candomblé: (Mark all that apply.)*
   a. include a belief in the ability of mediums to make contact with the Holy Spirit.
   b. draw upon religious beliefs that came to the Americas with enslaved Africans during the seventeenth and eighteenth centuries.
   c. have attracted many adherents through their emphasis on direct contact with the spirit world.
   d. are especially prominent in Nicaragua and elsewhere in Central America.

____ 7. Vatican II:
   a. was called by Pope John Paul II to reassert traditional Catholic stances on personal moral issues.
   b. was part of the Catholic Church's response to the need for greater institutional relevance to the modern world.
   c. was never accepted by the majority of Latin American Catholics, who preferred the traditional Latin masses.
   d. began a move of the Catholic hierarchy in Latin America away from their earlier stance on behalf of social change.

____ 8. The appeal of spiritist and Pentecostal churches: *(Mark all that apply.)*
   a. is linked to the active stands that those churches have taken against oppressive social and political structures.
   b. is due in part to the absence of Catholic and Protestant churches from some rural areas.
   c. is already on the decline throughout most of Latin America.

d. indicates the desire of many Latin Americans for a more personal and direct connection between their religion and their daily lives.

____ 9. In general, CEBs share which of the following characteristics with liberation theology? *(Mark all that apply.)*
   a. Both represent innovative responses to the challenges facing religion in modern society.
   b. Both are examples of efforts to connect religious beliefs and practices more directly with the concerns of the poor.
   c. Both resulted from the Catholic Church's self-examination under the leadership of Pope John Paul II.
   d. Both have emphasized the failures of socialist and Marxist societies to achieve greater socioeconomic justice.

____ 10. Which of the following is true of the position of the Catholic Church in El Salvador's civil war?
   a. There was a split between the popular church and Archbishop Romero, who remained allied with the country's elites.
   b. Church leaders were rebuked by the Vatican for their involvement in the country's political situation.
   c. Church activism on behalf of the poor led to Church members' becoming targets for repression and assassination.
   d. The Catholic Church lost so many members to Pentecostal movements that it became irrelevant during El Salvador's civil war.

____ 11. Religious trends in Brazil are important because: *(Mark all that apply.)*
   a. Brazil is the largest Catholic country in the world and is quite influential within Latin America.
   b. the Catholic Church in Brazil has been one of the region's most conservative organizations and has affected stands taken by CELAM.

c. Pope John Paul II has been very influential in directing the course of the Brazilian Catholic Church.
d. Brazil's size and cultural diversity have made it a site for religious experimentation and innovation.

_____ 12. Nicaraguan Christians were active in the movement to overthrow Somoza because:
a. they were outraged by the murder of Archbishop Romero.
b. they viewed the Somoza government as corrupt and immoral.
c. Somoza had made the Catholic Church a particular target of state-sponsored repression.
d. the pope and other religious figures called on Christians to join the Sandinistas.

_____ 13. Liberation theology was criticized for: *(Mark all that apply.)*
a. sanctioning class conflict.
b. favoring the middle classes.
c. relying on the capitalist system to eliminate poverty.
d. ignoring internal oppression, such as racism and sexism, within the Church.

_____ 14. Which of the following represents an important effect of repression against church leaders in El Salvador? *(Mark all that apply.)*
a. Greater international attention was drawn to human rights abuses by the military and paramilitary death squads.
b. Church leaders tended to overcome their internal disagreements to unite in opposition to government repression.
c. The martyrdom of major religious figures was successful in silencing official Church criticism of human rights violations.
d. The repression of church workers undermined the legitimacy of U.S. policy in El Salvador.

_____ 15. Which of the following actions have earned the Brazilian Catholic Church a reputation as one of Latin America's most progressive? *(Mark all that apply.)*
a. Participation in the reformist military government that took power after the 1964 coup
b. Outspoken criticism of government abuse of human rights, especially in the 1970s
c. The creation of a Catholic political party, which was able to put Fernando Collor de Mello in the presidency in 1990
d. Support for greater access to land for the rural poor

True or False

_____ 16. The Catholic Church, the religion of about 90 percent of all Latin Americans, is the exclusive authority in religious matters throughout most of the region.

_____ 17. Until Vatican II, church people in Latin America were uninterested and uninvolved with the situation of the poor in their countries.

_____ 18. The wealth and power of the Catholic Church in Latin America prompted concern among many republican governments in the postindependence period.

_____ 19. The shrine of the Virgin of Guadalupe is located at a spot held sacred by the Aztecs and dedicated to their goddess Tonantzín.

_____ 20. There has been relatively little diversity of opinion or internal dissent within the Catholic Church on major moral issues during most of its history in Latin America.

_____ 21. The fact that so many Brazilians choose to baptize their children Catholic means the children will in all likelihood grow up to be active, practicing members of the Catholic Church.

_____ 22. The spiritist religions of *Umbanda* and *Candomblé* are practiced mostly in Central America, particularly by Nicaraguans.

Identification/Short Answer

Define or describe the following terms, concepts, or persons, or answer the following questions. Answers should be no longer than a few sentences.

23. Popol Vuh:

24. The Valladolid debate:

25. Pope John XXIII:

26. Liberation theology:

27. What was the significance of CELAM II?

28. What does the celebration of Holy Week in Brazil reveal?

29. Oscar Romero:

30. What was the significance of Ernesto Cardenal's participation in the Sandinista government?

QUESTIONS TO CONSIDER

1. The anthology excerpt from Gustavo Gutierrez's *A Theology of Liberation* (Reading 8.5) on the Church's obligation to take the side of the poor in their struggle against oppression provoked both deep fears and great hopes among different sectors of Latin American society. Why was this idea so controversial? Why does it continue to be so influential?

2. How are some Latin Americans able to participate in more than one religious tradition when their beliefs and practices may conflict with one another? What might this indicate about the role of religion in their lives?

3. Should churches and religious persons take sides in revolutionary upheavals in their countries? What are some of the arguments that favor their staying out of politics? Why might some feel a moral obligation to become involved? How is church activism linked to liberation theology and the image of the "guerrilla priest"?

RESOURCES

Nonfiction

Brown, Diana DeGroat. *Umbanda: Religion and Politics in Urban Brazil.* Ann Arbor, Mich.: University Microfilms International Research Press, 1986. A basic textbook on contemporary *Umbanda.*

Bruneau, Thomas C., Chester E. Gabriel, and Mary Mooney, eds. *The Catholic Church and Religions in*

Latin America. Montreal: McGill University Center for Developing-Area Studies, 1984. Examines the influence of Catholicism on non-Catholic religious practices and vice versa.

Cole, Jeffrey A. *The Church and Society in Latin America.* New Orleans: Tulane University Press, 1984. A collection of essays covering Protestantism and Catholicism in both the colonial and national periods.

Dorr, Donal. *Option for the Poor: A Hundred Years of Vatican Social Teaching.* Maryknoll, N.Y.: Orbis Books, 1983. A survey of Catholic positions on social issues since the late nineteenth century, including an analysis of Vatican II and Medellín.

Gannon, Thomas M., S.J., ed. *World Catholicism in Transition.* New York: Macmillan, 1988. A collection of essays analyzing the role of the Catholic Church in the modern world with special attention to Asia, Africa, and Latin America.

Gutierrez, Gustavo. *The Truth Shall Make You Free: Confrontations.* Maryknoll, N.Y.: Orbis Books, 1990. The most current of the leading liberation theologian's works available in English. Reflects some modifications of Gutierrez's earlier positions.

Hennelly, Alfred T., S.J., ed. *Liberation Theology: A Documentary History.* Maryknoll, N.Y.: Orbis Books, 1990. Contains selections from the most influential liberation theologians, as well as responses to their work.

Levine, Daniel H. "Is Religion Being Politicized? And Other Pressing Questions Latin America Poses." *Political Sociology* (Fall 1986): 825–31. Tackles the issues involved in the charges that religion in Latin America, and particularly the Catholic Church, is becoming too political.

Levine, Daniel H. *Religion and Political Conflict in Latin America.* Chapel Hill: University of North Carolina Press, 1986. Focuses on grassroots Catholicism and popular religiosity.

Mainwaring, Scott. *The Catholic Church and Politics in Brazil, 1916–1985.* Stanford, Calif.: Stanford University Press, 1986. First-rate analysis of Catholicism in twentieth- century Brazil.

Mainwaring, Scott, and Alexander Wilde, eds. *Progressive Church in Latin America.* Notre Dame, Ind.: University of Notre Dame Press, 1988. Examines progressive church movements in Central America, Brazil, and Peru and their evolution over time.

McGovern, Arthur F. *Liberation Theology and Its Critics.* Maryknoll, N.Y.: Orbis Books, 1989. Contains a brief history and analysis of liberation theology and then examines the principal controversial issues it generated.

Murphy, Joseph M. *Santería: An African Religion in America.* Boston: Beacon Press, 1988. Describes the spiritist religion of *Santería* and its influence in the Cuban-American communities in Miami and New York.

Sigmund, Paul E. *Liberation Theology at the Crossroads: Democracy or Revolution?* New York: Oxford University Press, 1990. An analysis of the origins and evolution of liberation theology in Latin America and some of the controversies generated by it.

Stoll, David. *Is Latin America Turning Protestant? The Politics of Evangelical Growth.* Berkeley: University of California Press, 1990. Argues that Protestantism, especially Pentecostalism, is spreading rapidly in Latin America. Stoll's statistics have been challenged by a good number of scholars as being overstated.

Tamez, Elsa, ed. *Through Her Eyes: Women's Theology from Latin America.* Maryknoll, N.Y.: Orbis Press, 1989. Collection of essays on women's views of liberation theology, particularly its relevance to the problems of women in Latin America.

van Duk, Frank Jan. "The Twelve Tribes of Israel: Rasta and the Middle Class," *New West Indian Guide* 62: 1, 2 (1988). This article describes the rise and growth of the Kingston-based Twelve Tribes of Israel—the largest, best-organized, and best-disciplined group within Rastafarianism.

Wafer, Jim. *The Taste of Blood: Spirit Possession in Brazilian Candomblé.* Philadelphia: University of Pennsylvania Press, 1991. An analysis of African-Brazilian spiritism and who is attracted to it.

Williams, Philip J. *The Catholic Church and Politics in Nicaragua and Costa Rica.* Pittsburgh: University of Pittsburgh Press, 1989. Examines contemporary trends within the Nicaraguan Catholic Church and compares them with those in the Church in Costa Rica.

Fiction

Carpentier, Alejo. *Explosion in a Cathedral.* Translated by John Shirrock. Boston: Little, Brown, 1963. This international best-seller by a Cuban author recounts the origins of the Haitian revolution and the interplay of various motivations, including the challenge of freemasonry to the Catholic Church and to traditional society.

Esquivel, Julia. "They Have Threatened Us with Resurrection: Parable." In *You Can't Drown the Fire: Latin American Women Writing in Exile,* edited by Alicia Partnoy, pp. 190–97. Pittsburgh: Cleis Press, 1988. A poem by a Guatemalan Protestant political activist about repression in her country.

Greene, Graham. *The Power and the Glory.* New York: Penguin Books, 1962. Graham Greene's classic novel set in Mexico after the 1910–17 revolution recounts the story of a priest caught up in the anticlericalism of the period.

Mistral, Gabriela. *Selected Poems of Gabriela Mistral.* Translated and edited by Foris Dana. Baltimore: Johns Hopkins University Press, 1971. Poems by the first Latin American writer to receive the Nobel Prize for literature. This Chilean poet's work is suffused with religious imagery and references as she discusses death, grief, children, and nature.

Partnoy, Alicia. *The Little School: Tales of Disappearance and Survival in Argentina.* Pittsburgh: Cleis Press, 1986. The chapter entitled "Religion" is a meditation on religion and political activism, and on the interplay of religions, as well as belief and nonbelief.

Films

Unless otherwise indicated, all films listed are available in VHS video format.

The Mission. 128 minutes, 1986. Robert De Niro and Jeremy Irons star in this epic tale of eighteenth-century Jesuit missionaries in Brazil and the disaster that results when they try to convert the indigenous tribes living in Brazil's interior. Available for rental from most video stores in the United States.

Popol Vuh: The Creation Myth of the Maya. 29 minutes, 1989. This animated film recounts the creation myth of the Maya in ancient Guatemala. Available for rental ($60 plus $7 shipping) from: University of California Extension Media Center, 2176 Shattuck Avenue, Berkeley, CA 94704; (510) 642–0460.

Unit 9

Builders of Images: Writers, Artists, and Popular Culture

Two of Puerto Rico's most prominent artists, writer Luis Rafael Sánchez and painter Nick Quijano, are concerned with the balance between local and international influences in Latin American culture today. © Juan Mandelbaum

UNIT SUMMARY

Unit 9 examines the diversity, vibrancy, and historical role of various forms of cultural expression in the Americas. The unit illustrates the complex roots of Latin American and Caribbean culture in indigenous, European, and African traditions. The television program and anthology profile different types of art and artists from the realms of literature, painting, music, theater, and cinema, and examine the political and social impact of art in the region.

The unit also includes a brief historical overview of the development and role of Latin American literature, and outlines some of the major questions facing artists throughout the continent today: Is there a distinct Latin American voice? Should art be autonomous or should it reflect social and political reality? How should artists respond to the pervasive influence of North American culture, as well as to the impact of locally produced mass TV and radio programming?

KEY ISSUES

· What are the historical and social roots of cultural expression in Latin America and the Caribbean, and how do they sometimes conflict with one another within various literary and artistic forms?

· What are some examples of attempts by modern authors and artists in the region to incorporate distinctly Latin American themes into their work?

· What is the relationship among literary and artistic expression, social questions, and political issues in Latin America and the Caribbean?

· Who are some of the region's most prominent authors, artists, and musicians, and how has their work reached a broader audience?

· How has Latin American and Caribbean culture been affected by the spread of literacy, the impact of modernization, and widespread access to modern means of mass communication?

GLOSSARY

blocos afro (BLOCK-ohs AH-froh): community music groups from Bahia, in northeastern Brazil, which affirm African heritage.

bossa nova (BOSS-ah NOH-va): a slow *samba* (see below) developed in Rio de Janeiro, some forms of which have been influenced by jazz.

Coatlicue (kwat-lee-kway): Aztec goddess who is mother of the earth and the sea; her statue is housed in the Museum of Anthropology in Mexico City.

magic realism: term coined by Cuban novelist Alejo Carpentier in the 1940s which refers to some authors' use of descriptive narrative in combination with fantasy and myth to define a new, Latin American vision of reality.

modernism: literary movement that emerged in Latin America in the late nineteenth century which proclaimed the autonomy of art and literature, especially poetry; influenced particularly by cultural developments in France.

muralism: modern art movement that began as a government-sponsored experiment in the 1920s in Mexico, using popular art, painted on walls, employing traditional and recognizable images, colors, and styles, to communicate with illiterate and semi-literate people. It is most notable for taking art out of private galleries into public spaces. Diego Rivera, David Alfaro Siqueiros, and José Clemente Orozco were some of the Mexican muralists whose large-scale works explored political and social themes.

Operation Bootstrap: U.S.-financed program, undertaken during the 1950s and 1960s, that accelerated industrialization in Puerto Rico.

samba (SAHM-bah): Brazilian popular music exhibiting African influence.

tropicalism: musical movement during the late 1960s in Brazil that re-examined Brazilian popular music and opened it to a variety of domestic and international influences; associated with Caetano Veloso, one of the movement's leaders.

OVERVIEW

The idea that there is a distinctive Latin American and Caribbean culture contains elements of both reality and myth. Certainly the variety of cultural forms present in countries throughout the region reflects a history, tradition, and current reality that distinguish the Americas from the rest of the world. However, in a region where seven official and dozens of indigenous languages are spoken, and where the arts draw from the different historical experiences of numerous countries and subregions, it is difficult to identify a single Latin American or Caribbean culture as particularly illustrative of the Americas as a whole.

At the same time, the countries and artists of the hemisphere are not isolated from one another or from the rest of the world. Important changes have occurred in the second half of the twentieth century, especially with the advent of modern communications technologies and a mass consumer culture. These changes have eroded the barriers that once divided culture along class, ethnic, national, and other lines. Although Latin American and Caribbean artists continue to struggle with the need to build authentic national images, their work in many cases has transcended national limits and achieved widespread international recognition.

An important theme of this unit is the complex relationship between artists of the region and U.S. culture and politics. Several of the artists profiled in the program and anthology voice concern about U.S. cultural and political domination, and describe their fierce desire to differentiate themselves and their work from U.S.-influenced mass culture. The textbook readings on Puerto Rico and interviews with Puerto Rican artists in the program provide some insight into how that island's unique historical relationship with the United States has affected its culture, politics, and society.

The Development of Latin American Literature

The authors, poets, and intellectuals of Latin America and the Caribbean have played a critical role in their nations' social and political development. Their influence dates back to the colonial period and the struggles for independence, when poetry, narratives, and letters praised the wonders of the New World. During the postindependence period of national formation, literature was considered by many to be an important instrument for expressing the spirit and identity of the emerging nations.

In conjunction with profound economic changes in the period from the 1890s to the 1920s, an era known as the "belle epoque," a new trend of modernism emerged in Latin American literature. Modernist artists attempted to assert a new independence for art. They were particularly influenced by trends in Western Europe, especially France, and their work encouraged Latin American involvement in the highest forms of "Western" culture.

The best-known example of a modernist artist is the poet Rubén Darío (1867–1916), a Nicaraguan who traveled extensively in Latin America and Europe. Darío's work began with an interest in Europe but gradually evolved to an interest more focused on the social realities of life in Latin America.

Throughout the early twentieth century, Latin American artists seemed caught between the desire to be "modern" and the need to remain true to their unique national and historical experience. Many asserted the inherent "otherness" of Latin America and its right to develop a distinctive cultural voice. They frequently used traditional, indigenous, and popular elements in their work as examples of the region's unique heritage. In Latin American literature, some of the many important movements that followed modernism include Brazilian regionalism, cultural nationalism, social realism, and numerous avant-garde trends such as ultraism and surrealism.

In the early 1960s, Latin American literature took off in many different directions. The works of authors such as Gabriel García Márquez, Mario Vargas Llosa, Carlos Fuentes, José Donoso, José Maria Arguedas, and Miguel Angel Asturias were translated and disseminated as never before. The literature of this period is notable for its innovative styles and complex language. Magic realism, a literary term that had first been coined by Cuban Alejo Carpentier in the 1940s, became one of Latin America's best known exports during this period. Magic realism refers to the intermingling of fantasy with reality within the narrative. Other au-

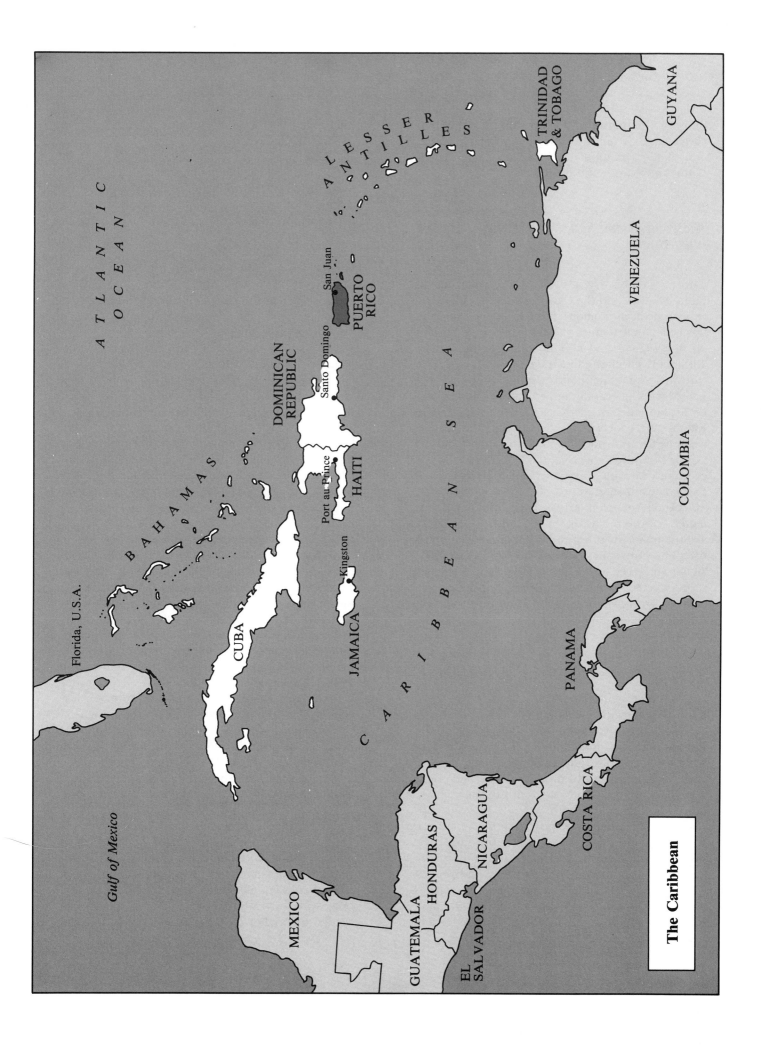

ATLANTIC OCEAN

Gulf of Mexico

Florida, U.S.A.

BAHAMAS

CUBA

MEXICO

GUATEMALA

HONDURAS

EL SALVADOR

NICARAGUA

COSTA RICA

PANAMA

CARIBBEAN SEA

JAMAICA

Kingston

HAITI

Port au Prince

DOMINICAN REPUBLIC

Santo Domingo

San Juan

PUERTO RICO

LESSER ANTILLES

TRINIDAD & TOBAGO

GUYANA

VENEZUELA

COLOMBIA

The Caribbean

thors of this period, known as the "boom," borrowed freely from indigenous myth or oral tradition. Their common desire was to create a new Latin American mode of expression.

The Political and Social Role of the Intellectual

Throughout history, authors and intellectuals in Latin America and the Caribbean have held widely varying political positions, but have tended to share the belief that writers should take a public stand on important social and political questions. The anthology selections illustrate this historical role with the proindependence writing of Cuban poet José Martí; the graphic and empathetic description of peasant life in northeast Brazil by Graciliano Ramos; the concern for the working class in the work of Chilean poet Pablo Neruda; and Gabriel García Márquez's speech at the Nobel Prize awards ceremony on contemporary Latin American social and political issues.

Latin American artists have also been intimately connected with their countries' struggles against political authoritarianism and social injustice. The efforts of Mexican director Jesusa Rodríguez and Argentine filmmaker Fernando Solanas to defy censorship and challenge convention are current examples of this long-standing tradition of political engagement.

Popular Cultures and Modern Mass Culture

Until well into the twentieth century, the impact and influence of Latin America's poets and authors was restricted by limited literacy in the region. The so-called high culture of the intellectuals, such as poetry, literature, and European-influenced opera and classical music, co-existed with theater, music, dance, and other forms known collectively as popular culture. There was no one popular culture but rather a variety of cultural expressions that reflected the history, language, and interests of many groups: urban slum dwellers, indigenous communities, rural farmers, black and *mulatto* descendants of enslaved Africans, and others. Many of these popular cultural forms had remained nearly

unchanged for centuries, usually quite isolated from the rest of the world.

With the advent of modern communications these local and regional cultures began to change. Many different forms began to intermingle as the diffusion of radio throughout the hemisphere and the enormous popularity of Latin cinema brought about major changes in popular music and other forms of popular expression. Some popular musicians in the 1960s and 1970s, for example, used indigenous instruments and melodies to create new sounds, such as Caetano Veloso's reworking of the Brazilian samba, or Chilean protest music based on Andean folk songs.

Today, popular cultures in the Americas are inspired by many different sources. Internationally recognized Brazilian and Caribbean music is a blend of African, European, and American styles; the samba, merengue, and other well-known dances are rooted in African rhythms and songs that have been transformed into truly Latin forms; modern theater and cinema draw upon indigenous oral traditions and urban street festivals for their material. Most recently, with the arrival of "salsa" music, formerly distinct styles have melded into a new, pan-American hybrid that cannot be attributed to any one country or tradition.

Throughout Latin America and the Caribbean, mass communications technology has also contributed to the development of an electronic media mass culture. The new popular culture has a far greater audience than that ever enjoyed by the region's novelists and poets. A U.S. influence on the region's mass culture became especially pronounced with the arrival of television in the 1950s, when the most widely watched programs were imports such as "Bonanza" and "Mission Impossible." Although many Latin American and Caribbean artists rejected this wave of "cultural imperialism" (and continue to do so today), there is no denying its enormous impact.

Later, locally based media conglomerates, such as Rede Globo in Brazil or Mexico's Televisa, capitalized on the popularity of *radionovelas* (radio programs that featured serialized stories) to create new forms of a particularly Latin American mass culture, which ultimately surpassed the U.S. imports in popularity. The soap operas *(telenovelas)*, comic books and illustrated books *(fotonovelas),* and other products of these media giants have succeeded in further burying former divisions along urban/rural, indigenous/Hispanic, popular/elite, and national/international lines.

Most recently, Latin American and Caribbean artistic, literary, and popular expression of all types has come to be more widely known and appreciated internationally as well as domestically, aided by the global reach of mass communications. Within the region's artistic communities, however, debate continues over whether there is indeed an authentic regional culture and, if so, how it should be expressed in today's society.

ASSIGNMENT

1. Before viewing the program, read:

   Modern Latin America, 3d ed., pp. 301–3.

   Puerto Rico: From Settler Colony to Capitalist Showcase, in chapter 9, "The Caribbean: Colonies and Mini-States," discusses Puerto Rico's unique relationship with the United States and the continuing controversy within the island over whether and how that relationship should be altered in the future.

2. View the program "Builders of Images."

3. After viewing the program, read:

   Americas: An Anthology, chapter 9, pp. 241–71.

   The anthology provides an overview of major trends in Latin American literary development. The selection of readings from various authors, periods, and literary genres is suggestive of the variety of styles produced by Latin American and Caribbean artists.

UNIT REVIEW

After viewing the program and reading the assignments, you should be able to:

· Recognize that the many different forms of cultural expression in Latin America and the

Caribbean draw upon a complex heritage of indigenous, African, European, national, and international influences.

· Cite ways in which modern authors and artists in the region have attempted to incorporate distinctly Latin American themes into their work.

· Explain the relationship among social questions, political issues, and literary and artistic expression in the Americas.

· Recognize the contributions of some of the region's most prominent authors, artists, and musicians.

· Understand the cultural impact of higher literacy levels, modernization, and the introduction of modern communications technology.

SELF-TEST QUESTIONS

Multiple Choice

*Mark the letter of the response that **best** answers the question or completes the statement.*

_____ 1. José Martí: *(Mark all that apply.)*
   a. was Cuba's most widely known painter.
   b. defended Spanish colonialism in Latin America.
   c. favored national liberation from Spain.
   d. admired the U.S. democratic system but feared U.S. expansion.

_____ 2. Which of the following statements is true of the Operation Bootstrap program? *(Mark all that apply.)*
   a. It was undertaken in Puerto Rico to eradicate the *favelas*.
   b. It accelerated the flow of Puerto Rican migrants to the U.S. mainland.
   c. It sought to encourage international investment in Puerto Rico.

d. It undermined the traditional peasant agricultural system.

_____ 3. About what percentage of Puerto Ricans have left their island to live on the U.S. mainland?
a. 5 percent
b. 20 percent
c. 40 percent
d. 70 percent

_____ 4. Throughout history, intellectuals in Latin America and the Caribbean:
a. looked to the dynamic society of the United States for their inspiration.
b. advocated the right of artists to remain aloof from social and political questions.
c. were particularly inspired by the oral traditions of the region's indigenous peoples.
d. were noted for taking a stand on the leading issues of their times.

_____ 5. Rubén Darío is:
a. a modernist poet from Nicaragua.
b. the first Brazilian poet to write in Portuguese.
c. a Cuban author widely known for his use of magic realism.
d. a Mexican painter associated with the muralist period.

_____ 6. The roots of cultural expression in Latin America and the Caribbean: *(Mark all that apply.)*
a. are found in the region's diverse ethnic and racial heritage.
b. are exclusively indigenous, with the Quechua-speaking peoples having the most influence.
c. are primarily European, emanating from the different countries' colonial experiences.
d. exhibit few examples of African influence except in isolated areas of Brazil's northeast region.

_____ 7. Gabriela Mistral was: *(Mark all that apply.)*

a. an Argentine feminist painter.
b. a former teacher who was very involved in education.
c. a Chilean poet.
d. the first Latin American to be awarded the Nobel Prize for literature.

_____ 8. Jorge Luis Borges was:
a. an Argentine writer criticized for his lack of identification with national themes.
b. a Chilean filmmaker who incorporated magic realism techniques into his films.
c. an Argentine writer admired for his emphasis on local and indigenous themes.
d. a Peruvian writer who primarily wrote long, elaborate, and complex novels.

_____ 9. The *blocos afro* are: *(Mark all that apply.)*
a. the names of various deities in *Candomblé*.
b. an affirmation of the Portuguese cultural legacy.
c. community music groups in northeastern Brazil.
d. an example of the African influence on Brazilian culture.

_____ 10. Which of the following is true of popular culture in Latin America today?
a. It is primarily identified with the award-winning literature of Latin America's "boom" period.
b. It exhibits little or no influence from popular television programs and movies from the United States.
c. It is dominated by national media conglomerates whose homogeneous programming is viewed in provincial towns as well as major cities.
d. It emphasizes the differences between people from urban and rural areas.

_____ 11. Which of the following statements is true of Gabriel García Márquez? *(Mark all that apply.)*

a. He has been an outspoken admirer of Fidel Castro.

b. His films have received widespread international recognition.

c. He called upon the United States to intervene to protect democracy in Latin America.

d. One of his most famous works is *One Hundred Years of Solitude*.

_____ 12. In general, artists from Latin America and the Caribbean are critical of U.S. influence on their culture because:

a. it tends to minimize the value and importance of the unique cultural heritage of the region.

b. it tends to exaggerate the similarities between North and South America.

c. it has not been able to overcome regional differences such as class, race, and language.

d. it has not developed a large audience outside of the English-speaking Caribbean.

_____ 13. According to Jesusa Rodríguez, the Mexican elite: *(Mark all that apply.)*

a. are very aware of their indigenous roots.

b. do not see the connection between the Aztec past and the fate of indigenous people in Mexico today.

c. are highly critical of her desire to use Aztec themes in her literature.

d. have relegated their indigenous past to the museums.

True or False

_____ 14. An important political issue in Puerto Rico continues to be the question of its future status in relation to the United States.

_____ 15. One of Latin America's earliest literary figures to achieve international recognition was a woman.

_____ 16. Caetano Veloso is one of the few Brazilian singers to emphasize the importance of Brazil's African legacy.

_____ 17. Culture in the Americas owes part of its tradition to the European colonizers—Portugal, Spain, England, Holland, and France.

_____ 18. The continued popularity of cultural events in Colombia, even under threats of political violence, is an example of the importance Latin Americans attach to cultural expression.

_____ 19. Most Latin American artists are grateful for the role U.S. mass culture has played in their countries.

_____ 20. U.S. popular culture has been influenced by Cuban dance, Brazilian music, and Mexican muralism.

_____ 21. Latin American artists have tended throughout history to resist commenting on important political and social issues of their time.

Identification/Short Answer

Define or describe the following terms, concepts, or persons, or answer the following questions. Answers should be no longer than a few sentences.

22. Give two examples of cultural forms in the Americas that have transcended local and national boundaries.

23. What are some of the problems that the popularity of U.S. mass culture poses for Latin American artists?

24. Why does actress and theater director Jesusa Rodríguez say that the goddess Coatlicue

should complain that her children are paying no attention to her?

25. The tropicalism movement in Brazil was:

26. Daniel Santos:

27. What kinds of concerns do Rubén Darío and José Martí express about the fate of Latin America?

28. Magic realism in Latin American literature is:

29. What are some of the factors that Latin American artists say make it difficult to build their own authentic cultural images?

30. Mexican muralism:

QUESTIONS TO CONSIDER

1. Why does Mexican actress Jesusa Rodríguez say that "art is a weapon, but one which works very slowly?" How does she use her own art as a weapon?

2. Why has Argentine filmmaker Fernando Solanas become a target of criticism and violence?

3. Has the role of North American artists in society been similar to or different from that played by artists in Latin America? Why?

RESOURCES

Nonfiction

Ades, Dawn. *Art in Latin America*. New Haven: Yale University Press, 1989. A historical overview of the art of the region.

Baddeley, Oriana, and Valerie Foster. *Drawing the Line: Art and Cultural Identity in Contemporary Latin America*. New York: Verso, 1989. By examining such diverse art forms as Mexican murals and Chilean *arpilleras*, the authors try to correct recent stereotypical interpretations of Latin American art while placing it in the context of contemporary modernist art movements.

Burton, Julianne. *Cinema and Social Change in Latin America*. Austin: University of Texas Press, 1986. Interviews with several Latin American filmmakers; includes annotated bibliography of Latin American cinema.

Foster, David William. *From Mafalda to Los Supermachos: Latin American Graphic Humor as Popular Culture*. Boulder, Colo.: Lynne Rienner, 1989. Exploration of Latin American popular literature as exemplified by comic books and strips.

Franco, Jean. *An Introduction to Spanish American Literature*. New York: Cambridge University Press, 1969. A historical account of the literary trends in Latin America from the conquest to magic realism, focusing on the social and political contexts.

Franco, Jean. "Remapping Culture." In *Americas: New Interpretive Essays*, edited by Alfred Stepan. New York: Oxford University Press, 1992. A description of the changing cultural terrain in the

Latin America and the Caribbean, written by a member of the *Americas* academic advisory board as an optional addition to this unit.

Franco, Jean. *The Modern Culture of Latin America.* London: Pall Mall Press, 1967. This book examines the relation of art and the sociopolitical context in Latin America since the nineteenth century. It focuses on the attitude of artists toward society, and on the ways in which this attitude is reflected in their artistic expressions.

Gazarian Gautier, Marie-Lise. *Interviews with Latin American Writers.* Naperville, Ill.: Dalkey Archive Press, 1989. Interviews with 15 Latin American writers, including Isabel Allende, Cabrera Infante, José Donoso, Carlos Fuentes, Mario Vargas Llosa, and Luis Rafael Sánchez. Includes selected bibliography.

King, John. *Magical Reels: A History of Cinema in Latin America.* New York: Verso, 1990. This survey of Latin American film examines the history of cinema in the region country by country, from the silent era to the present, and shows how Latin American filmmakers have had to compete with the North American movie industry and, often, overcome censorship by the state.

Martin, Gerald. *Journey Through the Labyrinth: Latin American Fiction in the Twentieth Century.* New York: Verso, 1990. In recent years, the works of Latin American writers have begun to reach a wider audience in English translations. This critique provides an overview of the works of Borges, García Márquez, Vargas Llosa, and others, and sets them in the context of the region's cultural and political history.

Rowe, William, and Vivian Schelling. *Memory and Modernity: Popular Culture in Latin America.* New York: Verso, 1991. An overview of Latin America's popular culture, including the samba, carnival, soap operas, oral poetry, and folk theater.

Fiction and Poetry

Agosin, Marjorie. *Women of Smoke.* Pittsburgh: Latin American Review Press, 1988. Collection of poems originally published as *Mujeres de Humo.*

Allende, Isabel. *The Stories of Eva Luna.* Translated by Margaret Sayers Peden. New York: Atheneum, 1991. While lying in bed with her lover, Eva Luna, the main character of Allende's third novel, narrates 23 interwoven stories. These stories about a myriad of characters, from fortunetellers to revolutionaries, are a good example of the highly imaginative, magical style that characterizes the Chilean author's writing.

Carpentier, Alejo. *The Kingdom of This World (El Reino de este Mundo).* Translated by Harriet de Onís. London: Deutsch, 1990. This Cuban novelist is one of Latin America's literary masters.

Donoso, José. *The Obscene Bird of the Night.* Translated by Hardie San Martin and Leonard Mades. New York: Knopf, 1973. In this novel, Donoso explores the remnants of traditional culture in contemporary Chilean society through the oppressive master-servant relationships.

Ferré, Rosario. *The Youngest Doll and Other Stories.* Translated by Marie-Lise Gazarian and Diana Vélez. Norman: University of Oklahoma Press, 1990. A collection of stories first published in Spanish in 1976, this book is an example of the new generation of Puerto Rican writers.

Flores, Angel. *Hispanic Feminist Poems from the Middle Ages to the Present: A Bilingual Anthology.* New York: Feminist Press at the City University of New York, 1986. An anthology of poetry by Latin American women.

Fuentes, Carlos. *The Death of Artemio Cruz.* Translated by Sam Hileman. New York: Farrar Straus Giroux, 1988. This novel conveys the sweep of modern Mexican history through the eyes of one man.

García Márquez, Gabriel. *One Hundred Years of Solitude.* Translated by Gregory Rabassa. London: Cape, 1991. Recounts the lives of the Buendía family in the mythical town of Macondo, Colombia, over a period of 100 years.

Manguel, Alberto, ed. *Other Fires: Short Fiction by Latin American Women.* New York: Crown, 1986. Foreword by Isabel Allende. A collection of short stories by 19 contemporary women writers from

Argentina, Brazil, Colombia, Cuba, Mexico, and Uruguay. Includes stories by Clarice Lispector, Silvina Ocampo, Elena Poniatowska, Lydia Cabrera, Beatriz Guido, Lygia Fagundes, Armonía Sommers, and Rosario Castellanos, among others.

Ramírez, Sergio. "To Jackie with All Our Heart." In *Stories*. Translated by Nick Caistor. New York: Readers International, 1986. This short story looks at Latin Americans who forsake their own culture in favor of North American culture.

Sánchez, Luis Rafael. *Macho Camacho's Beat.* Translated by Gregory Rabassa. New York: Pantheon, 1980. Novel about the problem of cultural assimilation and its negative impact on Puerto Rican society.

Santos, Rosario, ed. *And We Sold the Rain: Contemporary Fiction from Central America.* New York: Four Walls Eight Windows Press, 1988. Collection includes title story by Costa Rican author Carmen Naranjo and work by writers from Guatemala, Honduras, Mexico, and other Latin American countries.

Vargas Llosa, Mario. *The Greenhouse.* Translated by Gregory Rabassa. New York: Harper and Row, 1975. This novel tells three apparently unrelated stories, set in Peru's desert, the Andes, and the rain forest. By juxtaposing lives as different as that of a prostitute and a member of an indigenous tribe, Vargas Llosa draws a sharp contrast between life in Peru's traditional societies and in its modern cities.

Vargas Llosa, Mario. *The Time of the Hero.* Translated by Lysander Kemp. New York: Grove Press, 1966. This novel tells the story of a group of cadets at the Leoncio Prado Military Academy in Lima. The actions of an "inner circle" of cadets set in motion a series of events that lead to murder and suicide. The novel exposes the rigid military code of honor and brutal mistreatment that govern life for military cadets at the academy.

Walcott, Derek. *Collected Poems, 1948–1984.* New York: Farrar Straus Giroux, 1986. The work of the Caribbean's foremost playwright and poet reflects the ethnic and cultural diversity of the islands.

Recordings

Blades, Rubén. *Buscando América.* Sarava/Elektra, 1984. *Agua de Luna.* Elektra, 1987. New York-based singer and composer Rubén Blades has been a leading figure in "salsa" music since the 1970s.

Buarque, Chico. *Convite para Ouvir.* RGE Records, 1988. *Chico Buarque and Maria Bethania.* Philips, 1975. Chico Buarque and Maria Bethania (Caetano Veloso's sister) are leading figures in contemporary Brazilian music.

Byrne, David. *Rei Momo.* Luaka Bop, 1989. This album is influenced by Brazilian rhythms.

Guerra, Juan Luis. *Bachata Rosa.* Karen Publishing, 1990. Dominican composer-singer Guerra and his group 440 are widely known in Latin America and the U.S. Latino community. Guerra, a U.S.-trained musician, combines traditional Dominican rhythms with international pop music.

Inti Illimani. *Fragments of a Dream.* CBS Masterworks, 1990. *Cancion para Matar Una Culebra.* Monitor, 1987. World-known Chilean group Inti Illimani combines folk-Andean music with contemporary music.

Nascimiento, Milton. *Txai.* Columbia, 1991. *Encontros e Despedidas* ("Meetings and Farewells"). Polydor, 1987. *Sentinela* (with Mercedes Sosa, a foremost Argentinean singer). Verve, 1991. Brazilian singer and composer Nascimiento is one of the most recognized contemporary musicians. His album *Txai* was nominated for a Grammy award in 1992.

Olodum. *10 Years: From the Northeast of the Sahara to the Northeast of Brazil.* Sound Wave/Tropical Storm, 1991. This Brazilian *blocos afro* band recorded with Paul Simon on *Rhythm of the Saints.* On this solo album, they play a variety of songs, including the political anthems "Olodum's Revolt" and "ANC's Hymn."

Palmieri, Charlie, prod. *The Cesta All-Star Salsa Festival.* Musical Productions, 1990. A collection of salsa music by musicians based in New York and

Puerto Rico, including Palmieri, Cheo Feliciano, and others.

Piazzolla, Astor. *Tango: Zero Hour*. Pangaea, 1988. Piazzolla was the master of innovative tangos influenced by jazz and other international modern music.

Puente, Tito. *The Mambo King*. RMM Records/Sony, 1991. *Dance Mania*. BGM Records, 1991 (reissue from the original RCA, 1958). Percussionist Tito Puente is a leading figure in Latin jazz.

Rodríguez, Silvio. *Canciones Urgentes. Los Grandes Exitos de Silvio Rodríguez*. Cuba Classics 1 (compiled by David Byrne). Luaka Bop/Warner Bros., 1991. Cuban composer and singer Rodríguez is the leading figure of the Nueva Trova Cubana, the socially engaged song movement that emerged with the Cuban Revolution.

Simon, Paul. *Rhythm of the Saints*. Warner Bros., 1990. Simon is joined on this recording by Olodum and Nana Vasconcelos, among others.

Sosa, Mercedes. *Gracias a la Vida*. Polydor, 1988. Argentinean singer Mercedes Sosa is a leading figure of the Latin American New Song movement. The title track is a song by Violetta Parra, the originator of the movement in Chile.

Veloso, Caetano. *Estrangeiro*. Elektra, 1989. *Cores Nomes* ("Colors/Names"). Verve, 1982. Featured in the program, Brazilian singer-composer Veloso has been a leading figure of the Brazilian song since the 1960s. He is widely known for his eclectic approach which assimilates traditional Brazilian music with international popular music.

Villa-Lobos, Heitor. *Bachianas Brasileiras*. EMI, 1987. In these classical compositions, Villa-Lobos blends Brazilian folk rhythms and tunes with his love of the music of Bach.

Unit 10

Get Up, Stand Up:
The Problems of Sovereignty

In their music, reggae poets like Mutabaruka express Jamaica's powerful sense of national identity. Courtesy Shanachie Records

UNIT SUMMARY

Unit 10 examines the issue of sovereignty and various challenges to it in Latin American and Caribbean countries. The unit concentrates on the struggles of Panama, Jamaica, and Colombia to maintain independence, autonomy, and the legitimacy of state authority while confronting a range of external and internal forces. The television program, text, and anthology explore the threats to sovereignty posed by military intervention, economic dependency, domestic guerrilla movements, and international narcotics trafficking. The unit also considers the history of the U.S. role in the region, the justifications given by the United States for its interventionist stance, and the reaction among Latin American and Caribbean states to this external threat to sovereignty.

KEY ISSUES

· What is sovereignty, and why it is such a crucial issue in the countries of Latin America and the Caribbean?

· How have Latin American and Caribbean nations attempted to assert and defend their sovereignty?

· What threats have Jamaicans perceived to their sovereignty, and how have they attempted to protect their autonomy?

· What is unique about Panama's struggle for sovereignty, and how has the United States responded?

· What are the major threats to Colombian sovereignty? What is the U.S. role in the Colombian case?

GLOSSARY

bauxite: red claylike ore used to make aluminum; large deposits are found on the island of Jamaica.

democratic socialism: Michael Manley's plan for social and economic reform in Jamaica. As he envisioned it, democratic socialism would combine public and private sector ownership of industry and property with a competitive multiparty electoral system. An important aspect was the imposition of a 7.5 percent levy on all bauxite produced in the country.

Garvey, Marcus A.: influential Jamaican (1887–1940) who advocated fraternal unity among all blacks and the establishment of one or more independent black nations, preferably in Africa (the "Back to Africa" Movement); active in the United States from 1916 to 1925.

Hay-Bunau-Varilla Treaty: a 1903 agreement between the U.S. government and French engineer Philippe Bunau-Varilla, acting as Panama's representative, which authorized permanent control by the United States of a 10–mile-wide canal zone in Panama.

la violencia (lah bee-oh-LEN-see-ah): civil war that raged in the late 1940s and 1950s in Colombia, claiming more than 200,000 lives. *La violencia* ended in a truce between Colombia's two major parties, the Liberals and the Conservatives, which resulted in political stability but also effectively excluded all other parties from power. This prompted the creation of a number of guerrilla movements in Colombia, including the Popular Army of Liberation (EPL), and the M-19.

maroon communities: communities of escaped slaves in seventeenth- and eighteenth-century Jamaica who lived in the mountains by relying on subsistence agriculture. The maroon communities signed legal treaties with the British government in 1739 and again in 1795 which guaranteed their semiautonomous existence.

Manley, Michael: prime minister of Jamaica from 1972 to 1980; re-elected in 1989. Controversial leader who attempted to create a system of "democratic socialism" for his country in the 1970s. Manley focused on increasing Jamaican power vis-à-vis the international bauxite and aluminum producers, and on improving Jamaica's self-image as a sovereign nation.

Monroe Doctrine: pronouncement by President James Monroe in 1823 which made clear that the

United States would look unfavorably upon any attempt by European powers—especially Great Britain, France, Spain, and Russia—to assert control over any nation in the Western Hemisphere, including their former colonies. The Monroe Doctrine eventually became a justification for U.S. military and political intervention in Latin America and the Caribbean.

Operation Just Cause: term used by the U.S. government to refer to the U.S. military invasion of Panama in December 1989. As a result of the invasion, General Manuel A. Noriega was removed from power and brought to the United States to stand trial on drug-trafficking charges, while Guillermo Endara, who had been unable to take office when elected in 1989, was placed in the presidency.

Organization of American States (OAS):   an inter-American organization established in 1948 to serve as the diplomatic decision-making body of the Western Hemisphere. According to the charter, OAS members are committed to the principles of nonintervention (sought by the Latin American members as protection for national sovereignty) and continental solidarity (sought by the United States as part of its strategy to resist Soviet expansionism), along with economic cooperation, social justice, democracy, and human rights. All independent Latin American and Caribbean nations except Cuba are members, along with the United States and Canada, but throughout most of its history the organization has served primarily to endorse the policies of its most powerful member, the United States.

Roosevelt Corollary: message of President Theodore Roosevelt to the U.S. Congress on December 6, 1904, in which he justified a U.S. role as international police power and debt-collecting agency in the Western Hemisphere. This role was based on Roosevelt's broad interpretation of the Monroe Doctrine; his message became known as a "corollary" to that doctrine.

Seaga, Edward: conservative prime minister of Jamaica from 1980 to 1989, who attempted a decisive break with the economic policies of his predecessor, Michael Manley. Seaga focused especially on restoring international investment and tourism.

sovereignty: supreme power; political concept that affirms the right of independent states to control their territories and shape policy without foreign interference. Sovereignty implies more than self-government; economic self-sufficiency, freedom of decision making, and the ability to defend oneself from internal and external threats to central state authority have all been viewed as key aspects of sovereignty.

OVERVIEW

Sovereignty is a critical issue for the countries of Latin America and the Caribbean. The notion of national sovereignty, meaning the ability of nations to act freely and without outside interference in their internal affairs, appears frequently in the political rhetoric of many Latin American and Caribbean nations. It plays a crucial role in the relationships between weaker and stronger states. Demonstrating and defending national sovereignty has historically been a major preoccupation of leaders in the region, and it continues to be of major importance today. Unit 10, "Get Up, Stand Up: The Problems of Sovereignty," illustrates the complexity of the internal and external threats to sovereignty in the Americas, and examines some of the measures Latin American and Caribbean nations have taken to protect their rights as independent states.

In the nineteenth century, some of the new states of Latin America and the Caribbean received help from the United States to defend their independence against the former colonial powers. However, as we saw in Unit 9, Latin Americans were wary of the "Colossus of the North" and feared its expansionist tendencies. In 1823, U.S. president James Monroe declared in his address to Congress that the United States would not tolerate the re-entry of European powers in the hemisphere. Some 20 years later, after a war with Mexico, the United States annexed more than one-half that country's former territory, gaining land that was later incorporated into the states of California, New Mexico, Arizona, Colorado, Utah, and Texas.

The Monroe Doctrine was later expanded upon by President Theodore Roosevelt, who in 1904 asserted for the United States self-appointed rights as the international police power and debt-collector for the hemisphere. The Roosevelt Corollary was used to justify numerous military interventions in Latin American and Caribbean states until 1935, when the United States agreed to a ban on unilateral intervention in the affairs of other American nations. After World War II, the new geo-political ideological conflict of the Cold War became Washington's primary concern. U.S. intervention continued, especially after the triumph of the Cuban Revolution in 1959, justified by the need to protect U.S. security interests against the perceived threat of international Communism.

Foreign military intervention is still the most overt threat to a nation's sovereignty, but it is not the only one. National sovereignty is affected by internal as well as external forces, ranging from economic vulnerabilities to international drug traffic. The program and readings use the examples of Panama, Jamaica, and Colombia to illustrate the range of issues confronted by Latin American and Caribbean states as they seek to promote and preserve their national sovereignty.

Panama

Since Panama first became a nation, its sovereignty has never been secure. It was carved out of Colombia's territory after the United States prevented Colombians from putting down a rebellion in the isthmus in 1903. The secessionist government immediately received U.S. recognition and signed the Hay-Bunau-Varilla Treaty, which not only authorized U.S. construction of the Panama Canal, but also gave the United States perpetual sovereignty over a 10–mile-wide zone across the isthmus. Until modifications to the treaty in 1935 and 1955, the United States reserved the right to intervene in Panama and to maintain order in the largest cities, Colón and Panama City, making Panama virtually a protectorate of the United States.

It wasn't until 1978 that Panamanian leader General Omar Torrijos and U.S. president Jimmy Carter signed an agreement that provided for eventual Panamanian sovereignty over the canal. The treaty came after years of increasingly nationalistic sentiment within Panama that had erupted several times into anti-U.S. violence. Even after the Panama Canal Treaty, however, the U.S. retained its military bases in the Canal Zone and continued to have concerns over secure access to the canal.

In the 1980s, U.S. suspicions grew that Panama was an important transit point for international narcotics trafficking with the approval and complicity of General Manuel Antonio Noriega, leader of the Panamanian armed forces. Beginning in 1988, the United States began a campaign to oust Noriega, who refused to recognize the 1989 election of Guillermo Endara as president of Panama despite his evident victory at the polls. The United States imposed a trade embargo and other financial pressures. When that failed, a U.S. military invasion was launched. The December 1989 "Operation Just Cause" succeeded in capturing Noriega, who was arrested and brought to Miami to face drug trafficking charges.

The action was popular in the United States as well as with many Panamanians who had hopes for political democracy and an economic recovery in their country once free of Noriega. But the invasion was also seen by many Latin Americans—including some Panamanians—as a patent violation of national sovereignty. Many Panamanians lost homes and property during the bombing that accompanied the invasion, and unofficial estimates of the civilian death toll range from 400 to 2,000. Panamanian enthusiasm for the invasion was further undermined by the delay in sending even small amounts of U.S. aid for Panama's reconstruction and by suspicions that the real U.S. goal was to retain control of the canal. Throughout the Americas, "Operation Just Cause" also raised concerns that the "war on drugs" and the defense of democracy would now replace the Cold War as justifications for U.S. intervention in Latin America and the Caribbean.

Jamaica

Jamaica was a colony of Great Britain until 1962, although it had begun to experiment with self-government after World War II. Even when formal independence did arrive, it did not mean full sovereignty for Jamaica.

When Michael Manley became prime minister in 1972, he saw his election as a mandate for

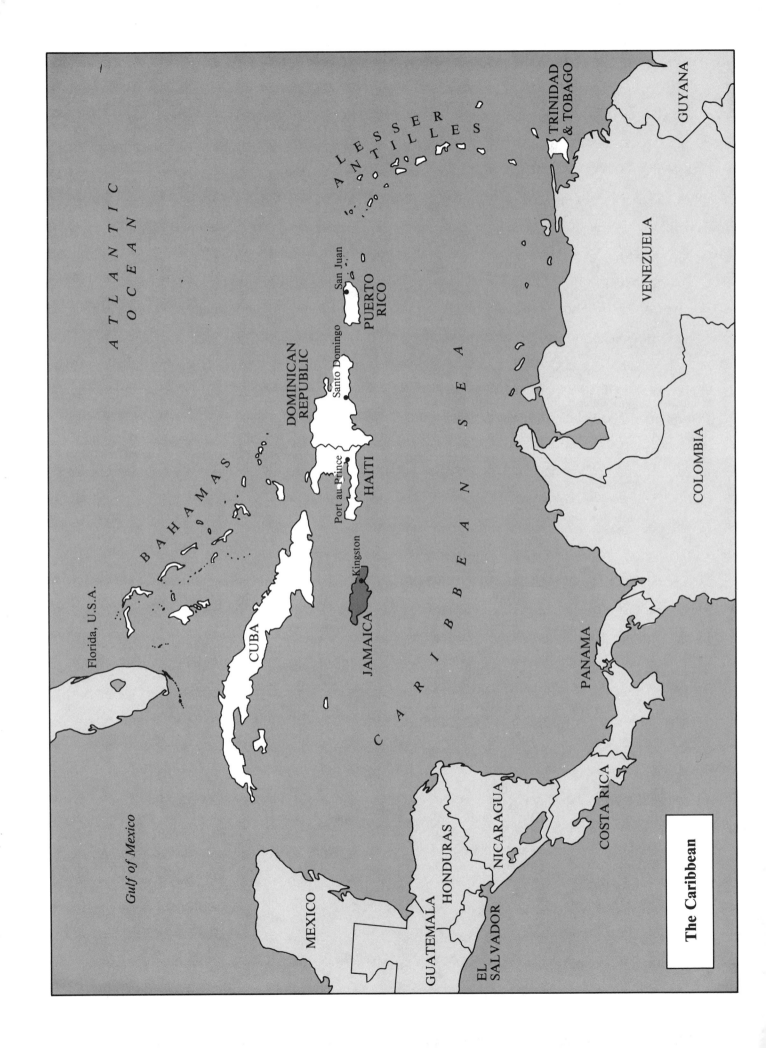

The Caribbean

fundamental change. Manley initiated far-reaching economic, social, and educational reforms—which he later developed into a policy of "democratic socialism"—designed to bolster Jamaican nationalism and improve conditions for the poorest sector of the population. He sought to strengthen government's role in the economy and to enlarge its control over Jamaica's resources, while retaining the democratic political system.

Bauxite, the country's most valuable natural resource, used to produce aluminum, was a symbolic reminder of Jamaica's lack of sovereignty because its production and export were controlled by five foreign companies, mainly from the United States and Canada. Although Jamaica was the world's largest bauxite producer, it received little compensation from the mining companies which, at the same time, were reaping healthy profits. Manley opened negotiations with the bauxite companies to press for higher returns for Jamaica. After those negotiations failed in 1974, the Manley government unilaterally imposed an increase in the levy, or tax, on the production of bauxite to 7.5 percent of the price of aluminum ingot for each ton of bauxite mined. In the first year under the new system, Jamaica's bauxite revenues shot up from $25 million to $200 million. The levy was widely seen within Jamaica as a firm and fair assertion of national autonomy.

But after Manley was re-elected in 1976, the country began four years of economic and social turmoil. The bauxite companies reduced the scale of their operations and shifted their investments to other countries. Public enthusiasm for Manley's government dwindled as the economy suffered a series of setbacks. An increase in oil prices, a shrinking bauxite market, and state overspending combined to undermine Jamaica's economy. Foreign investment and U.S. assistance also became increasingly scarce after Manley established close ties with Fidel Castro of Cuba. With another election approaching, Jamaican society was polarized between Manley's supporters and opponents, political violence escalated, and thousands from Jamaica's middle and upper classes left the country.

Manley was replaced as prime minister in 1980 by the conservative Edward Seaga of the Jamaica Labour party. Although he had the backing of a relieved U.S. government, and seemed popular at first in Jamaica, Seaga could not restore general confidence in the economy. His decisions to welcome foreign investment and revitalize the tourist industry led many Jamaicans to accuse Seaga of undermining their national sovereignty.

Jamaicans turned back to Manley in 1989, only to discover that the once defiant champion of democratic socialism was now a convert to the free market approach. The new, more pragmatic Manley abandoned attempts to carry out economic redistribution and, to the despair of some supporters, placed his faith in the private sector and foreign capital.

As shown in the program, Jamaica continues to strive for economic independence. Today, much of the country shares a sobering awareness of the practical limits to a small nation's sovereignty.

Colombia

Despite its larger size and more lengthy history as an independent nation, Colombia also faces a number of serious threats to its national sovereignty. Central government authority is weak, and numerous rival guerrilla bands operating within the country exert great power in the zones they control. Perhaps most seriously, armed, powerful, and rich drug cartels have established themselves as virtual states within the state, and have brought a reign of violence that has paralyzed the judicial, legal, and political systems.

Colombia's history has frequently been marked by political violence. The most infamous period was the uncontrollable violence that spread throughout the country from 1948 to 1958. Colombians still refer to this as *la violencia*, the violence. In rural areas *la violencia* was primarily a conflict between the two major political factions of Liberals and Conservatives. But the war was also marked by social conflicts over land and labor, personal vendettas, and banditry. By the time the two main parties declared a truce in 1958, there was massive destruction of property throughout the country, and about 200,000 Colombians—approximately 2 percent of the population—had been killed.

Some guerrilla groups refused to accept the political arrangement worked out by the Conservatives and Liberals to alternate the presidency between them, achieving political stability but effectively excluding all others from power. The

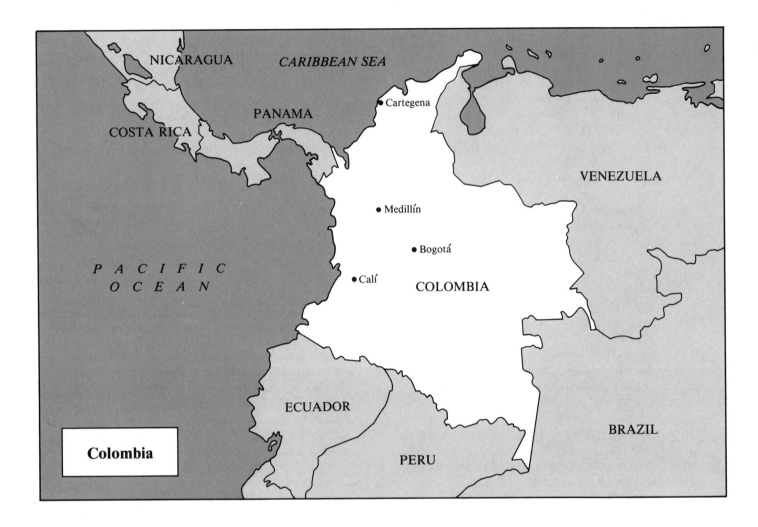

Colombia

Cuban Revolution gave some of these guerrillas military and ideological reinforcement, and they soon expanded their territorial control. Through the 1970s they became strong enough to create their own autonomous zones within the larger state, directly challenging the army and the government. Their struggle and their ability to win popular support among the rural poor were facilitated by a national government that concentrated its efforts on the country's cities, especially Bogotá, and an elite that was insensitive to the inequalities that pervaded the country.

Colombia's internal situation became even more complex during the 1980s as powerful drug cartels based in Medellín developed control of an extensive area of the middle Magdalena River valley. Sometimes the drug lords worked together with the guerrillas against the government; at other times they allied with local officials against the

guerrillas or fought both guerrillas and the government. Their violence and intimidation penetrated all levels of society, further undermining government authority and legitimacy. Much of the demand for cocaine originated in the United States, which was engaged in its own "war on drugs." As part of that effort, the United States helped destroy thousands of acres of coca fields, many of them worked by small peasant farmers. In 1989, outright war broke out between the drug cartels and the government. Narcotraffickers killed politicians, judges, journalists, policemen, military personnel, and any who dared to speak out against them.

In 1989, with the Colombian legal and judicial system seemingly unable to handle the threats posed by the drug cartels, President Virgilio Barco agreed to U.S. demands for the extradition of narcotraffickers to face trial and serve prison sentences in the United States. However, this presented new dilemmas for the state, especially on the sensitive issue of sovereignty. Medellín's drug lords increased the violence, and included state officials and political candidates among their targets. Their violent tactics reached a peak with the assassination of popular candidate Luis Carlos Galán during the 1989 presidential campaign. In the all-out war that followed, terrorist attacks in public places such as supermarkets and schools traumatized Colombia's cities and citizens. In 1990, reflecting a war-weary nation tired of the violence, the newly elected government of President Cesar Gaviria Trujillo terminated extradition in order to negotiate a peace with the drug traffickers. The most famous drug dealers, Pablo Escobar and the Ochoa brothers, turned themselves in and agreed to stand trial, but received sentences that have been criticized as too lenient. Critics argue that the Colombian justice system is still incapable of punishing the drug dealers, some of whom may still be operating international drug networks from luxurious prisons. Moreover, the problems of the Medellín cartel have not led to a decrease in cocaine trafficking, but merely an increase in the activities and market share of the rival Cali cartel.

Gaviria also called a constitutional convention aimed at restoring the legitimacy and authority of the national government, which included assurances of access to Colombia's political process for drug dealers, guerrillas, and other politically excluded sectors. Many have accepted the government's proposal, laid down their arms, and are now organized as political parties. The decisions to reject U.S. pressures for extradition and to devise local solutions have brought a measure of peace to Colombia. It is not clear, however, whether Colombia will be able to overcome its violent past and establish itself as a fully sovereign state with a legitimate national government that represents the majority of its people.

ASSIGNMENT

1. Before viewing the program, read:

   Modern Latin America, 3d ed. pp. 298–301, 321–24, 374–75.

Jamaica: Runaways and Revolutionary Socialism, (pp. 298–301) in chapter 9, "The Caribbean: Colonies and Mini-States," provides a very brief overview of Jamaican history and the country's route to independence. The reading also notes Jamaica's difficulties in asserting political and economic autonomy in today's complex world system.

Panama: A Nation and a Zone, (pp.321–24) in chapter 10, "Central America: Colonialism, Dictatorship, and Revolution," describes Panama's history as that of a nation trying to create and protect its own identity. The text examines the history and important role of the Panama Canal, the growth of Panamanian nationalism, and the most recent episodes in the U.S.-Panama relationship.

In chapter 11, "Latin America, the United States, and the World," the assigned section (pp. 374–75) contains a brief discussion of the impact of illicit narcotics trade on the relationship between Latin America and the United States. The text highlights the dramatic impact of drug trafficking on both domestic and international affairs in affected countries.

2. View the program "Get Up, Stand Up."

3. After viewing the program, read:

   Americas: An Anthology, chapter 10, pp. 272–98.

   The introduction and readings in the anthology explain the historic justification given by the United States for its intervention in Latin America and the Caribbean. The anthology contains excerpts from the Monroe Doctrine and the Roosevelt Corollary. The readings also provide insight into the very different perspective on that role held by Latin American and Caribbean leaders.

UNIT REVIEW

After viewing the program and doing the assigned readings, you should be able to:

- Define sovereignty and understand why it is such a crucial issue in the countries of Latin America and the Caribbean.

- Identify and describe various measures Latin American and Caribbean nations have relied on to assert and defend their sovereignty.

- Understand the threats that Jamaicans have perceived to their sovereignty and the measures they have taken to protect their national autonomy.

- Explain the unique aspects of Panama's struggle for sovereignty and discuss the role of the United States in that country.

- Name three major domestic and international threats to Colombian sovereignty and explain the role of the United States in that country.

SELF-TEST QUESTIONS

Multiple Choice

*Mark the letter of the response that **best** answers the question or completes the statement.*

_____ 1. The presidential message that expanded upon earlier policies to justify U.S. military action within the Western Hemisphere was:
   a. the Roosevelt Corollary.
   b. the OAS Charter.
   c. the Monroe Doctrine.
   d. the Hay-Bunau-Varilla Treaty.

_____ 2. The U.S. invasion of Panama in 1989:
   a. was the first use of U.S. military forces in that country.
   b. was requested by Panama's neighbors, who feared Panama's expansionist tendencies.
   c. was necessary to remove dictator General Omar Torrijos from power.
   d. was justified as part of the U.S. government's "war on drugs."

_____ 3. Reggae music in Jamaica:
   a. is an imported phenomenon that has only become popular in Jamaica in recent years.
   b. has been used as an outlet for popular expression, including discussion of political issues.
   c. has not been accepted outside of Jamaica because of its highly local characteristics.
   d. has tended to avoid political commentary and focused instead on escapist themes.

_____ 4. Which of the following statements about Jamaican prime minister Michael Manley are true? *(Mark all that apply.)*
   a. He established closer ties between Jamaica and Cuba.
   b. He used the issue of bauxite to assert Jamaican sovereignty.
   c. He returned to power still convinced that democratic socialism would help Jamaica's economic development.
   d. He saw Jamaica's struggles as linked to other Third World nations' efforts to defend their rights.

_____ 5. U.S. government demands that Colombia extradite drug traffickers: *(Mark all that apply.)*
   a. were seen by many Colombians as an affront to national sovereignty.
   b. were successful at eliminating the power of the drug cartels.
   c. led to an upsurge in drug-related violence.
   d. were rejected by Colombian president Virgilio Barco.

_____ 6. Which of the following presents a threat to Panama's sovereignty today? *(Mark all that apply.)*
   a. Internal corruption due to the impact of international drug traffic.
   b. Attempts by European colonial powers to reassert authority over the country.
   c. Foreign governments' interests in the Panama Canal.

____ d. Attempts by Colombia to reincorporate Panama into its territory.

____ 7. The 1898 speech by Argentinean Roque Saenz Peña (anthology reading 10.2) characterized the Monroe Doctrine as:
   a. an ineffectual statement that had little impact on Latin America.
   b. a helpful pledge of U.S. assistance to protect Latin American independence.
   c. a worrisome indicator of U.S. expansionist tendencies in the hemisphere.
   d. a statement of genuine U.S. support and respect for Latin American sovereignty.

____ 8. Which of the following is an example of Colombia's efforts to defend its sovereignty? *(Mark all that apply.)*
   a. The demand for a higher levy on bauxite.
   b. The decision to revoke the extradition policy.
   c. The decision to accept U.S. assistance in destroying the coca fields.
   d. The decision to call a constitutional convention.

____ 9. Jamaican prime minister Edward Seaga:
   a. successfully restored long-term economic prosperity and domestic confidence to Jamaica.
   b. defended Jamaican sovereignty by imposing a bauxite levy.
   c. called for Jamaican autonomy, opposing any influx of foreign investment.
   d. received support from the U.S. and international financial institutions.

____ 10. Political violence in Colombia:
   a. has been a common occurrence throughout the country's history.
   b. began with the rise of armed guerrilla movements in the 1960s.
   c. was largely eliminated after the agreement to extradite drug lords to the United States.
   d. has been restricted to certain affected neighborhoods in Medellín.

____ 11. Which of the following have been criticized by some Latin Americans as a breach of sovereignty? *(Mark all that apply.)*
   a. The 1989 U.S. invasion of Panama.
   b. U.S. pressure on Colombia to extradite drug dealers.
   c. U.S. efforts to undermine democratic socialism in Jamaica.
   d. U.S. membership in the Organization of American States.

____ 12. Armed guerrillas in Colombia agreed to the government's amnesty offer because:
   a. the high death toll of *la violencia* had made them too weak to continue resistance.
   b. they came under pressure from the drug lords to end political violence in Colombia.
   c. they had lost the support of the rural poor.
   d. they decided to seek power through participation in the political process.

____ 13. Jamaica's decision to impose a levy on bauxite:
   a. was the result of a negotiated agreement with the foreign aluminum companies.
   b. was opposed by the bauxite workers who feared losing their jobs.
   c. was an attempt by Edward Seaga to prove that he would defend Jamaican sovereignty.
   d. brought pride to most Jamaicans and raised concern among foreign investors.

True or False

____ 14. A huge foreign debt is one of the main factors limiting Jamaica's attempts to defend sovereignty.

____ 15. The United States and Canada are members of the Organization of American States.

_____ 16. The United States has repeatedly apologized for its intervention in Panama and sworn in a recent conference to respect Panama's, and all Latin America's, autonomy in the future.

_____ 17. After much pressure from the United States, Colombia finally agreed to plans to construct an interoceanic canal in Panama.

_____ 18. Since the War of the Thousand Days, Colombia has feared another military invasion by the United States.

_____ 19. The Roosevelt Corollary justifies U.S. involvement in the internal affairs of Latin American and Caribbean countries.

_____ 20. After World War II, the United States tended to justify its intervention in Latin America by citing the threat of Communist expansion in the region.

_____ 21. Unlike Argentinean Roque Saenz Peña, most Latin Americans welcomed the Monroe Doctrine as a sincere expression of the U.S. desire to protect their independence.

_____ 22. Bauxite companies symbolized Jamaica's lack of sovereignty because they were using violence to break up workers' attempts to strike.

Identification/Short Answer

Define or describe the following terms, concepts, or persons, or answer the following questions. Answers should be no longer than a few sentences.

23. Operation Just Cause:

24. The Monroe Doctrine:

25. Why was Jamaica's imposition of a 7.5 percent bauxite levy perceived as an indicator of sovereignty?

26. Hay-Bunau-Varilla Treaty:

27. What was the significance of the constitutional convention called by Colombian president Cesar Gaviria Trujillo?

28. As portrayed in the program, what measures have residents of poor neighborhoods in Medellín taken to protect themselves from drug-related violence?

29. General Omar Torrijos:

30. democratic socialism:

QUESTIONS TO CONSIDER

1. Poet Rubén Darío, in his turn-of-the-century work "To Roosevelt," said, "The United States is grand and powerful. Whenever it trembles, a profound shudder runs down the enormous

backbone of the Andes." How does this illustrate the history of U.S.–Latin American relations? Was Darío referring only to issues of sovereignty?

2. What do you think of Latin Americans' argument that the drug trade is caused by the pull of U.S. demand, not the push of supply? Is the United States justified in seeking to use its military forces in the destruction and interdiction of drug supplies in other countries? Why or why not?

3. Now that the era of the Cold War is over, is U.S. interest and action in Latin America and the Caribbean likely to increase, decrease, or remain about the same? Why?

4. In 1991, the country of Haiti began to experience a political crisis when popularly elected president Jean-Bertrand Aristide was driven from power in a military coup. The country returned to violent and repressive government under a dictator. The United States and the OAS attempted various measures to pressure the military government to restore Aristide to power: negotiations, economic sanctions, and a threat of military intervention. Do you think this was an interference in Haitian sovereignty? Should foreign governments be allowed to intercede in other countries' internal affairs in this type of situation? What are the limits of intervention and nonintervention?

RESOURCES

Nonfiction

Barry, Tom. *Panama: A Country Guide.* Albuquerque, New Mexico: The Resource Center, 1990. This excellent reference work contains valuable information on society, history, economics, politics, religion, and the environment.

Dinges, John. "The Case Against Noriega." *Washington Post Magazine.* January 28, 1990. Details the indictments against Noriega, the extent of corruption during his reign in Panama, and his alleged involvement in narcotrafficking.

Dinges, John. *Our Man in Panama.* New York: Random House, 1990. This study of Manual Noriega by an experienced journalist follows Noriega's tangled connections to both the U.S. government and the Colombian drug cartels. Dinges concludes that the United States' efforts to unseat Noriega using propaganda and military force reflect basic flaws in the theory and practice of U.S. foreign policy in the region.

Gauhar, Altaf. "Manley Rides the New Wave." *South: The Third World Magazine.* July 1989, pp. 10–11. Gauhar, editor-in-chief of the magazine, interviewed Manley as he was installed back in power after nearly a decade.

Goodwin, Paul, ed. *Global Studies: Latin America.* Guilford, Conn.: Dushkin, 1990. A convenient source for short histories and summaries of important historical data on all the Latin American and Caribbean states. The regional introduction and extracts from press publications provide extremely useful information on current themes.

Gugliotta, Guy, and Jeff Leen. *Kings of Cocaine: Inside the Medellín Cartel—An Astonishing True Story of Murder, Money, and International Corruption.* New York: Simon and Schuster, 1989. A dramatic exposé of the Medellín cartel.

Hart, Richard. *Slaves Who Abolished Slavery: Blacks in Rebellion.* vol. 2. University of the West Indies, Jamaica: Institute of Social and Economic Research, 1985. This second volume is an in-depth study of the maroon wars and of the many slave revolts that were a feature of Jamaica's struggle against slavery.

Kaufman, Michael. *Jamaica Under Manley: Dilemmas of Socialism and Democracy.* Westport, Conn.: Lawrence Hill, 1985. No other study does a better job of exposing the obstacles to change faced by small countries with dependent economies and a privileged economic class supported by the United States. Particularly good on the strengths and weaknesses of the People's National Movement in Jamaica.

Knight, Franklin W. *The Caribbean: The Genesis of a Fragmented Nationalism,* 2d ed. New York: Oxford

University Press, 1990. This study is useful for placing the history of Jamaica in a wider regional context. The final chapter reflects on issues of state and nationalism throughout the Caribbean and suggests that without greater regional cooperation the chances of success for those dependent economies and sovereign ministates will remain dim.

Knight, Franklin W. "The State of Sovereignty and the Sovereignty of States." In *Americas: New Interpretive Essays,* edited by Alfred Stepan. New York: Oxford University Press, 1992. An analysis of the ideas of sovereignty, written by a member of the *Americas* academic advisory board as an optional addition to this unit.

LeFeber, Walter. *The Panama Canal: The Crisis in Historical Perspective.* New York: Oxford University Press, 1989. This short, perceptive review of the relations between Panama and the United States by a leading U.S. diplomatic historian sorts through the record reaction and rising nationalism with the canal as the focus.

Levi, Darrell E. *Michael Manley: The Making of a Leader.* Athens: University of Georgia Press, 1989. This, the first thoroughly researched biography of Michael Manley, is good both on the principal subject and on the fascinating changes in Jamaican politics, culture, and society during the twentieth century.

Lowenthal, Abraham. *Partners in Conflict: The United States and Latin America.* Baltimore: Johns Hopkins University Press, 1987. A revisionist view of U.S.–Latin American relations, with a stress on recent decades.

Manley, Michael. *Jamaica: Struggle in the Periphery.* London: Third World Media, 1982. This sober evaluation of Jamaica's triumphs and failures in the period 1972–80 was produced by the man who was in charge. Essential to Manley's politics is the quest for respect for individual sovereignty.

Manley, Michael. *The Politics of Change,* rev. ed. Washington, D.C.: Howard University Press, 1990. Manley, a prolific writer, first published this idealistic book in 1973. The revised edition reflects the sobering experience of his political fortunes, both his successes and his failures.

Painter, James. "Bolivians Protest U.S. Militarization of Drug War." *Christian Science Monitor,* April 15, 1991, p. 5. Representatives from Bolivia and the Roman Catholic Church protest U.S. Army instructors' being sent in to train Bolivian infantry battalions to enter the drug war. In the same issue, see Sally Bowen's article, "Leading Peruvians Spurn Antidrug Pact with United States."

Parenti, Michael. "What Will It Really Take To Win The Drug War?" *Political Affairs,* November 1989. (An excerpted version appeared in the May–June 1991 issue of the *Utne Reader.*) This essay takes a critical view of U.S. policy in international narcotrafficking.

Ugarte, Manuel. *The Destiny of a Continent.* New York: AMS Press, 1970. In this book, originally published in 1925, the Argentine author sets forth his observations and concerns after visiting the United States and Mexico. He was convinced that Latin America was "in danger of being absorbed and dominated" by the United States. His perspective offers an alternative Latin American viewpoint on North American intervention.

Yarbro, Stan. "Colombian Justice System Falters." *Christian Science Monitor.* January 24, 1991, p. 3. This article claims that although drug traffickers turn themselves in as part of a new program encouraging suspects to surrender, judges still face intimidation and the country's judicial system is strained to its limits.

Fiction

Adisa, Opal Palmer. *Bake-Face and Other Guava Stories.* Berkeley, Calif.: Kelsey Street Press, 1986. Collection of short stories set in Jamaica.

Kincaid, Jamaica. *At the Bottom of the River.* New York: Aventura/Vintage Books, 1985. This collection of short stories includes selections that recount the history of the maroons.

Mordecai, Pam, and Mervyn Morris. *Jamaica Woman: An Anthology of Poems.* Portsmouth, N.H.: Heinemann Educational Books, 1980. Poems by 15 contemporary Jamaican women, both well- and lesser-known.

Reid, V. S. *The Leopard.* Portsmouth, N.H.: Heinemann Educational Books, 1980. This brief tale by a renowned Jamaican novelist is set during Kenya's Mau Mau revolution of the late 1940s and 1950s, during which many Kikuyu people were jailed by the colonial administration for participating in the activities of the Kenya African Union.

Films

Unless otherwise indicated, all films listed are available in VHS video format.

Giving Up the Canal. 60 minutes, 1990. This film explores Operation Just Cause as the latest chapter in a saga that represents the glory of the United States technological achievement and the dark vestiges of U.S. colonialism in Central America. Available for purchase ($59.95) from PBS Video, (800) 424–7963; fax: (703) 739–5269.

The Noriega Connection. 60 minutes, 1991. Originally aired as part of the "FRONTLINE" series, this film examines Manuel Noriega's involvement with the United States. Available for rental ($95) from PBS Video, (800) 424–7963; fax: (703) 739–5269.

Recordings

Marley, Bob, and the Wailers. *Legend: The Best of Bob Marley and the Wailers.* Island Records, 1984. Includes renditions of "One Love" and "Get Up, Stand Up," both of which are featured in the program.

Marley, Rita. *We Must Carry On.* Shanachie, 1991. After Bob Marley's death, his widow, Rita, emerged as an artist in her own right. On this album, she performs songs written by her late husband.

Mowatt, Judy. *Black Woman.* Shanachie, 1988. This is a classic recording by the woman who is widely recognized as reggae's greatest female artist. A longtime backup vocalist with Bob Marley and the Wailers, Mowatt sings inspirational songs about Black Liberation, women's rights, and Rastafarianism.

Mutabaruka. *Outcry.* Shanachie, 1987. One of Jamaica's most outspoken "dub poets"—artists who recite political poetry over reggae music—Mutabaruka sings about racism, political oppression, war, and hunger.

Unit 11

Fire in the Mind:
Revolutions and Revolutionaries

This soldier is part of the forces of Cuba's Fidel Castro, who led the first socialist revolution in the Americas. © Alberto Korda, Havana/Courtesy Center for Cuban Studies

UNIT SUMMARY

Unit 11 examines major revolutions in twentieth-century Latin America using the examples of Mexico (1910–17), Cuba (1959), and Nicaragua (1979), as well as contemporary revolutionary processes in El Salvador, Guatemala, and Peru. The textbook and anthology readings consider the roots of revolution, similarities and differences among revolutionary movements, and the policies of the revolutionary governments that assumed power in Mexico, Cuba, and Nicaragua. The television program looks at those who participate in revolutionary movements, and examines their reasons for engaging in prolonged, difficult struggles to transform their nations.

The program is set primarily in El Salvador, where a stalemate between guerrilla forces and the military contributed to a negotiated settlement in early 1992 to end the country's civil war. The program also travels to Peru to explore the objectives and activities of the Sendero Luminoso, or Shining Path, guerrilla movement.

KEY ISSUES

· What are some of the common factors that contributed to revolutionary movements in Mexico, Cuba, Nicaragua, Guatemala, El Salvador, and Peru?

· Are revolutionary movements one-time events, or are they processes that develop over many years? Why are revolutions' courses or eventual outcomes difficult to predict?

· What has been the role of Marxist ideology in Latin American revolutionary movements, and how did Marxism affect the policies of the revolutionary governments that came to power in Cuba and Nicaragua?

· What was the nature of the coalitions that led revolutionary movements in twentieth-century Latin America, and why did they split apart after taking power?

· What was the U.S. response to revolutionary movements in Cuba, Nicaragua, and El Salvador?

· What are the key features that distinguish Peru's revolutionary movement from others in the region? How might a government led by the Shining Path in Peru differ from other revolutionary regimes in the Americas?

· How has the end of the Cold War affected revolutions and revolutionary movements in Latin America?

GLOSSARY

Arbenz, Jacobo: Guatemalan president from 1950 to 1954, whose agrarian reform program included the expropriation of properties owned by the United Fruit Company. Arbenz was considered a Communist by the Eisenhower government, which organized a CIA-backed coup to remove him from office. The 1954 coup was a turning point in Guatemalan history. It diminished the possibility of center-left political reform and was followed by decades of military governments and human rights abuses, which in turn prompted new revolutionary movements.

Bay of Pigs invasion: the April 17, 1961, unsuccessful CIA-backed exile invasion of Cuba, organized and financed by the U.S. government. The defeat was an embarrassment for U.S. president John F. Kennedy and helped to consolidate support for Castro both domestically and in the USSR.

Castro, Fidel: Latin America's most important contemporary revolutionary; Cuban leader who headed the movement to oust dictator Fulgencio Batista and transformed Cuba into a socialist country; has governed the country since the revolution began in 1959.

Chamorro, Violeta Barrios de: president of Nicaragua since 1990 when the anti-Sandinista coalition she headed, UNO, defeated the Sandinistas in internationally supervised elections. She is the widow of prominent journalist and outspoken Somoza opponent Pedro Joaquín Chamorro, whose assassination in 1978 triggered the insurrection in Nicaragua.

contras: Nicaraguan slang for *contra-revolucionarios* or counterrevolutionaries. Term given to the exiles funded by the United States and commanded in part by former Somoza army officers who fought against the Nicaraguan Sandinistas for most of the 1980s. Reagan administration military support for the *contras* in contravention of a congressional ban contributed to the Iran-Contra scandal, which rocked the Reagan government in the mid-1980s.

Cristiani, Alfredo: president of El Salvador, elected in 1989 as leader of the Nationalist Republican Alliance (ARENA), a far-right party originally associated with death squad violence and with El Salvador's business and landowning elites. Cristiani agreed to UN-sponsored peace talks, which resulted in an end to the Salvadoran civil war in early 1992.

Cuban missile crisis: 1962 confrontation between the United States and the Soviet Union over the USSR's placement of nuclear missiles on Cuban soil; led to a naval blockade of Cuba by the U.S. Navy and appeared to bring the two superpowers to the brink of nuclear war. The Soviet missiles were withdrawn after a secret understanding between Soviet leader Khrushchev and U.S. president Kennedy which also brought assurances that the United States would not invade Cuba.

death squads: name given to paramilitary groups, typically on the far right, known for kidnapping, torture, and murder. Death squads have been particularly active in the Central American and Southern Cone countries; two of the oldest and most notorious are Guatemala's "Mano Blanca" and "Ojo por Ojo." Roberto D'Aubuisson, a founder of El Salvador's ARENA party, was widely regarded as connected to death squad activity, including the 1980 assassination of San Salvador's archbishop Oscar Romero.

Duarte, José Napoleón: founder of the Salvadoran Christian Democratic Party, prevented from taking office as president in 1972 when the military intervened after the elections. Duarte headed a civilian-military junta in 1980, then became the elected president when the Christian Democrats won elections in 1984. Although he remained in office until 1989, Duarte was unable to complete the agrarian reform, stop military abuse of human rights, or end the Salvadoran civil war.

Esquipulas (or Arias) Plan: Central American peace plan based on negotiated settlements and elections agreed to in a meeting of the Central American presidents in Guatemala in 1987. The plan was stimulated by Costa Rican president Oscar Arias, who won the 1987 Nobel Peace Prize for his role.

FMLN (Farabundo Martí Front for National Liberation):   Salvadoran guerrilla army; named for the leader of the 1932 peasant uprising, which resulted in a massacre of an estimated 10,000–30,000 peasants. The inability of either the FMLN or the Salvadoran army to win a military victory contributed to a negotiated settlement to the country's 12–year civil war. The FMLN dominated the Salvadoran revolutionary coalition, which also included former civilian politicians and several popular organizations (see below).

Granma: name of the small, dilapidated boat that brought Fidel Castro and a band of fellow revolutionaries from exile in Mexico to Cuba in 1956 to begin a new phase as rural guerrillas in the rebellion against the Batista dictatorship. Later became the title of the official Cuban newspaper.

guerrilla: may refer to the individual soldiers involved in a revolutionary movement or to the act of revolutionary civil war itself. Guerrilla armies typically seek to overcome the regular army's superior supplies and number of troops through unconventional tactics such as harassment, mobilization of popular support, superior knowledge of the terrain, and destruction of supplies, transportation networks, and power facilities.

Guevara, Ernesto ("Ché"):   Argentine physician, guerrilla leader, and revolutionary theorist who worked closely with Fidel Castro in designing the early policies of revolutionary Cuba. Guevara called for similar movements throughout Latin America and for "many Vietnams" in the region; he was killed while attempting to inspire revolutionary sentiment among Bolivia's peasants in 1967.

Maoism: theory of revolution named for Chairman Mao Ze-Dong of the Chinese Communist Party. Following the Chinese example, Maoists view revolution as possible even in a preindustrial society that lacks a modern working class, and they look to the peasantry to provide the revolutionary foot soldiers.

Marxism: ideology that views capitalism as inherently flawed, and relies on class struggle to transform society into a Communist system. Marxists expect the working class or proletariat to be the focus of revolutionary sentiment, led by a revolutionary vanguard composed of intellectual elites and others. Named for nineteenth-century German political theorist and activist Karl Marx, Marxism is most closely associated with the 1917 Russian Revolution and the system which subsequently came to power in the Soviet Union. Marxism contains a theory of revolution that became influential in Asia, Africa, and Latin America, particularly in the 1960s, and inspired revolutionaries such as Ché Guevara and Fidel Castro in Cuba and the Sandinistas in Nicaragua.

Plan de Ayala: program issued by Emiliano Zapata in 1911 outlining his demands that Francisco Madero leave the presidency of Mexico; the plan also called for the expropriation and redistribution of large land-holdings as a vital part of the Mexican Revolution.

Plan of San Luis Potosí: 1910 document generally viewed as the beginning of the Mexican Revolution, written by revolutionary leader Francisco Madero from a prison in San Luis Potosí, Mexico. Madero called for Porfirio Díaz to resign or face armed revolt, and proposed the outlines of a new government.

Platt Amendment: U.S.-sponsored amendment to the Cuban Constitution adopted over Cuban objections after Cuba's independence from Spain in 1898. The amendment gave the United States the right to oversee the Cuban economy, veto international commitments, and intervene in domestic politics, making Cuba a virtual protectorate of the United States. It remained in force until 1934.

popular organizations: in El Salvador, term given to grassroots groups, usually of the poor, formed to advocate social and economic reforms through nonviolent means.

revolution: seizure of power, usually by violent means, for the purpose of bringing about rapid and radical change in political, economic, and social structures.

Sandinistas (Sandinista National Liberation Front, or FSLN): named after Nicaragua's nationalist and anti-imperialist leader Augusto César Sandino, who led a guerrilla movement against the U.S. Marine's occupation of Nicaragua in the late 1920s and early 1930s. The FSLN guerrilla movement led the military struggle against dictator Anastasio Somoza Debayle and assumed power in Nicaragua in 1979. Although it lost in national elections in 1990, the FSLN remained the largest single party in Nicaragua and retained control over the army and the police.

Sendero Luminoso (sen-DARE-oh loo-mee-NO-so): Peru's Shining Path revolutionary movement, which has been fighting since 1980 to destroy the state and to rebuild Peruvian society on a completely new model. The Shining Path operates with a high level of secrecy, an adherence to a modified Maoist doctrine, and a use of calculated terror against civilians to discourage rivals and enhance its own control. Its leader, Abimael Guzman, called "Chairman Gonzalo" by his followers, is revered as the "Fourth Sword of Marxism" after Marx, Lenin, and Mao; the Sendero Luminoso is also known as the Peruvian Communist Party.

26th of July Movement: name given to the revolutionary force led by Fidel Castro; refers to the 1953 attack Castro led against a provincial army barracks in southeastern Cuba. The 1953 attack was crushed, but the 26th of July Movement ultimately took power in Cuba in January 1959.

Zapatistas: followers of Emiliano Zapata, the revolutionary leader of landless peasants in Mexico. Zapata issued the 1911 Plan de Ayala, calling for land reform, and rebelled against the government of Francisco Madero after helping Madero to oust Porfirio Díaz.

OVERVIEW

Many North Americans have the impression that Latin America is a "hotbed" of revolutionary sentiment. It is true that economic dislocation, social inequality, and authoritarian rule in many Latin American countries have led to numerous revolutionary movements. Revolutions have been attempted in nearly every country of the region, beginning in Haiti in 1791 and continuing up to the present. However, remarkably few have actually succeeded in overthrowing the government and taking power.

While the common image of a revolution is that of a dramatic, one-time event, closer study reveals that revolutions are really processes that develop over many years. Revolutionary movements in Latin America have usually triumphed as coalitions of diverse social and political forces, which often dissolved into warring factions once the rebellion succeeded in taking power. The outcome of these power struggles reflects the internal dynamics of the revolutionary coalition and determines the future shape of the revolutionary government.

"Fire in the Mind: Revolutions and Revolutionaries" is concerned with understanding the roots of revolution in Latin America, the similarities and differences among revolutionary movements, and the broad changes implemented by twentieth-century revolutionary governments. It also looks at the impact revolutionary governments have had beyond their own borders, both elsewhere in the region and in relations with the United States.

The program addresses contemporary revolutionary processes in El Salvador and Peru which are continuing to unfold. The unit also includes information on Guatemala, where years of repression, particularly of the indigenous population, have failed to eradicate the revolutionary movements or bring an end to the country's civil unrest.

What Makes a Revolution?

The three most important revolutions in twentieth-century Latin America—those in Mexico (1910–17), Cuba (1959), and Nicaragua (1979)—took place in countries with many differences in their geography, demography, history, politics, and socioeconomic conditions. However, they share several important features that contributed to the growth of revolutionary sentiment and mobilization. Each experienced a long-term authoritarian regime: Porfirio Díaz in Mexico (1876–1910), Fulgencio Batista in Cuba (1934–59), and the Somoza dynasty in Nicaragua (1936–79). In each case, the regime's tendency to become increasingly repressive in response to growing pressures for change ultimately hastened its downfall.

Although their economic situations differed, in each country the revolutionaries were able to use appeals to nationalism and anti-imperialism to capitalize on public concerns about vulnerability to outside economic and political pressures. Government corruption and fiscal mismanagement in all three countries also undercut the regimes' support among important sectors of society, widening the base of discontent.

The three successful Latin American revolutions studied here were led by ideologically diverse, multiclass coalitions. Their leaders tended to be individuals from the middle and upper sectors who preached social justice and improved conditions for the poor, but whose alliance was not necessarily based on a shared blueprint for the future. The revolutionary coalitions were united, in large measure, by their opposition to authoritarian rule and by their desire to open up their countries' political systems and to carry out certain social and economic reforms.

Once they took power, however, these revolutionary coalitions did not hold together for long. In each case, the most cohesive elements within the original group solidified their power and were able to control the ultimate direction of the revolutionary process.

In Mexico, dissatisfaction with the government's lack of concern for the peasantry led Emiliano Zapata and Pancho Villa to turn against their former ally, Francisco Madero. The Mexican Revolution was eventually consolidated after seven years of civil war, and the most long-standing one-party government in Latin America was then installed. In the case of Cuba and Nicaragua, the dissolution of the original coalitions that had led their countries' revolutions meant a turn toward a socialist system inspired by Marxist-Leninist ideology.

Although revolutionaries may be inspired by nationalism, socialism, or other ideologies, such appeals are insufficient to prompt them to take up arms against their government. The existence of inequalities and injustices, or the experience of authoritarian rule, is also only part of the picture. Revolutionary movements occur when individuals become convinced that only the seizure of power through the use of violence will enable them to carry out essential reforms. Marxism had little to do with the success of Latin America's revolutionary movements, although it did help mold the regimes that took power in Cuba and Nicaragua. Marxism also influenced the thinking of revolutionary leadership in other countries. The history of revolutionary processes in El Salvador and Peru, examined more closely in the program "Fire in the Mind," provides further examples of the role and limitations of ideology in revolutionary conflicts.

Latin American Revolutionary Movements Since 1960

Cuba

The Cuban Revolution inaugurated a three-decade cycle of revolution in Latin America and the Caribbean. In the early years after his successful rebellion ushered in the Cuban Revolution, Fidel Castro and the Cuban Socialist (later Communist) Party consolidated power at the head of the revolutionary government. The CIA-backed Bay of Pigs invasion in 1961, along with the 1962 Cuban missile crisis and its aftermath, had an important impact on the internal dynamics of the revolution. The two events accelerated the process that had been developing since 1960, bringing the United States and Cuba into increasing conflict while simultaneously drawing Cuba closer to a new patron, the Soviet Union.

The Cuban revolutionary regime has been a significant focus of U.S. foreign policy for more than three decades. Cuban ties to Moscow and support—moral, military, and technical—for other revolutionary movements in Latin American and Africa, together with hostility toward the United States, nationalization of private property (including that owned by U.S. companies), military buildup, and repression of domestic political opposition, have been ongoing points of contention with the United States.

U.S. responses since the early 1960s have taken a variety of forms. Although no further military measures were attempted after the failed Bay of Pigs invasion, U.S.-led pressure on Cuba has included a trade embargo, a ban on visits to Cuba by U.S. citizens, sanctions by the Organization of American States, and denial of credit through the international financial organizations of the IMF and the World Bank.

Despite significant subsidies from the Soviet Union and the Eastern bloc (one estimate of Soviet aid in 1989 exceeded $4 billion, more than one-quarter of the Cuban GNP), Cuba's revolutionary government has failed to make much progress in diversifying the nation's exports or increasing its self-sufficiency. However, the Cuban government points with pride to its success in improving social indicators, such as literacy and infant mortality, and in creating a socialist society in the country. Although many observers believe that the Cuban Revolution is too deeply ingrained and institutionalized to be easily reversed, the pressures on Cuba in the post–Cold War era may make it impossible for the revolutionary regime to survive without significant changes.

Nicaragua

The Government of National Reconstruction, which took power in Nicaragua in July 1979, began as a multiclass coalition with broad-based support throughout society. Ultimately, though, it was dominated by the Sandinista National Liberation Front (FSLN), a Marxist-led group committed to radical socioeconomic change and a foreign policy of nonalignment. The Sandinistas' suspicions of the United States, their close relationship with Cuba, and their aid to the revolutionary movement in El Salvador undermined the initial efforts of some in the U.S. government to adopt a conciliatory approach.

Soon after the 1980 election of Ronald Reagan as president, the United States began a major effort to topple the Sandinistas, beginning with a cutoff of economic aid. In 1981 the Reagan administration approved covert funding for counter-revolutionaries, known as *contras*. Over the next several years, conflict with the *contras* absorbed an increasing proportion of Nicaragua's limited resources and caused tremendous destruction of infrastructure and many casualties among soldiers and civilians.

After the failure of numerous attempts at ending the war, the presidents of all the Central American countries agreed in 1987 to the Esquipulas, or Arias, Plan, initiated by Costa Rican president Oscar Arias. The plan, which called for negotiated settlements to the region's civil wars, internal democratization, and noninterference by foreign powers, led to a 1988 cease-fire in Nicaragua and national elections in 1990. The Sandinistas lost the elections to a coalition led by Violeta Barrios de Chamorro, a member of the first revolutionary government and the widow of one of Somoza's principal opponents.

The opposition victory ended U.S. support for the *contras,* but brought neither peace nor prosperity to Nicaragua. Postwar reconstruction proceeded slowly and their dissatisfaction with the Chamorro government's progress led some demobilized *contras* and former members of the Sandinista army to take up arms again. In the early 1990s it was unclear what was next for Nicaragua or its revolutionary process.

El Salvador and Guatemala

In El Salvador and Guatemala repression has been common for decades, particularly of the rural population, and the facade of elected governments has not been able to disguise the lack of real democracy or the ongoing repression by the military. Although rebellions by peasant groups date back to the early part of this century, the most recent civil wars began in Guatemala in the 1960s and in El Salvador in the late 1970s, inspired and supported, in part, by revolutionary regimes in Cuba and later Nicaragua. Long years of war, however, did not produce a clear military outcome in either country.

The program "Fire in the Mind" focuses particularly on El Salvador, where the repression of popular organizations and the failure of reformist military officers to bring about significant change after a 1979 coup spurred the growth of the Salvadoran revolutionary movement. The Salvadoran revolutionary coalition was dominated by the Farabundo Martí Liberation Front (FMLN), a Marxist group that joined forces with civilian reformers and some of the major popular movements.

During the 1980s the United States became deeply involved in the counterinsurgency effort and provided more than $4 billion in military and economic aid to the Salvadoran government. Despite the influx of aid, the Salvadoran military was unable to reach a decisive victory over the guerrilla forces, which were able to control certain areas of the country but were unable to win national power by the force of arms.

At the end of the 1980s three events came together to enhance the prospects for a successful negotiated settlement to the war. The end of the Cold War and the disintegration of the USSR, coming on top of the Esquipulas efforts, prompted a strategic reassessment by the FMLN, which put forward a new, more acceptable slate of conditions for peace. A similar reassessment took place in Guatemala, where negotiations were also under way, although the combination of a more intransigent government and a weaker guerrilla army made the possibility of success seem dimmer.

In El Salvador, the conservative Cristiani government was encouraged by the United States to accept UN mediation and pursue negotiations, and it signaled its willingness to do so. Finally, the failure of the FMLN's last major military offensive in 1989 emphasized the military stalemate, while the much publicized assassinations by a U.S.-trained army battalion of six Jesuit priests, their housekeeper, and her daughter in the midst of the rebel offensive placed continued U.S. support for the Salvadoran government in jeopardy.

Peace accords ending the Salvadoran civil war were signed in early 1992 under the auspices of the United Nations. The accords, which were greeted with a mixture of relief and joy by the exhausted Salvadoran public, committed the government to an unprecedented set of far-reaching reforms of the security, judicial, and political systems. The FMLN, for its part, agreed to demobilize its forces and participate as a political party in future national elections.

Observers on all sides hoped that the accords would contribute to the peaceful restructuring of El Salvador's security forces and the reduction of socioeconomic inequalities. Within months of the accords' signing, however, accusations were raised of noncompliance and delays in implementing the timetable. Peace will ultimately depend on the willingness of both sides to compromise and share power, the ability of the UN observer team to enforce compliance with the accords, and contin-

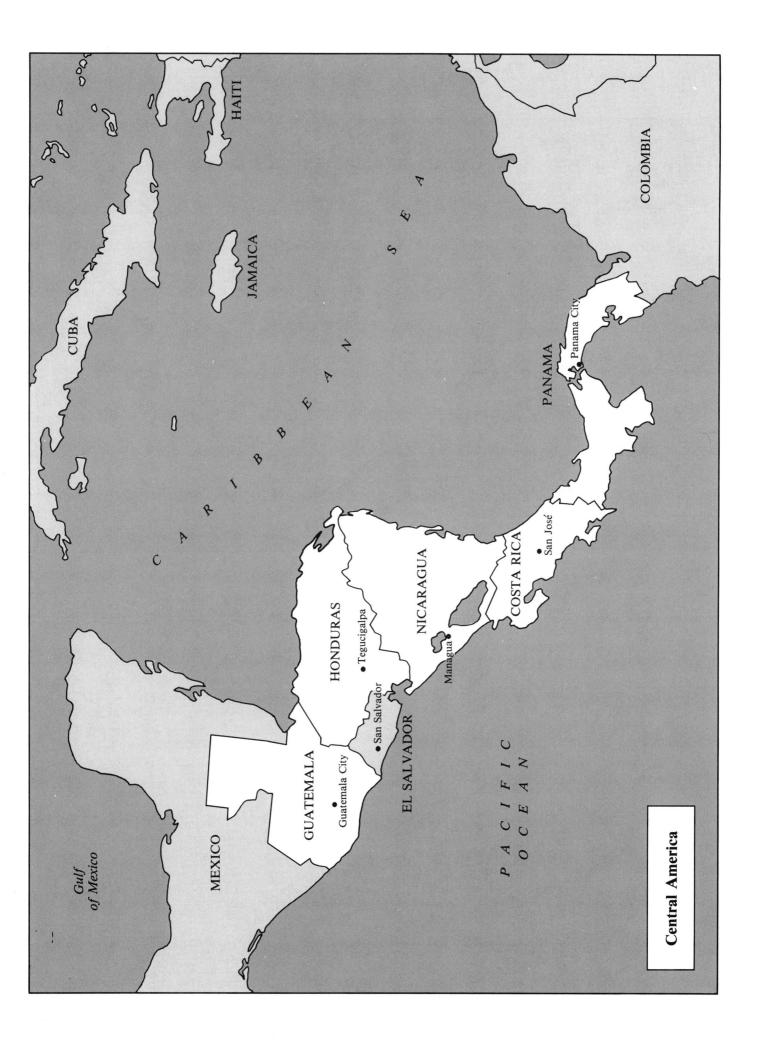

Gulf
of Mexico

CUBA

HAITI

JAMAICA

C A R I B B E A N   S E A

COLOMBIA

PANAMA

Panama City

San José

COSTA RICA

NICARAGUA

Managua

HONDURAS

Tegucigalpa

San Salvador

MEXICO

GUATEMALA

Guatemala City

EL SALVADOR

P A C I F I C
O C E A N

Central America

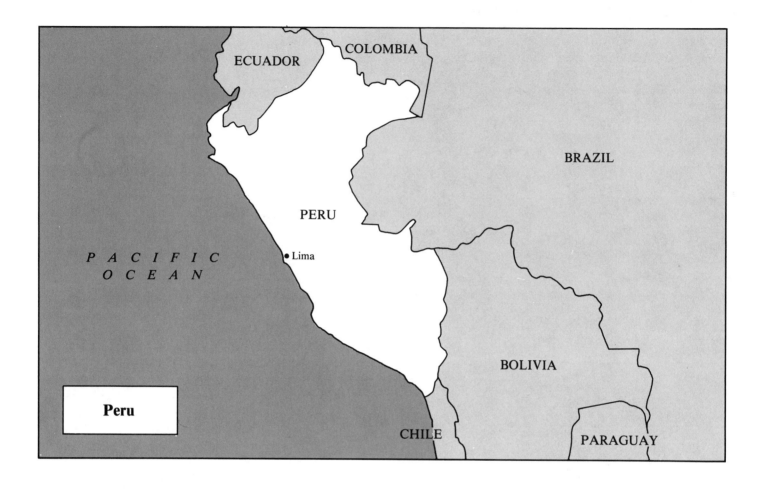

Peru

ued aid from the United States and other countries to rebuild the country's devastated economy.

Peru

The revolutionary movement Sendero Luminoso, or Shining Path, emerged in 1980 just as Peru returned to civilian government after 12 years of military rule. Sendero began with a campaign of violence in Peru's Ayacucho province directed against rival peasant leaders and local police. After 12 years, it controlled significant rural areas of Peru and had gained a substantial presence in the capital, Lima.

Although its appeal within some sectors of Peruvian society stems from the experience of oppression, poverty, and alienation from the state which characterized earlier revolutionary movements in the Americas, Sendero's methods and ideology distinguish it as something new. Unlike the other movements studied here, Sendero's support is not based on a broad, multiclass coalition but is largely working class and peasant based. Its leaders call themselves Maoists, after China's revolutionary leader, and their ideology is based on the modified Maoism of their leader, Abimael Guzman, known as "Chairman Gonzalo." Sendero tries to convert peasants, workers, and students to its cause and uses terror to intimidate those who oppose the movement. Its ruthless use of systematic violence has raised fears in Latin America, as well as within the United States, about the kind of revolutionary government that might arise from a Sendero seizure of power.

As the insurgency has grown—by the early 1990s it claimed to have 6,000 fighters and to control a large part of Peru—so has the intensity of the official response, but neither sustained military campaigns and repression nor a state of emergency imposed over nearly half the national territory has succeeded in stopping the Sendero advance. In early 1992, after an estimated 20,000–25,000 deaths in 12 years of civil war, Peru's president Alberto Fujimori took radical steps, suspending the constitution and dissolving the legislature. It was by no means certain that Fujimori's crackdown would end the years of conflict that have so devastated Peru's social, economic, and political systems.

Although most observers view Sendero as a peculiarly Peruvian phenomenon, in the post–Cold War era it remains to be seen whether the Shining Path heralds a new form of revolutionary threat that will be replicated elsewhere in the region. What its emergence and growth does underscore is that the end of the Cold War does not mean the end of revolutionary movements in Latin America and the Caribbean, although the revolutionaries of the future may be very different from those of the past.

ASSIGNMENT

1. Before you view the program, read:

Modern Latin America, 3d ed., pp. 201–3, 213–20, 254–56, 263–82, and 337–43.

In chapter 6, "Peru: Soldiers, Oligarchs, and Indians," the section entitled *Oligarchic Rule* (pp. 201–03), and the rest of the chapter assigned (pp. 213–20), provide an abbreviated look at Peru's struggles to achieve political stability and improve socioeconomic conditions, especially during the period since 1980.

In chapter 8, "Cuba: Late Colony, First Socialist State," the sections assigned (pp. 254–56 and 263–82) follow Cuba from the colonial period to the present. The assignment is especially focused on the evolution of revolutionary Cuba under the leadership of Fidel Castro.

In chapter 10, the section entitled *Guatemala: Reaction and Repression* (pp, 337–43) is a brief overview of Guatemala since the late 1800s, concentrating on the period since 1950. This selection highlights Guatemala's long history of strong-man rule, the U.S. role in deposing Jacobo Arbenz, and the subsequent years of

human rights abuse and social and political turmoil.

You should also review the following previously assigned readings:

The Mexican Revolution (pp. 228–33), covered in Unit 5; *Nicaragua: From Dynasty to Revolution* (pp. 326–30), and *El Salvador: From Stability to Insurgence* (pp. 332–37), from Unit 8; and pp. 185–87 from "Peru," covered in Unit 9.

2. View the program "Fire in the Mind."

3. After you view the program, read:

Americas: An Anthology, chapter 11, pp. 299–334.

Introduction and readings in the anthology provide the reader with insight into the basis for revolutionary movements. Excerpts are included from the writings and speeches of revolutionary leaders in Mexico, Cuba, Nicaragua, and El Salvador. The anthology also covers peace efforts in Central America, such as the Esquipulas Plan and the peace negotiations in El Salvador and Guatemala.

UNIT REVIEW

After viewing the program and reading the assignments, you should be able to:

· Name some of the common factors that contributed to revolutionary movements in Mexico, Cuba, Nicaragua, Guatemala, El Salvador, and Peru.

· Recognize that revolutions are not one-time events but instead are processes that develop over many years and do not have a predetermined course or outcome.

· Understand the role of Marxist ideology in most of these revolutionary movements and its effect on the policies of the revolutionary governments in Cuba and Nicaragua.

- Analyze the nature of revolutionary coalitions in Latin America in the twentieth century and explain the reasons for their difficulties in holding together after taking power.

- Describe the U.S. response to revolutionary movements in Cuba, Nicaragua, and El Salvador.

- List the key features that distinguish Peru's revolutionary movement from others in the region, and discuss how a government led by the Shining Path in Peru could differ from other revolutionary regimes in the Americas.

- Explain the impact of the end of the Cold War on revolutions and revolutionary movements in Latin America.

SELF-TEST QUESTIONS

Multiple Choice

*Mark the letter of the response that **best** answers the question or completes the statement.*

_____ 1. Which of the following describes similarities among revolutionary movements in Mexico, Cuba, Nicaragua, and El Salvador? *(Mark all that apply.)*
   a. They were generally led by middle- and upper-class individuals heading broad and ideologically diverse coalitions.
   b. They were characterized by intense competition between Communism and capitalism.
   c. They were a response to the brutality, corruption, and mismanagement of long-standing authoritarian governments.
   d. They encountered implacable hostility from the United States and forged close alliances with the Soviet Union.

_____ 2. Emiliano Zapata and Pancho Villa:
   a. were allies of Porfirio Díaz who resisted the rebel Francisco Madero in the Mexican Revolution.
   b. led rebel movements in the south and north of Mexico which sought greater attention to the issues of land reform and rural poverty.
   c. wrote the Plan de San Luis Potosí in a call for a general uprising against the Díaz government.
   d. received significant support from the United States, which hoped to create a new protectorate in alliance with the revolutionary government.

_____ 3. Farabundo Martí was:
   a. a one-time president of El Salvador who pushed through significant agrarian reform.
   b. an internationally known revolutionary from Argentina who called for "many Vietnams" in Latin America.
   c. the promoter of a 1932 peasant uprising whose name was chosen by El Salvador's main guerrilla army in the late 1970s.
   d. a Cuban patriot who struggled to achieve independence from Spain and inspired many later revolutionaries throughout the region.

_____ 4. Which of the following is true of the April 1961 Bay of Pigs invasion?
   a. President Kennedy committed U.S. forces to guarantee the invasion's success.
   b. The exiles were able to make it to the Cuban hills from where they launched a guerrilla war against Castro.
   c. U.S. sponsorship of the invasion reinforced Castro's popularity and helped solidify a Cuban alliance with the USSR.
   d. The invasion sparked spontaneous popular uprisings against Castro throughout rural parts of Cuba.

_____ 5. The Somoza dynasty in Nicaragua: *(Mark all that apply.)*
   a. brought about significant reforms in the country during its 40 years in power.
   b. earned near universal condemnation for its corruption, especially in its use of the 1972 earthquake relief aid.
   c. retained popularity for many years by using the rhetoric of anti-imperialism.
   d. used the National Guard as a personal army which became known for brutality and terrorism.

_____ 6. The 1979 Nicaraguan Revolution:
   a. relied on significant support from Sendero Luminoso.
   b. was a civil war pitting the Sandinistas against the *contras*.
   c. succeeded in forcing Somoza out of power by means of the agreements signed at Esquipulas.
   d. was supported by a diverse, multi-class coalition including the FSLN.

_____ 7. Which of the following are considered by the Cuban revolutionary government to be important achievements? *(Mark all that apply.)*
   a. The near elimination of illiteracy and reduction in infant mortality figures.
   b. The diversification of the Cuban economy away from dependence on sugar.
   c. Increased economic self-sufficiency, especially in industrial goods.
   d. Moral and technical support for other revolutionary movements in Africa and Latin America.

_____ 8. The guerrilla movement in El Salvador is notable because:
   a. it was the first rebel army in Latin America to obtain the support of the Catholic Church.
   b. it was vehemently opposed to Marxist ideology.

   c. it drew its support primarily from the urban elite, who opposed the concentration of wealth in the hands of the "Fourteen Families."
   d. after 12 years of civil war, it agreed to pursue its aims via a negotiated settlement rather than through continued fighting.

_____ 9. Which of the following is true of the U.S. response to the revolution in El Salvador?
   a. The tiny country of El Salvador was judged not important enough to warrant U.S. concern.
   b. U.S. policy toward El Salvador became a highly divisive domestic issue.
   c. U.S. support for the Salvadoran government against the wishes of Congress led to the Iran-Contra affair.
   d. The United States opposed President Alfredo Cristiani's efforts to seek a negotiated end to the war.

_____ 10. The Nicaraguan elections of 1990:
   a. gave the Sandinistas the electoral mandate they needed to legitimize their power.
   b. brought the widow of a prominent Somoza opponent to the presidency at the head of an anti-Sandinista coalition.
   c. were opposed by the United States, whose official policy was to continue pushing for a *contra* victory.
   d. were nullified by the Sandinistas, who used their control over the army to back up their refusal to leave office.

_____ 11. Which is true of Guatemala's indigenous people? *(Mark all that apply.)*
   a. In general, they suffer high rates of illiteracy, unemployment, landlessness, hunger, and infant and child mortality.
   b. Their situation has been markedly improved by the Guatemalan government's reform programs, de-

signed to eliminate the rural population's support for guerrillas.

c. Although they are the majority of Guatemala's population, their poverty has been a low-priority item for the country's military governments.

d. They have been the target of severe repression by the army in its fight against Guatemala's guerrilla movement.

_____ 12. Which of the following is considered a highly unusual guerrilla movement without real precedent in Latin America?

a. Sendero Luminoso
b. ARENA
c. Sandinista National Liberation Front
d. The 26th of July Movement

_____ 13. The U.S. response to revolutionary movements in Latin America has included which of the following measures? *(Mark all that apply.)*

a. Covert support for exile armies.
b. Financial and military support for embattled governments.
c. Economic sanctions and trade embargos against revolutionary governments.
d. Pressuring the Soviet Union to provide military and economic support to revolutionary movements.

_____ 14. The shift in strategy of some major revolutionary movements in Latin America from armed struggle to negotiations may be partly due to the fact that:

a. revolutionaries have abandoned the struggle for radical change in their societies.
b. guerrilla armies' clear military superiority has convinced repressive governments that they must agree to a negotiated settlement.
c. the changed international climate has reduced the levels of external

aid to both sides, limiting their ability to continue fighting.
d. Latin American armies have been able to achieve decisive military victories over the guerrilla forces.

_____ 15. Which of the following is true of Peruvian president Alberto Fujimori?

a. He was Peru's first civilian president after 12 years of military rule.
b. He suspended the consitition and disbanded the legislature in 1992.
c. He is a former army general who took power in a coup in 1980.
d. He sought United Nations assistance to broker negotiations with the Sendero Luminoso to end Peru's civil war.

_____ 16. The Shining Path in Peru is noted for: *(Mark all that apply.)*

a. persuading a broad-based coalition of Peruvians to back its radical revolutionary program.
b. continuing to grow in strength despite increasingly severe repression by the Peruvian military.
c. using the domestic and foreign news media to obtain widespread international support for its objectives.
d. using brutality and intimidation to enhance its control over large areas of the country.

True or False

_____ 17. Revolutionary leadership usually emerges as a grassroots phenomenon based within the peasantry.

_____ 18. Latin American revolutionaries have tended to use the themes of nationalism and anti-imperialism, and are typically opposed to foreign economic domination.

_____ 19. The National Bipartisan Commission on Central America argued that Soviet and Cuban influence had little to do with the revolutionary movements in El Salvador and Guatemala.

_____ 20. The Platt Amendment in effect converted Cuba into a U.S. protectorate by allowing the United States to intervene in Cuban internal affairs.

_____ 21. Marxism has had no effect on the policies of revolutionary governments that took power in Cuba and Nicaragua in the late twentieth century.

_____ 22. During the 1962 Cuban missile crisis, Castro was the architect of the agreement that ended the U.S.-USSR standoff and averted nuclear war.

_____ 23. In 1991 the FMLN rejected United Nations attempts to mediate in El Salvador's civil war and vowed to fight on for a military victory.

Identification/Short Answer

Define or describe the following terms, concepts, or persons, or answer the following questions. Answers should be no longer than a few sentences.

24. Augusto César Sandino:

25. Plan de Ayala:

26. Alfredo Cristiani:

27. Ojo por Ojo:

28. Name two important differences between the Mexican Revolution and other revolutionary movements in twentieth-century Latin America:

29. Ché Guevara:

30. Explain what Jesús Silva Herzog meant when he wrote in 1949, "The Mexican Revolution no longer exists. It ceased to be, died quietly . . . The Revolution has failed."

QUESTIONS TO CONSIDER

1. Why hasn't the Mexican Revolution been more successful at carrying out a complete transformation of society? What is likely to happen to Mexican politics in the 1990s and beyond?

2. What distinguishes Sendero Luminoso from other revolutionary movements in Latin America? Why does its continued growth provoke such fears in the United States and elsewhere in Latin America? What do you think the U.S. response should be to this new revolutionary threat? What is it likely to be, in your opinion?

3. Is the end of the Cold War likely to change future U.S. government reaction to revolutions in this hemisphere? Is it likely to change the U.S. government's attitude toward the existing revolutionary regime in Cuba? Or will revolutionaries' tendency to equate lack of sovereignty with U.S. influence continue to put revolutionary governments on a collision course with their powerful northern neighbor?

RESOURCES

Nonfiction

Arnson, Cynthia J. *Crossroads: Congress, the Reagan Administration, and Central America*. New York: Pantheon, 1989. An account by a former congressional staff member of the struggles between the Congress and the Reagan administration over U.S. policy toward Nicaragua and El Salvador.

Black, George. *Triumph of the People: the Sandinista Revolution in Nicaragua*. Austin: University of Texas Press, 1971. An account and analysis of Sandinista struggle and victory.

Cabezas, Omar. *Fire from the Mountain: The Making of a Sandinista*. New York: New American Library, 1985. A personal account by a leading Sandinista of his experience. A former Nicaraguan student leader, Cabezas joined the Sandinista guerrillas in the 1970s and discovered that being a successful revolutionary is much more difficult than he had imagined.

Castro, Fidel. *History Will Absolve Me*. New York: Lyle Stuart, 1961. A transcript of Fidel Castro's speech in his own defense at his trial after a 1953 attack on the Cuban army's Moncada barracks. Castro articulated the demands of the revolutionaries. The title is taken from the final phrase of his speech, "Condemn me. History will absolve me."

Costain, Pam. "What Ever Happened to Nicaragua?" *Utne Reader*, May/June 1991. The author argues that although Nicaragua was at the center of U.S. foreign policy in the 1980s, attention to the country has dissipated considerably although the country's political and economic problems continue.

Crahan, Margaret E., and Peter H. Smith. "The State of Revolution." In *Americas: New Interpretive Essays*, edited by Alfred Stepan. A study of the consequences and future of revolutionary movements in the Americas, written by two members of the *Americas* academic advisory board as an optional addition to this unit.

Cuban Studies/Estudios Cubanos. Periodical focused on Cuba, published annually by the University of Pittsburgh Press. A collection of essays; contains some of the best of recent research. Each issue includes a bibliography of current books and articles, and commentary on past issues of the periodical.

Dalton, Roque. *Miguel Marmol*. Willimantic, Conn.: Curbstone Press, 1987. Thirty thousand peasants and workers were killed in a month-long massacre when General Maximiliano Hernández Martinez attempted to wipe out "subversion" in El Salvador in 1932. One of the founder's of El Salvador's Communist Party, Miguel Mármol, survived, and continued to lead and organize the Communist Party. Fellow Communist Roque Dalton began this three-week interview about revolutionary advice, history, and adventure, in an effort to clear the Communist Party of blame for the 1932 massacre, and to educate future rebels.

Debray, Regis. *Revolution in the Revolution? Armed Struggle and Political Struggle in Latin America*. Westport, Conn.: Greenwood Press, 1980. Primer of the Cuban model of guerrilla revolution, intended to serve as a "how-to" guide for revolutionaries elsewhere in Latin America.

Domínguez, Jorge. *Cuba: Order and Revolution*. Cambridge: Belknap Press, Harvard University Press, 1978. The most detailed study of the Cuban Revolution and its evolution to the end of the 1970s.

Eckstein, Susan, ed. *Power and Popular Protest: Latin American Social Movements*. Berkeley: University of California Press, 1989. A survey of the origins and characteristics of both revolutionary and nonrevolutionary movements in Latin America.

Franqui, Carlos. *Diary of the Cuban Revolution*. New York: Viking, 1980. Documents tracing the origin and rise to power of Fidel Castro's revolutionary movement.

Gould, Jeffrey L. *To Lead as Equals: Rural Protest and Political Consciousness in Chinandega, Nicaragua, 1912–1979*. Chapel Hill: University of North Carolina Press, 1990. Excellent study of how ordinary people reacted to both dictatorship and revolution in Nicaragua.

Guevara, Ernesto Ché. *Handbook for Guerrilla Warfare.* New York: Vintage Books, 1968. Personal opinion of a leader of the Cuban Revolution on how to organize and lead a successful revolutionary movement.

Kinzer, Stephen. *Blood of Brother.* New York: Putnam, 1991. A U.S. journalist's view of where the Nicaraguan Revolution went wrong.

Knight, Franklin W. "Cuba." In *The Modern Caribbean,* edited by Franklin W. Knight and Colin A. Palmer. Chapel Hill: University of North Carolina Press, 1989. Examines the politics, economy, and culture in Cuba from the end of Spanish colonialism in 1898, to 1985, covering the acts and influence of the United States at the turn of the century, periods of democracy and repression, and Fidel Castro's revolution.

LaFeber, Walter. *Inevitable Revolutions: The United States in Central America.* New York: Norton, 1983. Covers U.S. intervention in Central America from Thomas Jefferson to Ronald Reagan. Author argues that the United States destabilized the region by subverting the leaders and institutions that could have brought peaceable change in Central America.

Perez, Louis A. Jr. *Cuba: Between Reform and Revolution.* New York: Oxford University Press, 1988. A very well written history of Cuba, emphasizing the twentieth century.

Perez, Louis A. Jr. *Cuba and the United States: Ties of Singular Intimacy.* Athens: University of Georgia Press, 1990. Focuses on Cuban history from 1810 to 1899 and on relations between the United States and the island nation.

Smith, Peter H. *Labyrinths of Power: Political Recruitment in Twentieth-Century Mexico.* Princeton: Princeton University Press, 1979. Examines the backgrounds of the political elite that emerged out of the 1910 Mexican Revolution.

Wilson Quarterly 12:1 (1988). This issue of the *Wilson Quarterly* focuses on Nicaragua. Selections in-

clude a systematic history of the nation by Richard L. Millet, a selection on democracy by Clifford Krauss, and an essay by Henry A. Kissinger on U.S. foreign policy in Nicaragua.

Womack, John, Jr. *Zapata and the Mexican Revolution.* New York: Vintage Books, 1968. An award-winning account of the role of Emiliano Zapata and his peasant movement in the Mexican Revolution.

Wyden, Peter. *Bay of Pigs: The Untold Story.* New York: Simon & Schuster, 1979. The most complete examination of the 1961 CIA-backed invasion of Cuba that contributed to the Cuban missile crisis.

Fiction and Poetry

Arenas, Reinaldo. *The Ill-fated Peregrinations of Fray Servand.* New York: Avon, 1987. Originally titled *Hallucinations* and banned in Cuba, the author's homeland, this comic picaresque novel is about a wandering Catholic priest, part rogue, part revolutionary.

Argueta, Manlio. *Cuzcatlán Where the Southern Sea Beats.* New York: Vintage, 1987. Traces the history of El Salvador, from the 1930s through the early 1980s, through one family's experiences.

Azuela, Mariano. *The Underdogs.* New York: NAL-Dutton, 1963. Translated by E. Munguia, Jr. The most famous novel about the Mexican Revolution; focuses on the rural population.

Cabrera Infante, Guillermo. *Three Trapped Tigers.* New York: Harper & Row, 1971. This sometimes humorous novel depicts Havana's corrupt and lively nightlife in the 1950s, just before Castro's rebellion overthrew the Batista regime.

Desnoes, Edmundo. *Memories of Underdevelopment; and, Inconsolable Memories* New Brunswick, N.J.: Rutgers University Press, 1990. Gripping novel of the reaction of a member of the bourgeoisie to the Cuban Revolution and 1962 missile crisis.

Guillen, Nicolás.*The Great Zoo and Other Poems.* New York: Monthly Review Press, 1972. Anthology of poetry by a Cuban revolutionary who emphasizes the contributions of the African heritage of many Cubans.

Lezama Lima, José. *Paradiso* (Paradise). Translated by Gregory Rabassa. New York: Farrar Straus Giroux, 1974. This story of Cuban José Cemí begins at the turn of the century and focuses on José's relationship with his mother after his father's death. She becomes the power behind José's creativity in his search for understanding of his father, love, and the power of the mind.

Sayles, John. *Gusanos*. New York: HarperCollins, 1991. This novel stretches over six decades in the history of a family and Cuba. It describes the corruption in Batista's Cuba as well as the fervor of Cuban exiles for recapturing their country.

Films

Unless otherwise indicated, all films listed are available in VHS video format.

Havana. 140 minutes, 1990. Set in Cuba under Batista's rule this film has been called a modern *Casablanca* and stars Robert Redford. Available in most video-rental outlets.

Portrait of Teresa (*Retrato de Teresa*). 103 minutes, 1990. (Spanish with English subtitles.) A housewife and mother who works in a textile factory displeases her husband when she gets involved in political and cultural groups in Cuba. Available in most video-rental outlets.

Salvador. 122 minutes, 1985. Feature film about a veteran war correspondent sent in 1980 to film the effects of civil war on the people in El Salvador. Directed by Oliver Stone. Available in most video-rental outlets.

Unit 12

The Americans: Latin American and Caribbean Peoples in the United States

There are 20 million people from Latin America and the Caribbean in the United States. Early in the next century, they will bypass African-Americans to become the country's largest minority. © Diana Walker/ Gamma Liaison

UNIT SUMMARY

Unit 12 considers the growth in numbers and importance of people of Latin American and Caribbean origin living in the United States. The unit addresses three sets of issues. First, what are the most important groups that make up communities of Latin American and Caribbean origin in the United States? What characteristics do they share, and in what key ways do they differ from one another? Second, what has been the experience of Latin American and Caribbean peoples who have migrated to the United States? How has the different reception accorded the various groups affected their subsequent adjustment to U.S. society? Finally, how has the growth of Latino and non-Hispanic Caribbean communities in the United States affected U.S. politics, culture, and society? How have these communities in turn adapted to and been changed by the realities of their experience in the United States?

By the end of this unit, you should understand that the terms *Hispanic* and *Latino* refer to a wide range of very diverse groups in this country. You should also be more familiar with the range of immigrant communities from the English- and French-speaking Caribbean, whose numbers and influence are particularly evident in the eastern United States. Finally, you should have a deeper appreciation for the many important contributions that Latin American and Caribbean communities have made to North American society, politics, and culture.

KEY ISSUES

- What are the major groups of Latin American and Caribbean origin in the United States, and how do they differ in terms of their histories, experiences, reasons for migration, and level of political activism?

- What factors have affected rates of emigration from Latin America and the Caribbean to the United States? What has been the reaction within the United States to Latin American and Caribbean immigrants in the 1980s and 1990s?

- How has their reception in the United States affected the ultimate success and adaptation of various immigrant groups from Latin America and the Caribbean?

- What are the main arguments in the controversy over the degree to which individuals and communities of Latin American and Caribbean origin should assimilate into North American society?

- To what extent have Latinos in particular evolved from being outside the U.S. mainstream to an increasing awareness and sophisticated use of their economic and political power?

- In what ways are the growing numbers of Latinos and non-Hispanic Caribbean peoples within the United States influencing and changing U.S. society, politics, and culture?

GLOSSARY

Anglo: term used by many Latinos (see below) to refer to white North Americans of European descent.

assimilation: the full integration of people into society, typically through the adoption of the language, culture, values, dress, and other social norms of the majority population. For non-English-speaking immigrants from Latin America and the Caribbean, assimilation has usually been associated with giving up their language and customs and conforming to the dominant social and cultural patterns of North American society.

bilingual education: educational method in which students are taught primarily in their native languages, while gradually increasing their use of English. The objective is to produce students who are fluent in both languages, while enabling non-English-speakers to maintain an appropriate grade level through subject instruction in their native tongue. It has been mandated by federal law since 1974 for schools with 20 or more students speaking any language other than English as their mother tongue.

Chicanos: Mexican-Americans born in the United States. The term was popularized during the 1960s.

Hispanic: term used to refer to all Spanish-speaking or Spanish-origin people living in the United States, including both immigrants and those who are U.S.-born. The term was first used by the U.S. Census Bureau in 1970, and has since become widely used as a catch-all term for all those of Spanish-American origin. It is viewed by some as unduly emphasizing the European element of Latin American and Caribbean culture while excluding those of African and/or indigenous descent.

Immigration Reform and Control (Simpson-Rodino) Act: U.S. law passed in 1986, targeted especially at illegal immigration from Mexico and Central America. While establishing tough sanctions for employers hiring undocumented workers, the law also provided amnesty from prosecution and an offer of legal residency for all who could prove they had been living continuously in the United States since 1981.

Latino: similar to Hispanic (above); a term used to refer to persons of Latin American origin living in the United States. *Latino* is preferred by some as a more inclusive term for the culturally diverse people of Latin America and the Spanish-speaking Caribbean.

Nuyorican: term coined to describe the dual identity of Puerto Ricans living in New York. About 40 percent of all Puerto Ricans live on the mainland. Over half of these (20 percent of the total) live in New York City.

OVERVIEW

The United States has always been a nation of immigrants, and it has been an important part of the nation's self-image to be seen as a haven of freedom and opportunity for peoples from many lands. Because close to three-quarters of U.S. citizens today are descended from the European immigrants who arrived in massive numbers during the nineteenth and early twentieth centuries, the growing numbers of Hispanic and Caribbean peo-

ples living in this country are perceived as newcomers, people quite different from other "Americans." Many North Americans might be surprised to learn that, in fact, Spanish-speaking peoples were the first nonnative settlers of the territory that is now the United States, and that the Hispanic presence antedated the establishment of an English colony in North America by a full century.

People of Latin American and Caribbean origin today are living not only in the southwestern territories that—until the 1848 Treaty of Guadalupe Hidalgo—belonged to Mexico. The states bordering Mexico still have some of the highest concentrations of Spanish-speaking people in the United States, but major urban areas across the country also now have significant minority populations of Hispanics, who are also known as Latinos. *Hispanics,* the term used by the U.S. Census Bureau to classify Spanish-speaking U.S. residents, now number more than 25 million, close to 10 percent of the total U.S. population. That figure does not include the 3.5 million Puerto Ricans living in the island of Puerto Rico, although they are U.S. citizens by birth and may move to the mainland at will. In addition, if undocumented migrants were included, the total numbers could be a few million higher. There are also significant communities of people from the English- and French-speaking Caribbean, especially in the eastern part of the United States.

There are three major groups within the broad spectrum of Latin American and Caribbean peoples now living in this country. People of Mexican descent constitute the largest single group, with 12.6 million people identified in the 1990 census. Mexican-Americans are the second-largest minority group in the United States, second only to African-Americans, and make up 63 percent of all U.S. Hispanics. Mexico is the largest single source for all migration, legal and illegal, to the United States, although an estimated third of those who enter the United States from Mexico may be Central Americans.

The next largest group of Hispanics is Puerto Ricans, at 2.3 million on the mainland alone. Most Puerto Ricans have settled in the northeastern United States, especially in New York. Puerto Ricans are, in fact, not migrants in the technical sense since they are U.S. citizens by birth—and have been since 1917. Nevertheless, their language, culture, and history link them to other Latin Americans, and they have retained a separate identity despite a presence in this country that dates back even prior to Puerto Rico's annexation by the United States as a result of the Spanish-American War of 1898. Puerto Rican migration was especially spurred by the social and economic changes wrought by Operation Bootstrap in the late 1940s and 1950s. More than 40 percent of all Puerto Ricans now live on the mainland, half of them in New York City alone. In fact, twice as many Puerto Ricans live in New York as in San Juan, the capital of Puerto Rico.

Finally, there are 1.1 million Cubans in the United States, over 60 percent of whom are in Florida, concentrated primarily in the greater Miami area. The Cuban population is highly visible despite its comparatively small size because of its high concentration in one location, the political nature of Cubans' migration to the United States, and the high skill and educational levels of many of the migrants, especially those who came immediately after the 1959 revolution.

These three groups have many important differences as well as certain similarities, which will be discussed below. It should be pointed out, however, that the Latino population within the United States is growing increasingly diverse, with significant numbers of newer migrants arriving from the Dominican Republic, Central America (especially El Salvador, Guatemala, and Nicaragua), and Colombia. The English-speaking Caribbean is also well represented, especially Jamaica and Guyana, while political turmoil and poverty in Haiti have led to significant migration from that country to the eastern seaboard, primarily to Miami and New York.

Latin American and Caribbean Peoples in the United States

The emergence of Hispanics as one of this country's largest minority groups has sparked debate among Hispanics and non-Hispanics alike on the probable impact of this trend on U.S. society, politics, and culture. But discussions of the potential impact of an emerging Latino vote, Latino support for a particular issue, or the impact of Latino culture on the United States tend to obscure the very real differences among the many migrants

from Latin America and the Caribbean. Most share the same language, the same history of colonialism, and the same goal of improving their lives by coming to the United States. Beyond that, Latinos are an extremely diverse group, with different social class origins, different motivations for coming, and different objectives once they arrive. Add to this the growth of non-Spanish-speaking immigrants from Haiti, Jamaica, Guyana, and the West Indies, and we begin to get a better idea of the complexity of peoples of the Americas in this country.

Mexicans have been living in the United States since before the midnineteenth century, when close to one-half of their national territory was incorporated into the United States after the Mexican-American War. Mexicans have also been actively recruited since the late nineteenth century to work as laborers in this country, under a variety of schemes described in earlier chapters (such as the *braceros* television program discussed in Unit 5). The nearly 2,000–mile-long border between the two countries, the longest point of contact in the world between an industrialized nation and a developing one, has also presented a readily accessible alternative for Mexicans looking for better wages, education, and living conditions. Many Mexicans move back and forth across the border frequently and retain close ties with home. At the same time, the 1990 U.S. Census revealed that about 75 percent of Mexican-Americans are U.S.-born (and thus U.S. citizens), a fact that says much about the lengthy history of immigration between the two countries.

As the largest single group, Mexicans tend to dominate the statistical profile of Hispanics in the United States. However, about three-fourths of all Mexican-Americans, or Chicanos, are in California and Texas alone, where their influence is most pronounced. Despite decades of U.S. residency, it is mainly since the 1960s that Chicanos have begun to organize themselves and become active participants in local and state politics. They have made some gains in representation at the local, state, and national levels, and have worked with other Latinos to define a common agenda. The controversy over the Bell Gardens rezoning plan from 1990 to 1992 depicted in the program is one example of the political muscle Mexican-Americans may be able to exert as their political awareness and activism increase.

The Puerto Rican community shares with Mexican-Americans a history of forced incorporation into the United States as a result of war, in this case the Spanish-American War in 1898. Puerto Ricans had been recruited as agricultural workers since the turn of the century, although the flow of migrants accelerated sharply after World War II. By comparison with other Latinos, though, Puerto Ricans have had far less success in this country. For example, although they have a higher educational level than Chicanos, Puerto Ricans have higher poverty rates and higher unemployment; they also have nearly double the rate of female-headed families (close to 40 percent, compared with 19 percent for both Mexican-American and Cuban-American communities).

Researchers attribute many of the difficulties of the Puerto Rican community to the fact that they tended to migrate to the northeastern United States, a region that has lost much of its manufacturing and industrial base since the 1970s. Not only have they lost access to well-paid manufacturing jobs, but Puerto Ricans have become displaced in recent years by the influx of new migrants from the Caribbean and South America who are willing to work for less pay and can be offered fewer benefits as noncitizens. Puerto Ricans have also been more likely to experience racial discrimination to the extent that they have been perceived as blacks.

At the same time, and despite the grave social and economic conditions in the inner cities where most of them live, Puerto Ricans on the mainland have made vital contributions to this country, particularly in the cultural sphere. New York's Puerto Rican community has been a dynamic and influential actor in the realms of art, theater, film, music, and language. Today, Puerto Rican artists of all types, ages, and backgrounds are gaining widespread recognition and popularity even outside the Puerto Rican and other Latino communities. For example, Puerto Rican rap artists Anthony Boston and Rick Rodriguez have gained new popularity for rap with their rhymes in "Spanglish," a mix of Spanish and English words, while *Hanging with the Homeboys*, a depiction of Hispanic and African-American teens in New York's South Bronx by Puerto Rican filmmaker Joseph Vásquez, has received widespread critical acclaim.

The permanence and influence of this blend of island and mainland cultures is captured for some in the term *Nuyorican*, referring to the unique sense of identity felt by those who are not fully of either society but simultaneously belong to both. The term recalls the story of Puerto Rican painter Nick Quijano, interviewed in the program "Builders of Images," who discussed his experiences growing up in New York, his desire to return to the island, and the effect the two cultures have had on his art. Puerto Ricans interviewed in "The Americans" provide important insights into the complexities of the Nuyorican self-image.

Puerto Ricans on the mainland have also formed active community associations that draw upon the family and neighborhood cohesiveness of traditional island community life. These associations, such as the Maplewood community organization described in the anthology, address common inner city problems such as crime, drugs, teenage pregnancy, and high school dropout rates, along with more uniquely Puerto Rican issues involving cultural and linguistic barriers to success. Within the larger Latino community in the United States, Puerto Ricans bring an important measure of sophistication gained through years of experience with political organizing and action.

The Cuban-American community, on the other hand, has had a surprisingly high rate of success in the United States and political influence far beyond their numbers. Their status as political refugees fleeing a Communist country brought them special assistance from the U.S. government, and the relatively high number of educated professionals among the migrants soon led to the development of a thriving entrepreneurial climate in Miami, where the vast majority ultimately settled, after early government efforts to disperse them throughout the country.

In recent years, upper- and middle-class Cubans who constituted the bulk of the immediate postrevolution migration have been followed to Miami by younger, less-educated, working-class Cubans. The strength of the social networks within the Cuban community has enabled many of these newer migrants to achieve significant mobility within a relatively short time; one study of Cubans who arrived in the Mariel boatlift of 1980 found that only six years after their arrival in Miami, 28 percent were self-employed and another 45 percent were employed by other Cubans.

For many, these figures are evidence that the relative insularity of the Cuban community, including Cubans' retention of their language and culture and their establishment of a thriving ethnic enclave, has been the key to their success. Non-Cuban immigrants to Miami have not shared equally in the relative affluence of the Cuban-Americans, leading to tensions and rivalries among Cuban-Americans, Puerto Ricans, Haitians, and African-Americans in southern Florida.

The Debate over Assimilation

For most Hispanics the question has never been *whether* to assimilate, but only *how*, and how quickly. It is only more recently that some within Latino and other Caribbean communities have raised the question of whether they must lose their language and cultural distinctiveness in order to integrate into North American society. By and large, non-English-speaking immigrants from Latin America and the Caribbean who remain in this country have followed the same pattern as migrants from other regions of the world: although the first generation tends to retain its language while learning "survival" English, their children speak both the native tongue and English, and the third generation is almost exclusively English-speaking. It is the continual arrival of new Spanish-speaking immigrants to pre-existing ethnic communities that promotes the popular perception that Hispanics are unwilling to learn English.

The debate over bilingual education has become symbolic of the broader issue of assimilation. Latinos have tended to support bilingual education, and their support has in turn been seen by critics as an indication of their unwillingness to assimilate. Proponents of bilingualism, including most Latinos, argue that it is actually a means of overcoming the linguistic and cultural barriers that prevent full integration. The debate has become even more complex with the addition of new factors, such as the desire of some third- and fourth-generation Latinos to regain the language of their grandparents and, along with the language, a sense of pride in their unique ethnic heritage. Their views are supported by research indicating that bilingual children have significant cognitive advantages over monolingual children, after controlling for social class and other demographic factors.

Although debate continues on the merits of Hispanic migration, integration, and political ac-

tivism, there is no denying the profound impact that people from Latin America and the Caribbean have already made in their new country. The Hispanic population is growing rapidly, both through natural increase and the continued arrival of new migrants. If current trends continue, Hispanics will overtake African-Americans by the end of the 1990s as the largest minority group in the United States.

The concentration of Latinos in particular regions of the country has not prevented their impact from being felt far beyond the confines of their major communities. From food to music, art, and language, Americans of every color and class are exposed on a daily basis to the cultural contributions brought to this country by Latin American and Caribbean peoples. Change is a two-way process—people of Latin America and the Caribbean are themselves adapting to and being influenced by North American society. The norms of Puerto Rican family life are replaced by individualistic, youth-oriented North American values; the sons of Mexican immigrants marry the daughters of Korean immigrants; the children of Cuban political exiles declare they are not willing to return to Cuba even if that were possible. At the same time, as illustrated by the 1992 Los Angeles riots, the process of cultural intermingling is far from tension free.

Latin American and Caribbean people are here to stay, and are beginning to acknowledge that they have a stake in the system and valid interests to defend. The coming decades may answer the question of whether a new, pan-Latino culture is emerging or whether the many diverse Latino groups will retain their individual languages, customs, and identities. In the process of adapting to the irresistible forces of U.S. popular culture, though, Latin American and Caribbean people are themselves having an important and irreversible effect on what it means to be truly "American."

ASSIGNMENT

1. Before viewing the program, read:

    Modern Latin America, 3d ed., pp. 378–81; review pp. 221–53, 254–82, 301–3.

    Hispanic Culture within the United States (pp. 378–81), in chapter 11, "Latin America, the

United States, and the World," focuses on the Hispanic population in various parts of the United States. The selection also discusses the issue of assimilation, focusing on the likelihood that Hispanics will manage to retain their language and separate identity longer than any other non-English-speaking immigrant group.

Chapter 9, "The Caribbean: Colonies and Mini-States" (pp. 283–307). This overview of the region includes previously assigned sections on Haiti, the Dominican Republic, Jamaica, and Puerto Rico.

You should also review the following previously assigned readings:

Chapter 7, "Mexico: The Taming of a Revolution" (pp. 221–53).

Chapter 8, "Cuba: Late Colony, First Socialist State" (pp. 254–82).

2. View the program "The Americans."

3. After viewing the program, read:

Americas: An Anthology, chapter 12, pp. 335–72.

The introduction and readings in the anthology illustrate the diversity of the people who have come to this country from Latin America and the Caribbean, and highlight the similarities and differences among their struggles, experiences, and challenges. One reading focuses on the impact of the West Indian community on local culture in New York. Three readings focus on Hispanic political activism, while the final selection considers the broad influence Hispanics have exerted on North American popular culture.

UNIT REVIEW

After viewing the program and reading the assignments, you should be able to:

· List the major groups of Latin American and Caribbean peoples in the United States, their

different histories, experiences, economic status, and levels of political activism.

· Understand the variety of factors underlying immigration from Latin America and the Caribbean to the United States, and explain the reasons for the mixed reaction that has greeted immigrants from Latin America and the Caribbean in the 1980s and 1990s.

· Recognize the effect that their reception in the United States has had on the ultimate success and adaptation of various immigrant groups from Latin America and the Caribbean.

· Explain the controversy over the degree to which Latin American and Caribbean peoples should assimilate into North American society or, instead, seek integration while retaining their identities as separate and unique social groups.

· Evaluate the extent to which Latinos in the United States have evolved from being outside the mainstream to becoming aware of and using their economic and political power.

· Indicate some of the important ways in which the growing numbers of Latinos and non-Hispanic Caribbean peoples within the United States are influencing and changing U.S. society, politics, and culture.

SELF-TEST QUESTIONS

Multiple Choice

*Mark the letter of the response that **best** answers the question or completes the statement.*

_____ 1. Cubans immigrating to the United States after Castro came to power were regarded as:
a. illegal immigrants.
b. economic migrants.
c. political refugees.
d. temporary residents.

_____ 2. In addition to the three major Hispanic groups, which of the following coun-

tries are well represented among contemporary immigrant groups in the United States? *(Mark all that apply.)*
a. Haiti
b. The Dominican Republic
c. Argentina
d. Nicaragua

_____ 3. The growth of non-Spanish-speaking communities of Caribbean origin: *(Mark all that apply.)*
a. has had little impact on the dominant North American culture.
b. has enhanced the effectiveness of Latinos' political activism.
c. has introduced some tensions with Latino groups and U.S.-born African-Americans.
d. is especially important in certain urban centers of the eastern United States.

_____ 4. Most Latin American and Caribbean immigrants to the United States: *(Mark all that apply.)*
a. leave their countries for economic reasons.
b. are the poorest and least skilled residents of their home countries.
c. have above-average levels of education and occupational skills in their home countries.
d. are concentrated in the northeastern part of the United States.

_____ 5. Which of the following are important reasons for Mexican migration to the United States? *(Mark all that apply.)*
a. A history of Mexican labor recruitment by U.S. businesses.
b. The influence of strong social and kinship networks in the United States.
c. The high level of political repression within Mexico.
d. The new policy measures contained in the 1986 Simpson-Rodino Act.

_____ 6. By comparison with Mexican-Americans and Cuban-Americans, Puerto Ricans living on the mainland:

a. exhibit the highest levels of income and employment.
b. are among the most recent arrivals to the United States.
c. have the highest levels of poverty.
d. have had the least impact on U.S. popular culture.

_____ 7. The concentration of Cubans in Miami has: *(Mark all that apply.)*
a. dramatically raised the levels of unemployment and poverty among Hispanics there.
b. given Miami a Spanish-speaking majority population.
c. assisted new migrants with a ready-made social and economic network.
d. limited their political effectiveness to the state of Florida.

_____ 8. Which of the following statements are true of the debate over Hispanics' assimilation into this country? *(Mark all that apply.)*
a. The majority of Spanish-speaking immigrants tend to be monolingual in English by the third generation.
b. Latinos place little importance on the need for their children to speak English.
c. Hispanic support for bilingual education is indicative of their unwillingness to assimilate.
d. Latinos' physical concentration in certain areas has created de facto bilingual societies.

_____ 9. The Bell Gardens controversy is indicative of:
a. the growing awareness among Chicanos of their political rights.
b. the inability of political activists to motivate the general Chicano population.
c. the responsiveness of Anglo government officials to Chicano concerns.
d. the continued lack of Chicano political influence.

_____ 10. The English-speaking Caribbean country with the largest number of migrants to the United States is:

    a. the Dominican Republic.
    b. Trinidad.
    c. Barbados.
    d. Jamaica.

_____ 11. Haitian and West Indian immigrants to the United States differ from Spanish-speaking immigrants because:
    a. their differences have prevented them from forming a united political front.
    b. many have been confined to low-wage jobs as domestics.
    c. they have received official protection as political refugees.
    d. they have encountered racial discrimination.

_____ 12. U.S. reaction to immigrants from Latin America and the Caribbean:
    a. is uniformly hostile, making it nearly impossible for them to integrate into North American society.
    b. is completely different from the reception given to immigrants from other regions of the world.
    c. varies depending on migrants' perceived race, country of origin, occupational skills, and reasons for migration.
    d. has been particularly hospitable since 1986, when Congress passed new legislation to attract more highly skilled Hispanics.

_____ 13. The women profiled in the program and anthology illustrate the fact that for women of Latin American origin:
    a. the persistence of machismo has completely inhibited their community activism.
    b. their experience as immigrants has enhanced their activism as community leaders and political organizers.
    c. there is an unwillingness to continue to be identified with the Latino community.
    d. their most common feature is the desire to return to their home countries.

_____ 14. Which of the following are examples of the impact of Latin American and Caribbean immigration on U.S. popular culture? *(Mark all that apply.)*
    a. The popularity of reggae music.
    b. The widespread availability of Mexican-style food.
    c. The fact that few U.S. high schools offer Spanish-language instruction.
    d. The decreasing popularity of Spanish-language television channels.

_____ 15. Which is true of likely future trends for U.S. Hispanics?
    a. If current trends continue, Asians will surpass Hispanics as the second-largest minority group in the United States.
    b. Although the U.S.-born Hispanic population is increasing, the number of migrants from Latin America and the Caribbean is dropping rapidly.
    c. If current trends continue, Hispanics will surpass African-Americans as the largest minority group in the United States.
    d. The Hispanic population is declining due to increased numbers' choosing to return to their countries of origin.

True or False

_____ 16. Mexico, Argentina, and Colombia are the only three countries in the Western Hemisphere with a larger Spanish-speaking population than the United States.

_____ 17. Hispanic presence and influence in the southwestern United States is a relatively recent phenomenon.

_____ 18. The reason migrants from Central and South America end up in low-wage jobs in the United States is that they are typically the poorest of the poor in their home countries.

_____ 19. North Americans have greeted recent migrants from Latin America and the Caribbean with the same mixture of fear, suspicion, and resentment that met European immigrants in earlier eras.

_____ 20. Racism has been cited as one of the important factors hindering the success of Puerto Ricans living on the mainland.

_____ 21. In general, Latinos share the same political views no matter what their original nationality.

_____ 22. International migration differs from internal migration in that it is for the most part unaffected by the existence of social networks.

Identification/Short Answer

Define or describe the following terms, concepts, or persons, or answer the following questions. Answers should be no longer than a few sentences.

23. Why are Central Americans more likely than Chicanos to be working as domestics in Los Angeles?

24. Briefly outline the major arguments for and against bilingual education for Spanish-speaking children.

25. The Simpson-Rodino Act:

26. Mexican-American writer and filmmaker Luis Valdés has said, "We did not, in fact, come to the United States at all. The United States came to us." Explain.

27. Summarize the arguments against further immigration as outlined by former Colorado governor Richard Lamm.

28. Assimilation:

29. Luis Botitol:

30. Who are the *Nuyoricans,* and why are they significant?

QUESTIONS TO CONSIDER

1. How encompassing is Latino identification? Are Latinos within the United States likely to become a significant political voice as a unified group? Or are the differences among the various groups of Latinos based on nationality, class, and length of residency in the United States too deep for them to be allied in one political movement?

2. Should the United States have a policy of unrestricted immigration? Why or why not? If you believe in limiting immigration levels, how restricted do you think immigration to this

country should be? What measures should be used to enforce the restrictions?

3. Some critics fear that the continued influence of Latin American and Caribbean culture on the United States is undermining the essential "American" characteristics of this country. Do you agree? Why or why not? What does it mean to be American in the 1990s?

RESOURCES

Nonfiction

Cardoso, Lawrence A. *Mexican Immigration to the United States, 1897–1931.* Tucson: University of Arizona Press, 1980. A Mexican scholar's history of Mexican immigration to the United States during three decades of active recruitment of Mexican labor by U.S. companies.

Chávez, Leo R. *Shadowed Lives: Undocumented Immigrants in American Society.* Fort Worth, Tex.: Harcourt Brace Jovanovich College Publishers, 1992. A thoughtful, well-documented ethnography of primarily Mexican undocumented immigrants in the contemporary United States, based on extensive fieldwork in California and Texas.

Fitzpatrick, Joseph P. *Puerto Rican Americans: The Meaning of Migration to the Mainland,* 2d ed. Englewood Cliffs, N.J.: Prentice-Hall, 1987. A standard text on Puerto Rican–Americans, focusing on history, culture, religion, family, and migration patterns to and from the island and the U.S. mainland.

Gómez Quiñones, Juan. *Chicano Politics: Reality and Promise, 1940–1990.* Albuquerque: University of New Mexico Press, 1990. A thorough and up-to-date analysis of the political development of the second-largest ethnic minority in the United States, both before and after the Chicano movement of the 1960s.

Grasmuck, Sherri, and Patricia Pessar. *Between Two Islands: Dominican International Immigration.* Berke-

ley: University of California Press, 1991. The best available study to date of Dominican migration between the "two islands" of Manhattan and the Dominican Republic. Includes insightful ethnographic materials from fieldwork conducted in the Dominican Republic, as well as more limited survey data collected in New York.

Jasso, Guillermina, and Mark R. Rosenzweig. *The New Chosen People: Immigrants in the United States.* New York: Russell Sage Foundation, 1990. A detailed study of contemporary immigration to the United States, focusing on the specifics of U.S. law and the development of "chain migration" patterns and networks among immigrant families.

Lamm, Richard D., and Gary Imhoff. *The Immigration Time Bomb: The Fragmenting of America.* New York: Dutton, 1985. Former Colorado governor Richard Lamm's critique of the impact of new immigration, especially that from Spanish America, in the United States as of the mid-1980s.

Lemann, Nicholas. "The Other Underclass." *The Atlantic,* December 1991, 96–110. A thoughtful journalistic inquiry into the status of the Puerto Rican community on the U.S. mainland today, focusing on New York City.

Levine, Barry B., ed. *The Caribbean Exodus.* New York: Praeger, 1987. An informed anthology of readings on what may be the world's most emigration-prone region: the Caribbean.

Moore, Joan, and Harry Pachón. *Hispanics in the United States.* Englewood Cliffs, N.J.: Prentice-Hall, 1985. A comprehensive descriptive text on the subject, focusing on the three largest Hispanic groups: Mexicans, Puerto Ricans, and Cubans.

Niess, Frank. *A Hemisphere to Itself: A History of US–Latin American Relations.* London: Zed, 1990. A critical historical assessment of two centuries of U.S. expansion and intervention in Latin America.

Pedraza-Bailey, Silvia. *Political and Economic Migrants in America: Cubans and Mexicans.* Austin: University of Texas Press, 1985. A comparative study of the adaptation of Cuban (political) and Mexican (economic) migrants in the United States, relying on demographic and socioeconomic data from the 1960, 1970, and 1980 censuses.

Portes, Alejandro, and Robert L. Bach. *Latin Journey: Cuban and Mexican Immigrants in the United States*. Berkeley: University of California Press, 1985. A superb longitudinal study based on surveys of samples of Cuban and Mexican immigrants who entered the United States in 1973 and who were followed through 1979.

Portes, Alejandro, and Rubén G. Rumbaut. *Immigrant America: A Portrait*. Berkeley: University of California Press, 1990. See especially chapters 4 and 6. A definitive portrait of contemporary immigration to the United States, primarily from Latin America and Asia. The book presents a typology of the new immigrants and chapters on patterns of settlement, economic and political incorporation, psychological consequences, acculturation, English-language acquisition, and the second generation.

Reimers, David M. *Still the Golden Door: The Third World Comes to America*. New York: Columbia University Press, 1985. A leading historian's analysis of the origins of the "new immigration" to the United States from Third World countries in Asia and Latin America.

Rieff, David. *Los Angeles: Capital of the Third World*. New York: Simon & Schuster, 1991. A journalist's sketch of the transformation of Los Angeles as a result of massive new immigration primarily from Asia and Latin America.

Rumbaut, Rubén G. "The Americans: Latin American and Caribbean Peoples in the United States." In *Americas: New Interpretive Essays*, edited by Alfred Stepan. New York: Oxford University Press, 1992. An up-to-date detailed review of Latin American and Caribbean groups in the United States today, relying on data from the 1980 and 1990 censuses.

Rumbaut, Rubén G. "The Hispanic Prologue." In *A Hispanic Look at the Bicentennial*, edited by David Cardús, pp. 5–22. Houston: Institute of Hispanic Culture, 1978. A detailed, fascinating, and highly readable look at the Hispanic presence in North America (which antedated by a century the formation of an English colony at Jamestown, Virginia and later at Plymouth, Massachusetts).

Rumbaut, Rubén G. "Passages to America: Perspectives on the New Immigration." In *America at Century's End*, edited by Alan Wolfe, pp. 208–244. Berkeley: University of California Press, 1991. An analysis of the national and class origins of recent immigration to the United States, and of its impact on economic and cultural institutions, with an extended section on the politics of bilingualism and linguistic assimilation.

Sánchez, Joseph P. "Hispanic American Heritage." In *Seeds of Change: A Quincentennial Commemoration*, edited by Herman J. Viola and Carolyn Margolis, pp. 173–85. Washington D.C.: Smithsonian Institution Press, 1991. A richly illustrated companion book to the Smithsonian Institution's "Seeds of Change" exhibition—a quincentennial commemoration of Columbus's "discovery" of the New World and the global forces it set in motion.

Fiction

Alvarez, Julia. *How the García Girls Lost Their Accents*. Chapel Hill, N.C.: Algonquin Books, 1991. This novel about a prominent family that flees the Dominican Republic portrays the intricacies of immigrant family life in the United States, the fracturing effects of assimilation, and the power of culture and language.

García, Cristina. *Dreaming in Cuban*. New York: Knopf, 1992. A story of three generations of Cuban women and their separate responses to Castro's revolution, this is a novel of and by the second generation, the U.S.-born children of Cuban exiles who came to the United States after 1959.

Hijuelos, Oscar. *The Mambo Kings Play Songs of Love*. New York: Farrar Straus Giroux, 1989. Winner of the Pulitzer Prize, this novel of two young Cuban musicians who make their way from Havana to New York in the late 1940s captures the social and cultural context of pre-Castro and pre-Miami Cuban immigration to the Big Apple.

Thomas, Piri. *Down These Mean Streets*. New York: Knopf, 1967. A story of Puerto Ricans in New York. A classic from the late 1960s.

Films

Unless otherwise indicated, all films listed are available in VHS video format.

Crossover Dreams. 86 minutes, 1985. Rubén Blades stars as a salsa artist who becomes overconfident and back-stabbing after cutting his first album. Available in most video-rental outlets.

El Norte. 139 minutes, 1984. Refugees emigrate to the United States fleeing horrendous civil war conditions in Guatemala. Available in most video-rental outlets.

Hanging with the Homeboys. 90 minutes, 1992. A depiction of Hispanic and African-American teens in New York's South Bronx by Puerto Rican filmmaker Joseph Vásquez. Available in most video-rental outlets.

La Bamba. 108 minutes, 1987. At age 17 with three rock 'n roll hits, Richie Valens died in the fatal plane crash that also killed Buddy Holly and the Big Bopper, changing rock 'n roll forever. Available in most video-rental outlets.

Milagro Beanfield War. 117 minutes, 1988. directed by Robert Redford. A comedy/drama about the citizens of rural Milagro Valley, New Mexico who attempt to preserve their way of life against intrusive big money interests. Available in most video-rental outlets.

Stand and Deliver. 103 minutes, 1988. True story of a math teacher in the Los Angeles public schools who inspires his students to increase their standardized test scores. Available in most video-rental outlets.

Unit 13

Course Review

This course has presented a study of Latin America and the Caribbean from a variety of perspectives. This map presents an unfamiliar perspective of the Americas. WGBH Design

UNIT SUMMARY

The main goal of Unit 13 is to review the material covered in the telecourse, considering how the examples of the various countries we have studied over the past 12 weeks illustrate the four major themes: first, Latin America and the Caribbean have a distinct historical relationship to the rest of the world; second, this external relationship in combination with domestic policy decisions has created significant internal tensions; third, people of Latin America and the Caribbean have developed many innovative responses to their economic, social, political, and cultural situation; and fourth, their innovations have had and continue to have an important impact on the world order and the region's relationship to it.

A second goal for the unit is to consider what the future may hold for the Americas: how the region is likely to develop, and what the main issues in Latin America and the Caribbean's relationship with the United States will be. There is no television program for Unit 13.

KEY ISSUES

· What is unique about the relationship of Latin America and the Caribbean with the rest of the world?

· Why has the history of the region been marked by frequent internal tensions?

· What are some of the innovations developed by people from Latin America and the Caribbean in response to their economic, social, political, and cultural realities?

· How will the region's relationship to the world order continue to evolve?

· How do the country examples we have studied illustrate the themes of the television course?

· In light of what we have learned, what reasonable predictions can we make about the future course of Latin American and Caribbean development?

· What are likely to be some of the most important issues in the continuing relationship of the countries of Latin America and the Caribbean, individually and as a region, with the United States and the rest of the world?

GLOSSARY

Note: Some of the following terms are repeated here from earlier units.

bureaucratic-authoritarian regimes: new form of military government that first emerged in Brazil after 1964 and was established in Chile and Uruguay in 1973, and in Argentina in 1976. Although the regimes differed from one another, key shared features are the role of the military as a governing institution and the exclusion from power of all popular sectors.

dependency theory: perspective on Latin American political and economic history developed by Latin American scholars in the 1970s and 1980s. Argues that the countries of the Americas have not been able to achieve independent development goals because their economies are tied to and are dependent on the growth of other nations, particularly the industrialized economies of North America and Western Europe. Some proponents of this view also maintain that economic dependency leads almost inevitably to political authoritarianism.

Economic Commission on Latin America (ECLA): United Nations organization created in 1948 to analyze the economic conditions in the region. ECLA's home site of Santiago, Chile, and its mostly Latin American staff signaled an emphasis on Latin American perspectives on and prescriptions for the region's economic difficulties. Under Argentine economist Raúl Prebisch, the agency's first director, ECLA took on an aggressive role in international economic affairs and promoted the theory that the world economy had systematically disadvantaged developing economies such as those in the Americas.

economic liberalism: ideology imported from Europe that became well established among Latin American and Caribbean elites in the nineteenth century, encouraging free trade and laissez-faire economic policies; economic liberalism justified the region's integration into the world economy as an exporter of foodstuffs and raw materials as the best means of achieving economic progress.

export diversification: the effort made by many Latin American countries in the mid- to late twentieth century to expand their economic growth through production of nontraditional exports.

export-import growth: economic model followed throughout the Americas from the late nineteenth century through the 1930s; based on the export of raw materials and agricultural goods, products believed to represent the region's "comparative advantage," in exchange for imports of manufactured goods, luxury items, and capital from the industrial powers of North America and Europe.

hegemony: the uncontested influence that one country has over others at a regional or international level. The influence may include one or more of the following types: military, economic, political, cultural, and/or ideological power. The United States exercised unparalleled hegemony over the Caribbean basin (those countries in and around the Caribbean Sea) during the first two decades of the twentieth century, when at various times it occupied Nicaragua, Haiti, the Dominican Republic, and Cuba, and constructed the Panama canal.

import-substituting industrialization (ISI):   economic strategy of reducing economic dependence and vulnerability to external economic fluctuations by developing local industries. The strategy, which sought to substitute locally produced manufactured goods for formerly imported goods, was adopted by many Latin American countries in the 1930s, 1940s, and 1950s.

the "lost decade":   term used by many Latin American analysts to describe the 1980s, a decade in which per capita GNP in the region fell by almost 10 percent, investment declined, public sector expenditures shrank, and many of the countries in the region struggled to meet payments on their massive foreign debts.

modernization theory: theory developed in the United States in the late 1950s and early 1960s which held that economic growth and industrialization had been delayed in the Americas but would ultimately bring about political democracy and greater social equity.

multinational corporation (MNC):   a company with bases of operation in more than one country, although the home office is generally in one of the advanced industrial countries. MNCs typically are both very large and highly mobile, able to take advantage of low wages, government incentives, trade conditions, or other favorable market conditions in different places around the world. MNCs also tend to be quite influential in developing country economies due to the magnitude of capital and technology they possess.

Organization of American States (OAS):   an inter-American organization established in 1948 to serve as the diplomatic decision-making body of the Western Hemisphere. According to the charter, OAS members are committed to the principles of nonintervention (sought by the Latin American members as protection for national sovereignty) and continental solidarity (sought by the United States as part of its strategy to resist Soviet expansionism), along with economic cooperation, social justice, democracy, and human rights. All independent Latin American and Caribbean nations except Cuba are members, along with the United States and Canada, but throughout most of its history the organization has served primarily to endorse the policies of its most powerful member, the United States.

popular classes: term used to refer to Latin America's lower classes of urban workers, rural laborers, and peasants, many of whom work in the informal economy.

populism: political model that emerged in many Latin American countries in the 1930s and 1940s as a response to the challenges and socioeconomic changes brought about by rapid industrialization. In general, populist leaders emphasized state involvement in promoting economic growth, based on a coalition of urban working classes, organized labor, the military, and nationalistic entrepreneurs. Nationalism and sovereignty were important themes to populists, who included Juan Perón in Argentina, Lázaro Cárdenas in Mexico, Getúlio Vargas in Brazil, and Victor Raúl Haya de la Torre in Peru.

revolution: seizure of state power, usually by violent means, for the purpose of bringing about radical change in political, economic, and social structures, relationships, and values.

The Rio Pact: collective defense treaty signed in 1947 in Rio de Janeiro by the United States and most Latin American countries; part of a U.S. effort to redesign the Pan-American system better to defend against international Communism. The Rio Pact defined an attack on any American state, from inside or outside the hemisphere, as an attack on all, requiring collective measures to counter the aggression.

structural adjustment policies: economic stabilization measures required by the IMF and the World Bank as a condition of extending new loans; typically these measures involve a reduction in the size of the public sector, elimination of government subsidies, devaluation of the national currency, promotion of exports, and elimination of most barriers to foreign investment.

OVERVIEW

The goal of this review chapter is to integrate the information we have gained over the past 12 weeks and examine how the many experiences of different countries we studied help to illustrate the themes of the *Americas* telecourse.

We were first introduced to the themes of the course in Unit 1. First, *Latin America and the Caribbean have a distinct historical relationship to the rest of the world* based on the experience of conquest, colonization, and settlement. In the first two units of the course, "The Introduction" and "Legacies

of Empire: From Conquest to Independence," we learned that the encounter of indigenous peoples with the Europeans and Africans, in combination with later processes of international migration, produced racially and culturally diverse societies with a mixed heritage from many ethnic groups. We also discovered how the mercantilist, export-oriented economic systems first established during the colonial period conditioned the options available to national policymakers in the early post-colonial period, and affected the shape of the region's subsequent economic development.

Throughout this course, we explored how Latin America and the Caribbean's unique relationship to the external world has been marked by:

1. a history of dependency on external powers, especially the industrial powers of Western Europe, the United States, and Japan, along with a corresponding vulnerability to events and decisions occurring outside the region;

2. delayed and/or partial industrialization in most countries of the region, with a heavy reliance on foreign capital and technology; and

3. the dependency of most of the region's economies on the production of exports, with a gradual move away from traditional exports of raw materials and agricultural products to modern manufactures and assembly products.

For these reasons, as we have seen, the issue of national sovereignty in all its forms has been especially important throughout the region. In "Get Up, Stand Up: The Problems of Sovereignty" (Unit 10) we saw how a natural resource, in this case Jamaican bauxite, may have tremendous value as a symbol of national sovereignty in the Americas. Examples from other units include copper in Chile, oil in Mexico and Argentina, and tin in Bolivia. But just as Latin American and Caribbean countries' sense of vulnerability is not restricted to the economic sphere, neither is the issue of sovereignty. Numerous direct and indirect interventions in their internal affairs by foreign powers, especially the United States, have been critical events in the history of nearly all the countries of the region.

A second overall theme explored in the course is that *these characteristics, along with key domestic political and economic choices, have created numerous internal tensions.* The social classes that make up contemporary Latin American and Caribbean societies have in most cases not shared equally in the benefits of economic development, leaving some groups with a life-style comparable to that of the middle and upper classes in the United States while others live in conditions of extreme poverty.

Struggles to gain a bigger share of the economic pie and to open up the political system are a recurrent theme in the history of the region. These struggles have led to many revolutionary efforts (for example, those we studied in El Salvador, Guatemala, and Peru) and have at times produced revolutionary regimes such as those in Mexico, Cuba, Nicaragua, and Grenada. These processes were the subject of "Fire in the Mind: Revolutions and Revolutionaries" (Unit 11). At other times the internal tensions of the region have produced political leaders committed to changing the distribution of economic and political power and benefits without violent revolution. Examples of such leaders covered in a number of the units of this course are Argentina's Juan Perón (Unit 3), Peru's Haya de la Torre (Unit 3), Getúlio Vargas in Brazil (Unit 4), Salvador Allende in Chile (Unit 7), Michael Manley in Jamaica (Unit 10), and Jacobo Arbenz in Guatemala (Unit 11).

Frequently, the military has reacted to internal tensions by imposing strict controls over political and civil liberties, supporting dictatorial rule, and, in the recent past, establishing bureaucratic-authoritarian states. The shift to bureaucratic-authoritarian states and the impact on Argentina, Brazil, and Chile were illustrated in "The Garden of Forking Paths: Dilemmas of National Development" (Unit 3), "Capital Sins: Authoritarianism and Democratization" (Unit 4), and "In Women's Hands: The Changing Roles of Women" (Unit 7).

A third theme of the course is that *the peoples of Latin America and the Caribbean have shown great creativity and have developed many innovative responses to their economic, social, political, and cultural situations.* Throughout the course we have been introduced to pioneering individuals, institutions, and groups that have made important contributions to improving the welfare of their communities and countries, and beyond. From revolutionaries to legislators, poor families to wealthy industrialists, community religious leaders to internationally recognized artists and writers, the people of Latin

America and the Caribbean share the important qualities of engagement, originality, imagination, and the determination to build a better future.

For example, Unit 7's program, "In Women's Hands," showed us poor women in Chile working together to create communal soup kitchens and to use their folk art to document human rights violations (the *arpilleras*). In "Builders of Images: Writers, Artists, and Popular Culture" (Unit 9), we learned of the many innovative cultural expressions of artists, musicians, writers, and filmmakers throughout the region. We also examined the relationship that contemporary and historical artists in the region have drawn between their work and important social and political issues and movements in the Americas.

"Mirrors of the Heart: Color, Class, and Identity" (Unit 6) explored the interaction of different races and ethnic groups in the Americas, and the realities of continued racial and ethnic prejudice within diverse and multicultural societies throughout the hemisphere. This unit, along with the others, illustrates the unique ways in which the different peoples of the region have managed to retain their individual cultures and identities while also living in close contact with one another. Across the Americas, religion, language, and local traditions mirror the interplay of a wide range of cultural influences.

In "Miracles Are Not Enough: Continuity and Change in Religion" (Unit 8), we studied the role of religion in the Americas, and saw how indigenous and African influences continue to play a critical role in Latin America's religious beliefs and practices. We also learned of the important contributions to theology and practice developed by Latin American Christians, and the role of the region's institutional churches, particularly during the last quarter of this century, on behalf of human rights and greater justice in their societies, including support for grassroots institutions that help people in their struggle for these goals.

Finally, we have seen that *the region's relationship to the world order continues to evolve,* in part because of these innovations and their impact. The nations of Latin America and the Caribbean are highly interdependent, not only on one another but also on political, social, and economic trends around the world. For example, in "Continent on the Move: Migration and Urbanization" (Unit 5) we learned how internal and international movements of people have been, and continue to be, tied to the forces unleashed by domestic and international economic development, as well as to more exclusively domestic factors such as civil war, revolution, and repression.

"The Americans: Latin American and Caribbean Peoples in the United States" (Unit 12) explored the impact on the United States of the more than 20 million people of Latin American and Caribbean origin now living in the nation. The cultural ties of these "new neighbors" to their countries of origin are another strand in the complex web of interdependence linking north and south in the Western Hemisphere. Those ties also include the effects of international narcotics traffic, portrayed in Unit 10's program, "Get Up, Stand Up"; the ongoing problem of paying for the region's high external debt, first introduced in Unit 4's program, "Capital Sins"; and the continuing importance given by the United States to political developments in the region, illustrated as recently as the 1980s and 1990s by U.S. involvement in El Salvador and Nicaragua's civil wars ("Fire in the Mind"), and the invasion of Panama and subsequent extradition and trial of General Manuel Antonio Noriega ("Get Up, Stand Up").

Prospects for Latin American and Caribbean Development

It is always somewhat risky to make predictions about the future, especially in a region with as great a degree of complexity as the Americas. However, there are certain trends in Latin American and Caribbean societies that we can expect to persist for the foreseeable future, and to continue to exert an important influence on the course of the region's development.

For example, we know that by the end of this century, Latin America will be primarily urban and will contain some of the largest cities in the world, Mexico City and São Paulo. The problems depicted in Unit 5 of unchecked urban growth, squatter developments, pollution, and marginal living conditions for many migrants which Mexico has experienced are already shared by its neighbors throughout the region, and these problems can be expected to become even more pressing as migration continues.

We also know that throughout the Americas a high percentage of the population (as much as half in some countries) is under the age of fifteen. Meeting the future needs of these millions of young people for education, jobs, housing, health care, and other essentials will pose an enormous challenge to the economies and political systems of the region. The burden is especially great as they seek to recover from the "lost decade" of the 1980s, during which per capita GNP actually fell by about 10 percent.

Based on our study of the region's history, we can also predict that internal struggles among its social classes and ethnic groups will continue to influence the course of each country's political development. The "Epilogue" chapter in the textbook provides a comparative framework for analyzing the different experiences of key countries we have studied. The authors classify the major actors within each society according to class, and discuss how at various times one or more of these social classes has allied itself with the main institutions (church, state, and military) and/or the foreign sector in order to obtain or hold on to political power. This analysis helps clarify the elements that many countries in the region hold in common, as well as the ways in which they differ from one another.

For the region as a whole, it is clear that its unique relationship to the world order, its economic development patterns, and the ongoing struggle among social classes and ethnic groups have produced deeply rooted tensions. No one social group or development "solution" is likely to be capable of eliminating such profound divisions, which are likely to pose as great a challenge and constraint for the region's future political leadership as for those in the past. The nations of the Americas also remain vulnerable to events and actors outside the region. To a large degree, economic and political development in each country, and in the region as a whole, must continue to respond to the pressures and opportunities presented by global economic trends.

There are also several "unknowns," important social actors and trends that will undoubtedly exert influence on the course of Latin American and Caribbean development, but whose effects we are not able to predict with much certainty. For example, Unit 7 explored the changing roles of women in the region, and made clear that women's choices, expectations, and participation in the social, economic, and political systems of their countries are continuing to evolve. The regional economic crisis over most of the past decade has led women to participate in the formal and informal labor markets in ever increasing numbers; that experience has been tapped by many in the region's feminist movements, especially at the grassroots levels. Although we can expect the changes in gender roles to continue, we can only guess as to the magnitude and direction of the subsequent changes women will effect throughout their societies.

Similarly, although we explored the impact of religion and the diversity of religious beliefs in the Americas in Unit 8, we reached no firm conclusion as to where the institutional and alternative churches are headed in the next century. Are the Americas likely to produce another important theological innovation with impact comparable to that of liberation theology? Is the influence of institutional churches likely to wane over time as more and more people respond to the appeal of Pentecostal churches? Will the movement toward spiritist religions we studied in Brazil become more widespread across the region? Religion will undoubtedly remain a major and influential force in the lives of many people in Latin America and the Caribbean, but the direction and impact of that force is not yet clear.

A third important category is the future of ethnic and race relations in the Americas. As was illustrated in Unit 6 and throughout the television course, the degree to which certain groups have benefited from economic growth has largely been governed by their race or ethnic heritage. It still remains true throughout much of the region that prospects for economic and social advancement are linked to the color of one's skin, and that those with whiter skin or more European features tend to be in the higher social strata.

But the multicultural diversity of Latin American and Caribbean societies has allowed for more complex perceptions of race than in North American society, as well as some mobility (recall the example of the physician Enrique Frías in the program "Mirrors of the Heart"). The question is whether the continued discrimination against people based on race and ethnicity will ultimately become a focus for profound discontent, even revolution. Some would argue, for example, that the alienation and oppression of Peru's indigenous

peoples has been partially responsible for the growth of that country's Shining Path guerrilla movement, examined in Unit 11.

The Future Course of U.S.–Latin American Relations

Finally, in considering the future of U.S. relations with the rest of the Americas, we need to remember the lengthy and complex history connecting the two parts of the hemisphere. Although the end of the Cold War has removed one rationale for U.S. involvement in regional affairs, the pressure of the many so-called transnational issues continues to build. Increasing global interdependence guarantees that neither the United States nor any one Latin American or Caribbean nation can by itself resolve the problems of international drug trafficking, rain forest destruction, air pollution, population growth, or foreign debt, to name just a few examples.

Similarly, economic self-interest ensures that international trade and investment will continue to be a driving force in the economies of the region, including that of the United States, which has become increasingly interested in a regional free trade agreement. Discussions on such an agreement have drawn public attention to the fact that a multinational corporation's decision to invest or move from one country to another has a major impact on labor migration, jobs creation, and economic prosperity in the United States as well as in the rest of the hemisphere. Finally, the large and growing population with Latin American and Caribbean roots now living in the United States ensures that a segment of North Americans will press for continued attention to the needs and aspirations of their families' countries of origin in the south, and that their influence over this country's foreign policy will likely increase in the future.

It seems clear, then, that the intricate and overlapping ties binding the Americas together will not only persist into the twenty-first century, but will probably grow. The world in the early 1990s seems poised between fracturing along nationalist and ethnic lines, and, perhaps simultaneously, uniting into major, regional blocs. It could be that the concept of national sovereignty which has been so critical in the history of the Americas will be consigned to the historical trash heap. Another possibility, however, is that the multipolar nature of the changing international environment will only reinforce the desire of individual nations in the region for sovereignty within the world community, and that economic integration will intensify the value placed on other dimensions of national sovereignty.

The challenge for the United States will be to fashion new rationales to govern its actions in the hemisphere, respecting the sovereignty of Latin American and Caribbean nations while also protecting U.S. interests and promoting common concerns. Similarly, Latin American and Caribbean nations will be challenged to respond to the changed international environment, seeking their own balance in an interdependent and multipolar world. One thing is clear: the issues you have studied in this course will remain the focus of public debate and individual decisions into the next century.

ASSIGNMENT

Read *Modern Latin America,* 3d ed., pp. 344–81, 382–406.

Chapter 11, "Latin America, the United States, and the World" (pp. 344–81), traces the history of U.S.–Latin American relations in their political, social, economic, and military dimensions.

The Epilogue, "What Future for Latin America" (pp. 382–406), provides a comparative analysis of political history in Argentina, Chile, Brazil, Peru, Mexico, Cuba, and El Salvador, and makes projections for future developments in the region based on past and current trends.

UNIT REVIEW

After reading the assignment, you should be able to:

· Understand the historical basis for the distinct relationship of Latin America and the Caribbean with the rest of the world.

· Explain the reasons for the region's history of serious and frequent internal tensions.

· Describe some of the innovations developed by Latin American and Caribbean peoples in response to their social and political realities.

· Recognize the parameters within which the relationship of Latin America and the Caribbean to the world order will most likely continue to evolve.

· Use several examples of different countries to illustrate the various themes of the television course.

· Make predictions about the future course of Latin American and Caribbean development.

· Identify some of the most important issues that will continue to characterize the relationship of the countries of Latin America and the Caribbean, individually and as a region, with the United States, and with the rest of the world.

SELF-TEST QUESTIONS

Multiple Choice

*Mark the letter of the response that **best** answers the question or completes the statement.*

_____ 1. Which of the following is/are no longer perceived as being of major concern for the United States in the Americas? *(Mark all that apply.)*
  a. Containment of international Communism
  b. Civil war and domestic instability
  c. Opportunities for foreign investment
  d. Illegal immigration to the United States

_____ 2. By the end of World War I, the United States exercised virtual hegemony in which part of Latin America?

a. The entire region
b. The Caribbean basin
c. The Southern Cone
d. The Andean region

_____ 3. Only one of the following is not an example of the unique position of Latin America and the Caribbean vis-à-vis the developed industrial powers. It is:
   a. the reliance of several countries, including Mexico and Brazil, on foreign laborers.
   b. the frequency of military intervention by outside powers in the Caribbean.
   c. the growth of agro-export industries in Central America.
   d. the historical association of nationalism with anti-imperialism in Cuba.

_____ 4. The theory of economic liberalism that dominated national policy making in the Americas until the 1930s was especially criticized by:
   a. foreign investors.
   b. Latin American nationalists.
   c. the landowning elites.
   d. the peasantry.

_____ 5. Internal tensions over the distribution of economic benefits have led to revolutionary movements since 1960 in which of the following countries? *(Mark all that apply.)*
   a. El Salvador
   b. Peru
   c. Grenada
   d. Costa Rica

_____ 6. Beginning with the Truman administration and continuing for close to 40 years, U.S. policy in Latin America: *(Mark all that apply.)*
   a. was based on the idea that events in the region had no impact on U.S. policy.
   b. included the negotiation of a series of bi- and multilateral mutual defense assistance pacts.
   c. used a variety of measures to mobilize Latin America in the fight to contain Soviet expansion.

   d. included the provision of economic aid in order to promote regional democratization.

_____ 7. As we learned in Units 9 and 12, authors and artists throughout the history of Latin America and the Caribbean have tended to:
   a. seek to emulate U.S. popular culture.
   b. remain aloof from the important social and political issues of their times.
   c. use their work to comment on important social and political issues of their times.
   d. make up the majority of the region's migrants to the United States due to the lack of free expression in their countries.

_____ 8. The Economic Commission for Latin America: *(Mark all that apply.)*
   a. was an OAS agency created in the 1980s to resolve the region's debt crisis.
   b. was a UN agency created in the 1940s to analyze the economic problems of the region.
   c. was a U.S. agency created in the 1950s to promote a regional free trade agreement.
   d. was an IMF committee created in the 1980s charged with overseeing structural adjustment in the region.

_____ 9. Which U.S. program in Latin America was widely viewed by 1970 as having failed?
   a. The war on drugs
   b. The Alliance for Progress
   c. Counter-insurgency training
   d. Debt repayment schemes

_____ 10. One of the greatest unknowns with regard to women in Latin America and the Caribbean is whether they will:
   a. continue to be restricted to the home and local community.
   b. play a larger role in their countries' political systems.

c. have any impact on the economies of their countries.

d. develop local and regional feminist organizations.

_____ 11. One of the key problems with massive foreign borrowing by Latin American countries in the mid- to late 1970s was:

a. much of the borrowed money was squandered by powerful national elites.

b. the loans weren't available on an equal basis to all countries.

c. the loans were made at very high interest rates.

d. the loans were invested in long-range projects to improve productivity.

_____ 12. The innovation and achievements of which of the following Latin American authors was recognized with the Nobel Prize for literature? *(Mark all that apply.)*

a. Jorge Luis Borges

b. Gabriel García Márquez

c. Gabriela Mistral

d. Pablo Neruda

_____ 13. The 1980s are known as the "lost decade" in Latin America because:

a. civilian governments throughout the region lost the opportunity to regain power.

b. respect for human rights generally took a step backward.

c. revolutionary movements became especially active in several countries.

d. per capita income declined and economic growth was slow or nonexistent.

_____ 14. According to the analytic framework presented in the textbook "Epilogue," the popular classes in Latin America include: *(Mark all that apply.)*

a. military officers.

b. urban students and professionals.

c. rural peasants.

d. industrial workers.

_____ 15. An important issue for political and economic development in the Americas for the 1990s and beyond is likely to be: *(Mark all that apply.)*

a. the possible decline of sovereignty as a major national policy priority.

b. the hardships involved in repaying the massive foreign debt.

c. the continued lack of work force participation by women.

d. the international appeal of Latin American music and dance.

_____ 16. The military in Latin America and the Caribbean: *(Mark all that apply.)*

a. is unlikely to resume its intervention in politics in the coming decades.

b. is solidly behind the civilian governments in many countries that once had bureaucratic-authoritarian regimes.

c. cannot be relied upon to stay out of politics if crisis conditions recur.

d. wields considerable power in many nominally democratic countries.

_____ 17. Which of the following is likely to remain true of the Caribbean island countries for the foreseeable future? They will continue to: *(Mark all that apply.)*

a. be heavily influenced by their large populations of indigenous people.

b. experience internalized racism without public segregation.

c. be economically vulnerable and dependent on the export of only a few products.

d. be the preferred destination for large numbers of migrants from elsewhere in the region.

True or False

_____ 18. Since the 1880s, the nations of the Americas have been systematically excluded from the capitalist world system.

_____ 19. The internationalization of the media has helped to extend the impact and influence of Latin American and Caribbean popular culture around the world.

_____ 20. Latin America's middle classes have tended to support military coups during periods of extreme crisis.

_____ 21. Politics in the Americas will continue to be decided by the interplay among key social groups.

_____ 22. The recent wave of change in women's roles throughout Latin America and the Caribbean seems to have come to an end.

_____ 23. Because birth rates are declining throughout much of Latin America and the Caribbean, the pressure of population growth is no longer of much concern to national leaders.

_____ 24. The war on drugs is seen by some Latin Americans as a reaffirmation of U.S. hegemony in the region.

which Latin America and the Caribbean were integrated into the world economy?

28. Give three examples from the course programs illustrating the types of internal tensions that characterize the nations of Latin America and the Caribbean and have had an important impact on domestic policy decisions.

29. Name two religious innovations that originated in Latin America.

30. Name three issues that are likely to be of growing importance in U.S. relations with Latin America and the Caribbean in the 1990s and beyond.

Identification/Short Answer

Define or describe the following terms, concepts, or persons, or answer the following questions. Answers should be no longer than a few sentences.

25. Raúl Prebisch:

26. Rio Pact:

27. What was the colonial policy of mercantilism and what was its impact on the manner in

QUESTIONS TO CONSIDER

1. Can Latin American and Caribbean countries eventually escape the legacy of conquest, foreign domination, and dependency which has continued to haunt them into the twentieth century? How? What kind of economic and political policies would you recommend to increase self-determination and self-sufficiency in the Americas?

2. Imagine you have just been appointed minister of finance for a Latin American or Caribbean country (select any one covered during this course). Your job is to advise the government on spending priorities. What are some

of the domestic tensions that will affect and limit your options in areas such as spending for health, housing, education, defense, industrial production? Given your country's limited financial resources and the many competing needs, how will you go about setting priorities and responding to these internal tensions? How do these factors change depending on the country you choose? For example, if you have been thinking of yourself as minister of finance for Brazil, how would your situation be different if you now became the minister of finance for Jamaica?

3. An important theme of this course is the many innovations developed by individuals and communities in Latin America and the Caribbean. What examples can you give of ways in which people of Latin American and Caribbean origin living in the United States have brought the tradition of innovation and creativity with them? Are your examples similar to those we have studied throughout the region during this course? Are there other examples that are unique to the situation of Latin American and Caribbean communities in this country?

4. In the aftermath of the Cold War and the dissolution of East-West blocs, Latin American and Caribbean nations have more freedom to build relationships with other parts of the world. To what extent will their relationships focus on the rest of the world in addition to or to the exclusion of the United States? For example, which region or regions will become more important to Latin American and Caribbean countries, and which region or regions will lose importance? What do you think will be the most important issues affecting the region's relationships with the rest of the world?

5. The textbook prologue is titled "Why Latin America?" Now that you have completed the telecourse, what reasons would you give for why it is important to increase our understanding of the Americas? In what ways has your own understanding been changed or reshaped?

Appendix

Answer Key

Answers indicate where information can be found for further review.

Unit 1, The Introduction

1. b (anthology, study guide)
2. b (textbook, study guide)
3. d (anthology, study guide)
4. a, d (anthology, study guide)
5. a, b, c (textbook, study guide)
6. a, b, c (anthology, study guide)
7. a (anthology, study guide)
8. c (anthology, textbook, study guide)
9. a, b, c (anthology, textbook, study guide)
10. d (anthology)
11. b, c (textbook, study guide)
12. a (anthology, study guide)
13. False (anthology, study guide)
14. True (anthology)
15. True (anthology, study guide)
16. True (textbook)
17. False (anthology, textbook)
18. False (study guide, textbook)
19. False (anthology, study guide)
20. False (anthology)
21. Europeans came first as colonizers in the late fifteenth and early sixteenth centuries; they later forcibly brought Africans as slaves beginning in the midsixteenth century. Asians came much later, most in the twentieth century, as laborers and settlers. (textbook, study guide)

22. Spanish, Portuguese, English, French, Dutch, Quechua, Creole. (anthology, textbook, study guide)
23. World's longest river, 3,300 miles long, which flows from Peru across Brazil to the Atlantic Ocean. (anthology, study guide)
24. A theory developed by North American scholars in the 1950s and early 1960s which proposed that economic growth had been delayed in Latin America and the Caribbean but would eventually occur there as it had in the United States. Proponents of this view also argued that the processes of growth and industrialization would bring about political democracy and greater social equity. (textbook, study guide)
25. Any three stereotypes could be correct; Smith and Skidmore list about 20 on page 4 of the textbook. The most common are dark-skinned, quick-tempered, emotional, religious, backward, and lazy. (textbook)
26. In the highlands of Central America, especially Guatemala, and in the rain forests of Central and South America. (anthology, study guide)
27. A perspective on Latin American political and economic history developed by Latin American scholars in the 1970s and 1980s. Argues that Latin American countries have not been able to pursue independent development goals because their economies are tied to and dependent on the growth of other nations, particularly the industrialized economies of North America and Western Eu-

rope. Many adherents of this view also maintain that economic dependency leads almost inevitably to political authoritarianism. (textbook, study guide)

28. GNP per capita is the total value of production of a country during the course of one year. GNP per capita is the total production divided by the number of citizens, giving a figure of average income per person that is a very rough estimate of the average standard of living in the country. (textbook, study guide)

Unit 2, Legacies of Empire: From Conquest to Independence

1. c (textbook)
2. a, b, c (textbook)
3. b (anthology)
4. a (anthology, study guide)
5. a, b, c (textbook, study guide)
6. b, c (anthology, textbook, study guide)
7. b (textbook, study guide)
8. a, d (anthology, textbook, study guide)
9. c (textbook, study guide)
10. c (anthology, study guide)
11. a, c (textbook, study guide)
12. d (anthology)
13. b (anthology, textbook, study guide)
14. a, c (textbook)
15. True (anthology, textbook, study guide)
16. False (textbook)
17. False (anthology, textbook, study guide)
18. True (anthology, textbook, study guide)
19. True (anthology)
20. True (anthology, textbook, study guide)
21. False (anthology, textbook, study guide)
22. False (textbook, study guide)
23. True (anthology, study guide)
24. The Spanish were able to conquer the Aztec and Inca empires due, in part, to the superiority of Spanish military equipment and tactics; the Aztecs' identification of Cortés with the god Quetzacoatl; the centralization of the Aztec and Inca empires; the hostility of many indigenous groups toward one another; and the outbreak of smallpox, which killed large numbers of the indigenous peoples. (textbook)

25. Spain relied largely on indigenous labor, Portugal largely on enslaved Africans; Spain emphasized both mining and agriculture, while Portugal relied more exclusively on agriculture, especially sugar cane, before the discovery of gold around 1695; Spain attempted to exert greater control over its colonies than did Portugal and more forcefully resisted their later attempts to become independent. (textbook)

26. Brazil: gold, sugar; Cuba: sugar; Mexico: cotton, silver; Peru: silver. (textbook)

27. Local governors responsible directly to the monarchy; part of a reformed system of colonial administration imposed by the Bourbon king Charles II in the late eighteenth century as a means of reasserting royal control over the colonies. Most intendants were born in Spain and sent to the Americas, rather than being chosen from among the *criollos*, as the *corregidores* they replaced often had been. (textbook, study guide)

28. Persons of mixed European and African ancestry. By 1825, *mulattos* in combination with black descendants of Africans constituted over half of the population of Brazil. (study guide, textbook)

29. Large agricultural estate in Spanish America. The *hacienda* system was sometimes semifeudal in nature, with the owner (which could be a family or an institution, such as a church or convent) controlling tracts of land of various sizes, sometimes substantial, along with entire villages of dependent laborers. The growth of *haciendas* throughout Spanish America was associated with the emergence of a native-born elite. (anthology, textbook, study guide)

30. Colonial administrative patterns had fostered the development of powerful local and regional authorities who exercised a great deal of autonomy. The wars for independence also elevated military leaders to positions of power and respect. Finally, the weakness of the state in the postindependance period and the ensuing struggles and civil wars made it more likely that strong local military leaders or *caudillos* would emerge to provide stability, some assuming national political control. (anthology, textbook, study guide)

Unit 3, *The Garden of Forking Paths: Dilemmas of National Development*

1. d (anthology, textbook, study guide)
2. a (textbook)
3. a, c (anthology, textbook)
4. b, c (anthology, textbook)
5. c (textbook)
6. a (textbook, study guide)
7. b (anthology, textbook, study guide)
8. c, d (textbook, study guide)
9. a, d (anthology, textbook, study guide)
10. d (anthology, textbook)
11. a, d (anthology, textbook, study guide)
12. c (program, anthology, textbook, study guide)
13. b (program, anthology, textbook)
14. a (program, anthology, study guide)
15. b (program, textbook)
16. a (anthology, textbook, study guide)
17. b, d (program, textbook)
18. False (textbook, study guide)
19. True (anthology, textbook, study guide)
20. False (anthology, textbook)
21. False (program, study guide)
22. False (textbook)
23. Disputed islands off the coast of Argentina which are controlled by the British and populated by British citizens. Argentina provoked war with Britain in 1982 in an attempt to remove what it perceived as a vestige of colonialism, but was badly defeated, leading to the resignation of General Galtieri, head of the military junta, and the military's decision to step down from power. (program, anthology, textbook, study guide)
24. Argentina's first civilian president after the bureaucratic-authoritarian regime of 1976–83. Alfonsín took on the challenges of prosecuting military personnel and police for human rights abuses and of addressing the country's serious economic problems. (textbook, study guide)
25. Argentine dictator from 1829 to 1852, responsible for defeating rival *caudillos* to unite the nation into a strong federalist union under Buenos Aires; Rosas later became an important patriotic symbol for Argentine nationalists. (textbook, study guide)
26. Agreement between the government of Costa Rica and U.S. citizen Minor Cooper Keith, according to which Keith renegotiated Costa Rica's debts in exchange for exclusive rights to develop and own (for 99 years) the railroad line into Costa Rica's coffee-growing region. The contract shows the dependent position in which many Latin American countries found themselves due to their reliance on foreign capital to develop badly needed infrastructure. (anthology)
27. Set of economic theories imported from Europe that became well established among Latin America's elites in the late nineteenth century, encouraging free trade and laissez-faire economic policies. Economic liberalism justified Latin America's integration into the world economy as exporter of raw materials and importer of manufactured goods. (anthology, textbook, study guide)
28. Argentine singer and composer whose rendition of the tango helped to transform it into a very popular song both in Argentina and throughout the world in the early decades of the twentieth century. (anthology, textbook, study guide)
29. Also known as "hard currency," this term refers to the few internationally accepted currencies used for international trade (such as the U.S. dollar, the German mark, the British pound, and the Japanese yen). All countries need reserves of foreign exchange, obtained by selling exports, in order to pay for imports. (textbook, study guide)
30. Any two of the following: their appeals to nationalism and anti-imperialism; their actions to expropriate foreign-owned industries; the fact that their political base was urban and multiclass, with particular appeal to the working class; their tendency to denigrate the elite, especially the landowning oligarchy. (anthology, textbook)

Unit 4, *Capital Sins: Authoritarianism and Democratization*

1. b, c, d (textbook)
2. c (textbook, study guide)
3. a, b, c (anthology, textbook, study guide)
4. c, d (anthology)

5. a, b, d (program, textbook, study guide)
6. a, c, d (program, anthology, textbook)
7. a (program, anthology)
8. b (anthology, textbook, study guide)
9. b, d (anthology, textbook, study guide)
10. a, b, c (anthology, textbook)
11. False (program, textbook, study guide)
12. False (textbook, study guide)
13. True (study guide)
14. False (textbook)
15. True (anthology, textbook)
16. False (textbook, study guide)
17. True (textbook)
18. True (program, textbook, study guide)
19. Government is by the military as an institution; the working class is demobilized and politically excluded; political activity is reduced drastically; and typically, the military government exhibits a welcoming attitude toward foreign investment and a focus on export-led growth. (textbook, study guide)
20. New capital city constructed in an underdeveloped region in Brazil's interior during the presidency of Juscelino Kubitschek. It was a symbol of prosperity and *grandeza.* (program, textbook, study guide)
21. Military rule involved the repression and suspension of political activity, such as the closure of legislatures, and the banning of political parties. After years of repression, many countries found their political institutions to be very weak once military rule ended. (textbook, study guide)
22. Luis Ignacio da Silva, dynamic labor leader and union organizer who headed the metalworkers union. Lula led a wave of strikes that paralyzed the industry in 1979 and 1980, and was narrowly defeated for the presidency in the 1989 presidential elections. (program, anthology, study guide)
23. Shantytowns and slum dwellings in and around major cities in Brazil; usually lack basic services such as water, sewers, and electricity. (textbook, study guide)
24. Brazil's first black congresswoman, born and raised in a *favela* outside Rio. (program)
25. The prosperity of Brazil's economic miracle was not shared by all Brazilians. The years of the "miracle" also brought an increasingly unequal distribution of income, a rise in urban poverty and in the rest of "social debt,"

such as neglect of education, housing, and health care. (anthology, textbook, study guide)

Unit 5, Continent on the Move: Migration and Urbanization

1. d (textbook)
2. c (program, textbook, study guide)
3. c (program, anthology, study guide)
4. b (program, textbook, study guide)
5. d (textbook, study guide)
6. a (anthology, study guide)
7. d (program, anthology, study guide)
8. a, b (program, anthology, study guide)
9. a, c (program, anthology, study guide)
10. b (program, textbook, study guide)
11. c (textbook, study guide)
12. b (textbook, study guide)
13. d (program, textbook, study guide)
14. a, c (program, anthology, study guide)
15. c, d (program, study guide)
16. d (program, study guide)
17. b (program, textbook, study guide)
18. False (program, anthology, study guide)
19. True (anthology)
20. True (anthology)
21. False (anthology)
22. True (program, anthology)
23. False (anthology)
24. False (program, study guide)
25. True (textbook)
26. During the years of rapid economic growth, Mexico City offered newly created industrial jobs, social services, entertainment, and a degree of social mobility to rural dwellers seeking a better life. (program, textbook, study guide)
27. The application and withdrawal of U.S. capital in different parts of the Caribbean basin was the major factor affecting migration patterns in the region. For example, the development of the sugar cane industry, with its seasonal demand for labor, led to massive flows of migrants following sugar around the Caribbean. The building of the Panama Canal between 1904 and 1914 had a similar effect. (anthology)
28. Term applied to Mexican manual laborers who were allowed to work in temporary ag-

ricultural and industrial jobs in the United States between World War II and the mid-1960s. (textbook, study guide)

29. The *pepenadores* are garbage pickers who make their meager livings by searching for salvageable trash and reselling it. Many also live in shacks on top of the garbage dumps. They symbolize the failure of Mexico City to absorb and provide for the huge numbers of migrants it attracted; they also illustrate the extremes of wealth and poverty that coexist in Mexico City today. (program, anthology)

30. The agreement proposed by U.S. president George Bush and Mexican president Carlos Salinas de Gortari in 1990 which would link the economies of the United States, Canada, and Mexico by lifting all trade barriers and allowing the free movement of capital, goods, and agricultural products within these three countries. (program, study guide)

Unit 6, Mirrors of the Heart: Color, Class, and Identity

1. c (textbook)
2. a (program, textbook)
3. c, d (program, textbook, study guide)
4. b (textbook, study guide)
5. a (anthology, study guide)
6. b (anthology)
7. d (anthology)
8. b (anthology)
9. b, c (anthology)
10. b (textbook)
11. a (anthology)
12. c, d (program, anthology, study guide)
13. c (program, anthology, textbook)
14. d (anthology)
15. b (program, study guide)
16. True (anthology, textbook, study guide)
17. True (textbook, study guide)
18. False (textbook)
19. True (textbook)
20. True (program, textbook)
21. True (textbook)
22. True (anthology, textbook, study guide)
23. True (program, study guide)
24. False (program, anthology, study guide)
25. False (program, anthology, study guide)

26. Bolivian revolution in which the most obvious remnants of the colonial legacy were finally removed. Mines were nationalized, the haciendas were broken up, and indigenous people were given the right to vote. (program, study guide)

27. Official policy promoted by Dominican dictator General Rafael Trujillo, who ruled from 1930 to 1961, which emphasized the country's cultural connection with Spain. (program, textbook, study guide)

28. For some Aymara the *pollera* is an important marker of their identity as a separate culture, and they are proud to wear it. It can also be a marker of higher economic achievement, as some *pollera* outfits, with jewelry, are quite expensive. But because it identifies them as indigenous, the *pollera* is also a symbol of domination by the Spanish, and of the history of discrimination. Many women who seek to become more modern by distancing themselves from rural Aymara culture no longer wear the *pollera*. (program)

29. Williams discusses the fact that although there is no visible segregation, there is near universal preoccupation with the issue of skin color. Racism has been internalized, he says, and lighter skin is viewed as far preferable to black. (anthology)

30. February 27 commemorates the end of 22 years of Haitian occupation rather than liberation from more than 400 years of Spanish colonialism. (textbook)

Unit 7, In Women's Hands: The Changing Roles of Women

1. c (anthology, study guide)
2. b (anthology)
3. a (anthology, study guide)
4. a, c (anthology)
5. d (program, textbook)
6. a, b, d (program, textbook)
7. b (program, textbook, study guide)
8. d (program, textbook, study guide)
9. b, c, d (program, study guide)
10. a, b (program)
11. a, c (program, anthology, textbook)
12. b (anthology)

13. a, b (program, anthology)
14. c, d (anthology)
15. a, c, d (program, anthology)
16. a, c (anthology)
17. True (program, anthology, study guide)
18. True (program, anthology)
19. True (anthology, study guide)
20. False (program, study guide)
21. False (program, textbook, study guide)
22. False (program, textbook, study guide)
23. False (program, anthology, study guide)
24. True (program, anthology)
25. Paternal authority; part of a legal framework derived from Roman law under which women were officially subordinated to the authority of their father or, if married, their husband. Women could not enter into contracts, own property, seek divorce or protection from domestic violence, or in general have any independent legal rights. (anthology, study guide)
26. At the time Maria Antonietta Saa was born, women were not even able to vote in Chile. Now, as an adult, she is the mayor of Chonchali, a city near Santiago. In the program she is shown talking with women building homes in a housing cooperative, another example of the new activism, organization, and non-traditional roles now opening up for women in the Americas. (program)
27. A cultural norm that idealizes women as the custodians of virtue, piety, morality, and spirituality. Traditionally, this feminine code was linked with *machismo* and precluded women from an independent life beyond their duties as wives and mothers. (From Maria, or Mary, the Virgin Mother of God in the Catholic tradition.) (program, textbook, study guide)
28. Long hours, no child care, unsafe working conditions, and the fact that work is only seasonal and not available year-round. (program)
29. They could not afford to feed their families individually. With the support of the Catholic Church and international organizations, the *ollas* appeared all over Chile during the Pinochet years as a response to poverty, unemployment, inflation, and hunger. (program, study guide)
30. Because the social, economic, and political turmoil of the recent past threatened their families, and women felt compelled to protest. For example, middle- and upper-class women marched in the streets banging on pots and pans to protest food shortages and inflation under Allende, and women demonstrated against the disappearance of their family members under Pinochet. (program, study guide)

Unit 8, Miracles Are Not Enough: Continuity and Change in Religion

1. a (anthology, study guide)
2. b, c (program, anthology, study guide)
3. a, d (program, anthology, study guide)
4. a, b, d (program, anthology, study guide)
5. c, d (anthology, study guide)
6. b, c (program, anthology, study guide)
7. b (anthology, study guide)
8. b, d (program, anthology, study guide)
9. a, b (program, anthology, study guide)
10. c (textbook)
11. a, d (program)
12. b (program, textbook)
13. a, d (anthology, study guide)
14. a, b, d (textbook)
15. b, d (program, textbook)
16. False (program, anthology, study guide)
17. False (anthology, study guide)
18. True (anthology, study guide)
19. True (study guide)
20. False (anthology, study guide)
21. False (program)
22. False (program, anthology)
23. The Holy Book of the Mayan religion, written down in script in the early sixteenth century; emphasizes the connection between humans and the natural world. (anthology, study guide)
24. Debate that took place in 1550 between Juan Ginés de Sepúlveda and Bartolomé de las Casas over the treatment of the indigenous peoples during the conquest. The debate indicated the concern of church people with the moral issues of the day, and illustrates that Catholic sympathy for the oppressed did not originate with the Medellín conference. (anthology)
25. Pope from 1958 to 1963 who began the im-

portant reform and revitalization of the Church that culminated in the Church council known as Vatican II. (anthology)

26. Liberation theology equates the teachings of Christ with a call for liberation of the poor. Gustavo Gutierrez, one of the earliest and most important liberation theologians, has argued since the 1960s that the Church has a responsibility to participate in class struggle, to take action against the various forms of oppression in society, and to work for the creation of greater socioeconomic justice. Some theologians have de-emphasized class struggle because of the conflict it presents between their religious values and potential support of violence. (anthology, study guide)

27. CELAM II was a meeting of the Catholic bishops of Latin America which took place in Medellín, Colombia, in 1968. It was notable especially for the bishops' decision to undertake public advocacy for the poor and oppressed. (anthology, study guide, textbook)

28. First, that Catholicism has more of a cultural than a religious significance for most Brazilians; second, that most Brazilians continue to participate in certain Catholic rituals although they may no longer be practicing Catholics; and third, that even this most Catholic of observances exhibits the influence of other religious traditions, especially those of indigenous and African origins. (program, study guide)

29. Catholic archbishop of San Salvador who became an outspoken critic of government repression and abuse of human rights. Romero's assassination while saying Mass in 1980 sparked international outrage. (textbook)

30. Cardenal, the minister of culture in the Sandinista government, was also a priest. He received a public rebuke from Pope John Paul II, who was increasingly dissatisfied with the Marxist orientation of the Sandinistas and forbade priests' involvement in politics. (program)

Unit 9, Builders of Images: Writers, Artists, and Popular Culture

1. c, d (anthology)
2. b, c, d (textbook)
3. c (textbook)
4. d (anthology, study guide)
5. a (anthology, study guide)
6. a (program, anthology, study guide)
7. b, c, d (anthology)
8. a (anthology)
9. c, d (program, study guide)
10. c (study guide)
11. a, d (anthology, study guide)
12. a (program, anthology, study guide)
13. b, d (program)
14. True (textbook)
15. True (anthology)
16. False (program, study guide)
17. True (program, anthology, study guide)
18. True (anthology)
19. False (program, anthology)
20. True (program, study guide)
21. False (program, anthology, study guide)
22. The *telenovelas* and other television programming produced by Latin American media conglomerates and viewed throughout the hemisphere; the creation of "salsa," a form of music that is universally popular and cannot be attributed to any one country; the international appeal and recognition accorded Latin American literature; the appearance of indigenous folk songs and/or instruments and of African–inspired melodies and folk rhythms in so-called "world beat" music. (program, anthology, study guide)
23. The idea that recognition from outside is somehow more valuable than that from within; lack of pride in being "the other"; a popular denial of the distinctiveness of Latin America and the Caribbean; and the importation of a consumer-oriented popular ideology. (program, study guide)
24. Because Coatlicue is only recognized as "dead history," a statue in a museum, not as a figure with importance for Mexicans in today's society. (program)
25. An attempt to open up popular music to influences from within and outside the country. It resulted in a redefinition of many traditional styles; Caetano Veloso was one of the leading singers associated with tropicalism. (program, study guide)
26. Puerto Rico's most famous singer, who reached the peak of his popularity in the 1950s. Luis Raphael Sánchez wrote a book about Santos

as an exploration of Puerto Rican culture. (program)

27. Both Darío and Martí were concerned with how their countries would withstand the pressures from the "giant neighbor to the North," and also wanted to emphasize pan-American solidarity rather than regional and national isolation. (anthology)

28. A term coined by Cuban novelist Alejo Carpentier in the 1940s, which refers to some authors' use of descriptive narrative in combination with fantasy and myth to define a new, Latin American vision of reality closely associated with the work of Nobel Prize-winning author Gabriel García Márquez. (anthology, study guide)

29. They must struggle to define what is truly national, since within each country there are many different histories, ethnicities, and classes, each with its own cultural forms. Also, they must struggle against the mass, homogeneous culture of consumerism popularized through TV, photo novels, and other media. Finally, they are not free to criticize convention or to challenge political authority without repercussions. (program, study guide)

30. Muralism was an experimental art movement sponsored by the Mexican government in the early twentieth century. The idea was to use popular art, painted on walls, employing traditional and recognizable images, colors, and styles, to communicate with illiterate and semiliterate people. The major artists associated with muralism are Diego Rivera, David Alfaro Siqueiros and José Clemente Orozco; Rivera and Orozco also painted in the United States. (anthology, study guide)

Unit 10, Get Up, Stand Up: The Problems of Sovereignty

1. a (anthology, study guide)
2. d (program, study guide)
3. b (program)
4. a, b, d (program, anthology, textbook, study guide)
5. a, c (program, study guide)
6. a, c (textbook, study guide)
7. c (anthology)
8. b, d (program, study guide)
9. d (program, textbook, study guide)
10. a (program, textbook, study guide)
11. a, b, c (program, anthology, textbook, study guide)
12. d (program, textbook, study guide)
13. d (program, textbook, study guide)
14. True (textbook)
15. True (anthology)
16. False (program, anthology, study guide)
17. False (textbook)
18. False (textbook, study guide)
19. True (anthology, study guide)
20. True (anthology, study guide)
21. False (anthology, study guide)
22. False (program, study guide)
23. U.S. term for its invasion of Panama in 1989 which drove dictator General Manuel Noriega from power and brought him to the United States to stand trial on drug trafficking charges. (program, textbook, study guide)
24. Pronouncement by President James Monroe in 1823 which made clear that the United States would look unfavorably upon any attempt by European powers—especially Great Britain, France, Spain, and Russia—to assert control over any nation in the Western Hemisphere. The Monroe Doctrine eventually became a justification for continued U.S. military and political intervention in Latin America and the Caribbean. (anthology, study guide)
25. Jamaica's imposition of a 7.5 percent bauxite levy was perceived as an indicator of sovereignty because bauxite was the country's most important resource and was monopolized by foreign companies; Jamaica would gain far greater income from the export of its bauxite after the levy was imposed; and Jamaica "stood up" to the power of foreign capital which had refused to agree to the higher tax. (program, anthology, textbook, study guide)
26. The 1903 agreement between the U.S. government and French engineer Philippe Bunau-Varilla, acting as Panama's representative, which authorized U.S. construction of the Panama Canal, and gave the United States permanent control of a 10–mile-wide zone bordering the canal. (textbook, study guide)
27. The Colombian government called the convention as a means of regaining government legitimacy and affirming national sovereignty. It led to amnesty for guerrillas and an end to the extradition of drug dealers.

Both measures have helped to restore greater civil peace to the country after years of increasing violence. (program, textbook, study guide)

28. Armed militias have set themselves up as vigilantes in order to eradicate the "killer kids" associated with the drug lords. (program)

29. Panamanian military dictator from 1968 until his death in a plane crash in 1981. Nationalist who negotiated with three U.S. administrations to secure sovereignty for Panama over the canal; signed the Panama Canal Treaty with President Carter in 1978. (textbook)

30. Ideology embraced by Jamaican prime minister Michael Manley, which called for a combination of a democratic political system with a mixed socialist and capitalist economic system. Manley's government took on a greater role in the economy and attempted to distribute a larger share of economic benefits to the country's poor. (program, textbook, study guide)

Unit 11, *Fire in the Mind: Revolutions and Revolutionaries*

1. a, c (textbook, study guide)
2. b (anthology, textbook)
3. c (textbook, study guide)
4. c (textbook, study guide)
5. b, d (textbook)
6. d (program, anthology, textbook, study guide)
7. a, d (anthology, textbook, study guide)
8. d (program, textbook, study guide)
9. b (program, anthology, textbook, study guide)
10. b (program, textbook, study guide)
11. a, c, d (anthology, textbook, study guide)
12. a (program, study guide)
13. a, b, c (program, textbook, study guide)
14. c (program, anthology, study guide)
15. b (program, study guide)
16. b, d (program, study guide)
17. False (study guide)
18. True (program, study guide)
19. False (anthology)
20. True (textbook, study guide)
21. False (program, anthology, textbook, study guide)
22. False (textbook)
23. False (program, anthology, textbook, study guide)
24. Nicaraguan guerrilla leader who waged a campaign against U.S. Marines stationed in Nicaragua in the late 1920s and early 1930s. Sandino was a nationalist and anti-imperialist leader. His name was taken by the Sandinistas, the rebel army fighting against Somoza in the Nicaraguan Revolution in 1979. (textbook, study guide)
25. Program issued by Emiliano Zapata in 1911 outlining his demands that Francisco Madero leave the presidency of Mexico and calling for the expropriation and redistribution of large land-holdings as a vital part of the Mexican Revolution. (anthology, study guide)
26. President of El Salvador elected in 1989 as leader of the Nationalist Republican Alliance (ARENA), a far-right party originally associated with death squad violence and with El Salvador's business and landowning elites. Cristiani agreed to UN-sponsored peace talks, which resulted in an end to the Salvadoran civil war in early 1992. (program, textbook, study guide)
27. One of the oldest and most notorious death squads in Central America, active in Guatemala in the 1970s. The name means "an eye for an eye." (anthology, study guide)
28. Any two of the following: the Mexican Revolution occurred prior to World War II and was unaffected by the Cold War or by superpower competition; the size, resource base and population were much larger at the start of the revolution in Mexico than they were in those countries where later revolutions occurred; the Mexican Revolution did not face the same degree of hostility from the United States that met later revolutions and revolutionary movements in the region. (textbook, study guide)
29. Argentine physician, guerrilla leader, and revolutionary theorist who worked closely with Fidel Castro in overthrowing Batista and in designing the policies of revolutionary Cuba. Guevara inspired guerrilla movements throughout the Americas and called for "many Vietnams"; he was killed while attempting to inspire revolutionary sentiment among Bolivian peasants in Bolivia in 1967. (textbook, study guide)

30. Herzog was arguing that the Mexican Revolution had lost its "creative vitality"; the Mexican government still called itself revolutionary but in fact was no longer the innovative and radical force for change it had once been. Herzog particularly criticized the political leadership, which had become dominated by an official party and was no longer committed, he said, to carrying out meaningful reform. (anthology)

Unit 12, The Americans:
Latin American and Caribbean Peoples in the United States

1. c (program, textbook, study guide)
2. a, b, d (anthology, textbook, study guide)
3. c, d (anthology)
4. a, c (anthology, study guide)
5. a, b (program, anthology, textbook, study guide)
6. c (program, anthology, study guide)
7. b, c (program, textbook, study guide)
8. a, d (anthology, textbook, study guide)
9. a (program, study guide)
10. d (anthology)
11. a (anthology, study guide)
12. c (anthology, study guide)
13. b (program, anthology)
14. a, b (anthology, textbook)
15. c (program, textbook, study guide)
16. True (textbook)
17. False (anthology, textbook, study guide)
18. False (anthology)
19. True (anthology)
20. True (anthology, study guide)
21. False (program, anthology, study guide)
22. False (program, anthology, study guide)
23. Because Chicanos have been in the Los Angeles area longer and have more extensive social networks for assisting new migrants, and because the Central Americans are in general less skilled than the Chicanos. Also, Central Americans have come farther and are more fearful of being deported than are most of the undocumented Mexicans, leading them to seek less risky (and less secure) employment in the informal economy. (program, anthology)
24. The arguments in favor are that bilingual education will help overcome language and cultural barriers, that it will speed integration of Latinos into society and enable Latino children to remain in school—thus helping break the cycle of being trapped in low-wage, low-skill jobs—and that research has shown cognitive advantages among bilingual children, compared with monolingual children. The arguments against bilingual education focus on the cost to communities of being forced to provide it, the fact that it enhances the separateness of Latinos and encourages them to retain their language rather than learning English, and that it produces children who are not competent in either English or Spanish. (anthology, textbook, study guide)
25. U.S. law passed in 1986 that implemented a two-pronged approach to immigration, especially illegal immigration from Mexico and Central America. While establishing tough sanctions for employers hiring undocumented workers, the law also provided amnesty from prosecution and an offer of legal residency for all who could prove they had been living continuously in the United States since 1981. (anthology, textbook, study guide)
26. He is referring to the fact that Mexicans first became U.S. residents when the United States took over the Mexican territory that is now the southwestern United States after the Mexican-American War. (anthology)
27. Lamm argues that immigration is making certain parts of the country too crowded and causing competition with U.S. nationals for jobs and services at a time when the United States is not able to expand the provision of those services. He also cites the fragmentation of North American culture, strains among immigrant groups, and the depression of wages as being risks from continued rapid immigration. (anthology)
28. The full integration of people into society, typically through the adoption of the language, culture, values, dress, and other social norms of the majority population. For non-English-speaking immigrants from Latin America and the Caribbean, assimilation has usually been associated with giving up their language and customs to become more fully accepted in North American society. (program, anthology, textbook, study guide)
29. President of Republic National Bank, the

largest local Hispanic bank in Miami. Botitol was involved in making loans to fellow Cuban businessmen that helped build the Miami Cuban economic enclave. (program)

30. *Nuyorican* is a term used to refer to the unique blending of North American and Puerto Rican cultures, exemplified by the Puerto Rican community in New York. The active cultural life of Puerto Ricans in New York has had a broad influence within the mainland Puerto Rican community, enhancing community cohesion and sense of pride and identity. Nuyoricans have also had an important impact on the culture of the island Puerto Ricans, due especially to their large numbers and to the frequent contact between the island and mainland communities. Finally, Nuyorican artists are gaining increased recognition and popularity among non-Latino North American groups, as exemplified by the popularity of Spanglish (mixed Spanish and English) rap groups, and of Puerto Rican films, plays, and music. (program, study guide)

Unit 13, Course Review

Note: Answers from the program, anthology, and study guide may be from any unit in the course.

1. a (textbook, study guide)
2. b (textbook)
3. a (program, anthology, textbook, study guide)
4. b (anthology, textbook, study guide)
5. a, b, c (program, textbook, study guide)
6. b, c, d (anthology, textbook)
7. c (program, anthology, study guide)
8. b (textbook, study guide)
9. b (textbook)
10. b (program, anthology, textbook, study guide)
11. a (textbook, study guide)
12. b, c, d (anthology, study guide)
13. d (textbook, study guide)
14. c, d (textbook, study guide)
15. a, b (study guide)
16. c, d (program, textbook, study guide)
17. b, c (program, anthology, textbook, study guide)
18. False (textbook, study guide)
19. True (program, anthology, study guide)
20. True (textbook, study guide)
21. True (textbook, study guide)
22. False (textbook, study guide)
23. False (textbook, study guide)
24. True (program, textbook, study guide)
25. Argentine economist who became the first head of ECLA, the Economic Commission on Latin America. Prebisch led the agency to a prominent role in advancing a Latin American analysis of the region's economic situation. (textbook, study guide)
26. Collective defense treaty signed in 1947 in Rio de Janeiro by the United States and most Latin American countries; part of a U.S. effort to redesign the Pan-American system better to defend against international Communism. The Rio Pact defined an attack on any American state, from inside or outside the hemisphere, as an attack on all, requiring collective measures to counter the aggression. (textbook, study guide)
27. You should recall from Units 1 and 2 that the colonial policy of mercantilism was designed to exploit the natural wealth of the colonies for the benefit of the imperial powers. Mercantilism specified that trade take place only between the colony and the colonial power (Spain or Portugal); trade among the colonies and between the colonies and other European powers was forbidden, although this policy could not be completely enforced. Under the mercantilist system, the Caribbean and Latin American colonies exported the products of plantations and mines, and received all their manufactured goods as imports from Europe. This system, which existed in at least modified form throughout the 300 years of colonialism, drastically affected the future patterns of the region's economic development. (anthology, textbook, study guide)
28. Each of the programs includes one or more examples of these tensions. To name just a few, you could consider the struggles over economic and political power that contributed to bureaucratic-authoritarianism in Chile, Argentina, and Brazil; the unequal participation in development by indigenous peoples (illustrated particularly in "Mirrors of the Heart" and "Fire in the Mind"); the

traditional restrictions on the roles of women and the tensions caused by women's recent social and political activism, depicted in "In Women's Hands" and "The Americans"; or the effect on internal and international migration of wide disparities between rural and urban areas ("Continent on the Move," and "The Americans"). (program)

29. You could cite any of the following: The interaction of Christianity with indigenous and African beliefs that has produced new religions *(Candomblé, vodún, Umbanda)* and affected the manner in which Christianity is practiced (for example, indigenous feast days often coincide with Christian holidays; Christian saints often have more than one identity). In recent decades, liberation theology and Christian base communities, both originating in Latin America, have had an important influence on the rest of the world. The social activism of institutional churches in the region, particularly on behalf of human rights under authoritarian governments, has also been very influential and widely publicized. (program, anthology, textbook, study guide)

30. Any of the following: migration within the region and to the United States; international drug trafficking and the power of drug cartels; adherence to international principles of respect for human rights; U.S. access to markets in the Americas, and vice versa; domestic conditions for foreign investment; repayment of the region's foreign debt; environmental protection; democracy and dictatorship. (program, anthology, textbook, study guide)